Leading HR

Leading HR

PAUL SPARROW, *Director, Centre for Performance-Led HR, Lancaster University*

MARTIN HIRD, *Executive Director, Centre for Performance-Led HR, Lancaster University*

ANTHONY HESKETH, *Deputy Director, Centre for Performance-Led HR, Lancaster University*

CARY COOPER, *Pro Vice Chancellor (External Relations) and Professor of Organizational Psychology and Health, Lancaster University*

First published 2010 by
PALGRAVE MACMILLAN

Palgrave Macmillan in the UK is an imprint of Macmillan Publishers Limited, registered in England, company number 785998, of Houndmills, Basingstoke, Hampshire RG21 6XS.

Palgrave Macmillan in the US is a division of St Martin's Press LLC, 175 Fifth Avenue, New York, NY 10010.

Palgrave Macmillan is the global academic imprint of the above companies and has companies and representatives throughout the world.

Palgrave® and Macmillan® are registered trademarks in the United States, the United Kingdom, Europe and other countries.

ISBN-13: 978–0–230–22259–5 hardback

This book is printed on paper suitable for recycling and made from fully managed and sustained forest sources. Logging, pulping and manufacturing processes are expected to conform to the environmental regulations of the country of origin.

A catalogue record for this book is available from the British Library.

A catalog record for this book is available from the Library of Congress.

10   9   8   7   6   5   4   3   2   1
19   18   17   16   15   14   13   12   11   10

Printed and bound by the MPG Books Group, Bodmin and Kings Lynn

To Sue, as always, for her insights and understanding. Paul
To Charlotte and Emily. Martin
To Helen, Thea, and Abby: my Golden Triangle! Ant
In the memory of Prof. Sir Roland Smith for his friendship and concerns about making business more humane. Cary

Contents

List of Figures and Tables

Figures

Tables

About the Authors

Paul Sparrow is the director of the Centre for Performance-Led HR and Professor of International Human Resource Management at Lancaster University Management School. He has worked as a Research Fellow at Aston University, Senior Research Fellow at Warwick University, Consultant/Principal Consultant at PA Consulting Group, Reader/Professor at Sheffield University and, whilst at Manchester Business School he took up the Ford Chair from 2002 to 2004 and was Director, Executive Education 2002–2005. He has consulted with major multinationals, public sector organizations and, intergovernmental agencies and was an Expert Advisory Panel member to the UK Government's Sector Skills Development Agency. His research interests include cross-cultural and international HRM, HR strategy, cognition at work, and changes in the employment relationship. He is on the Editorial Boards of a number of leading HR journals and has published over 100 journal articles and chapters and several books. In 2009 he was voted amongst the Top 15 Most Influential HR Thinkers by *Human Resources Magazine*.

Martin Hird is Executive Director at the Centre for Performance-led HR. Martin has held a range of managerial and educational roles. Following graduation and initial employment with the Dunlop Group he entered higher education becoming Dean of the Business School at Humberside Polytechnic whilst also operating an OD/Development consultancy. From 1988 to 2005 he worked for BAE Systems, McLaren Group, and Royal Mail in a series of HR Director roles which included responsibility for senior-level talent management and leadership development. He is a Fellow at the Centre for Leadership Studies at Exeter University. In addition to research and teaching within the Centre, his role focuses on client liaison and responding to business development opportunities. Martin has had a number of books, articles, and white papers published in recent years with particular emphasis on HR Delivery Systems and Talent Management.

Dr Anthony Hesketh is Senior Lecturer in the Management School at Lancaster University. His research focuses on capturing the impact of people and strategy on organizational performance. Anthony researches and consults with some of the world's leading organizations on strategic human capital management and its measurement, and outsourcing. Recent books include *The Mismanagement of Talent* (2004) and, with Steve Fleetwood, *Understanding the Performance of HR* (2009). He is the deputy director of the Centre for Performance-Led HR at Lancaster, a founding member of the HROA Europe Board, and for which he heads the Research & Publications Committee. Anthony regularly speaks at international conferences and sits on a number of advisory boards in the HR space and is Editor of the *Human Resources Business Review* (HRBR) and sits on the editorial board of *The HR Director*.

Cary Cooper is Professor of Organizational Psychology and Health, Lancaster University Management School and Pro Vice Chancellor (External Relations) at Lancaster University. He is the author of over 100 books (on occupational stress, women at work, and industrial and organizational psychology), has written over 400 scholarly articles, and is a frequent contributor to national newspapers, TV, and radio. He is a Fellow of the British Academy of Management and also of the Academy of Management (having also won the 1998 Distinguished Service Award). In 2001 he was awarded a CBE in the Queen's Birthday Honours List for his contribution to organizational health. He is Chair of The Sunningdale Institute, a think tank on management/organizational issues, in the National School of Government. He was also the lead scientist to the UK Government Office for Science on their Foresight programme on Mental Capital and Well Being (2007–2008), and was appointed a member of the expert group on establishing guidance for the National Institute for Health and Clinical Excellence on 'promoting mental well-being through productive and healthy working conditions,' 2009. He is Chair of the United Kingdom's Academy of Social Sciences. Professor Cooper is also the President of the Institute of Welfare, President of the British Association of Counselling and Psychotherapy, a national Ambassador of The Samaritans, a Patron of the Anxiety UK, and Patron of the National Bullying Helpline. *HR Magazine* named him the 6th Most Influential Thinker in HR in 2009.

Acknowledgments

The authors would like to thank all of the sponsor organizations for the Centre for Performance-Led HR for their research access and openness in discussing the issues facing HR: Britannia Building Society; Co-operative Financial Services; Hanson plc; IBM; McDonald's Restaurants Ltd; NG Bailey; Nestlé UK; North West Development Agency; Royal Bank of Scotland; Royal Mail; Sellafield Ltd; Shell International; United Utilities; and Vodafone.

In particular we would like to thank the HR Directors who have cowritten the case study chapters in this book, for the additional access that they have provided and for the way that their knowledge and expertise has helped us shape the academic agendas that must be faced.

We would also like to give a special mention to Shashi Balain and Craig Marsh, who as Researchers in the Centre, and notable authors on many of the chapters, have contributed significant intellectual capital to the ideas in this book and to our academic journey.

Finally, we would like to give an especial thanks to Teresa for her help in keeping the Centre show on the road and organizing both ourselves and our sponsors.

Notes on Contributors

Paul Chesworth: Paul has 23 years HR management experience within the commercial vehicles, defense and latterly telecoms sectors. He is currently HR Director, Vodafone Europe and Chairman of the Centre for Performance-Led HR at Lancaster University Management School.

David Fairhurst: Senior Vice President and Chief People Officer (Northern Europe), McDonald's Restaurants – Having been European Director of Recruitment and Leadership Planning for SmithKline Beecham, and Corporate HR Director for Tesco, David joined McDonald's in May 2005 and has board-level responsibility for HR, Training, Education, Customer Services, and Environment. He is a fellow of Lancaster University Management School, and in 2007 was awarded an honorary Doctorate in Business Administration by Manchester Metropolitan University Business School where he is a visiting professor. In 2007 and 2008, he secured the No. 1 position in Personnel Today's Top 40 HR Power Players list; and in June 2009, he was voted the United Kingdom's 'Most Influential Practitioner' by readers of HR Magazine for the second consecutive year.

Sherief Hammady: Sherief is an associate director with Hay Group UK and is a member of the private sector consultancy leadership team. He has a PhD in organizational studies from the University of St Andrews.

Matt Stripe: Matt is currently Assistant Vice President Human Resources for Nestlé SA, with responsibility for Human Resources and Global Talent Management for Nestlé's Strategic Business Units, Sales and Marketing, Finance, and Head office. Prior to this Matt was the HR Director for Nestlé Confectionery Division having previously held a number of Senior HR roles for BAE SYSTEMS and MBD.

Helen Sweeney: Helen is Group HR director at national building services provider, NG Bailey. Her responsibilities include developing and delivering a people-focused strategy in support of the business, as well as overseeing all other HR activity. Helen has also held senior HR positions at Co-operative Financial Services, Barclays Bank, and Unilever. She is passionate about developing talent and has an impressive background in introducing leading edge talent initiatives in the organizations she works for.

John Whelan: John is currently the HR director for the United Kingdom (Programmes and Support) business of BAE Systems. He has over 20 years of HR experience in large industrial companies in the UK and Europe.

Rob Woolley: Rob has worked for Co-operative Financial Services for 22 years working at all levels within the company and has also worked as a director for the last 7 years. He moved into the HR arena after running the company's call centers for 5 years and has a passion about people and culture.

CHAPTER 1

Introduction: Performance-Led HR

PAUL SPARROW, ANTHONY HESKETH, MARTIN HIRD, AND CARY COOPER

1.1. Introduction

By some accounts the human resource (HR) function's very existence is under threat. It must, the story goes, increase its strategic capability. This means unlocking and understanding what strategy is within businesses, and understanding the business and people models put in place to underpin strategic execution and delivery. This challenge lies at the heart of *Leading HR*. We have used this phrase to signal three imperatives:

1. There are a range of business issues that are *Leading HR* into *new roles and new contributions*;
2. There are some *Leading HR* processes and *practices that are highly embedded in the business*, not just technically sophisticated in HR terms, that can assist in the meeting of this business challenge;
3. But both of the above are highly dependent upon *Leading HR* as a capability within the organization – notably the *leadership provided by HR Directors*, but also as evidenced by other key players throughout the business.

What skills does such leadership require? What business languages does HR need to be fluent in? How can their social and political capital be used at boardroom level to influence strategic implementation?

The central question of strategic capability that is addressed throughout the book turns on how HR helps organizations understand the implementation of strategy from a people perspective, without insisting that HR is the common denominator to all things strategic. In this opening chapter we address two questions:

1. How should we think about people strategy in the context of business model change?
2. How should we look at strategy and understand the kind of people models that are associated with the emerging business models?

These are important questions, not least because the potential problems and risks associated with innovation in business models can be very high – events at Enron and then during the credit crunch attest to this.

In July 2008, we launched the first of a series of what we call White Papers in the field of performance-led HR, called Reversing the Arrow. Based on our analysis of what was taking place inside organizations over the preceding year, we asked the question:

> ... Many organisations within a sector can essentially pursue the same strategy. If organisations get it wrong, do they all go down like a pack of cards? Or are they capable of executing their business models differently?[1]

Despite our concerns, we, along with so many commentators, had but a faint fear of what might be possible in the business world when organizations got it wrong. The events of the subsequent months demonstrated to all the level of risk that exists. The questions that everyone in the field of HR should ask today, as were asked many years earlier about Enron, are as follows:

1. Did organizations fail not just despite of their HR, but because of their HR?[2]
2. How does HR – how must HR – position itself as organizations move forward?
3. How can it assist in the building of strategic capability?
4. What might this strategic capability look like?

We argue that the answer to these questions is to focus less on the HR for HR side of the equation, and to better understand the HR for the Business, or Performance-Led HR equation.

Throughout the book we draw upon the findings from the research agenda that has been pursued by the Centre for Performance-Led HR from 2006 to 2009. The Centre is focused on exploring ways to enhance the experience of the workforce and the productivity and performance of both employees and HR functions. We believe that this is a central issue for innovation and growth in businesses. This book is based on our work with HR Directors from 15 organizations – BAE Systems, the Cabinet Office, Co-operative Financial Services/Britannia Building Society, Hanson plc, IBM, McDonald's Restaurants Ltd, NG Bailey, Nestlé, North West Development Agency, Royal Bank of Scotland, Royal Mail, Sellafield Ltd, Shell International, United Utilities, and Vodafone.

The research methodology

The various projects, analyses, and case studies developed in this book are based upon data collected over the period from late 2006 until mid-2009. This has allowed us to gather a longitudinal picture of the realities of strategic HR, capturing changing events and priorities though a two-and-a-half-year window that ran from a period of high growth through to HR in tougher times as the credit crunch had its impact. We draw upon:

1. Over 100 primary interviews conducted in 15 organizations. A key priority has been to gain a line as well as HR perspective on the challenges for *Leading HR*. The line perspective is based on interviews with Chief Executive Officers, Managing Directors, a Chief Information Officer, Finance Directors, Marketing Director, Transformation Director, Capability Director, Head of Transition, Superintendant Major Projects, Strategy and Marketing Managers. The HR perspective is based on interviews with Group HR Directors and VPs, HR Directors for Operations, Transformation, Organizational Capability and Development, Capability Management, Shared Services, Employee Engagement, and a number of HR business partners.

2. Secondary material on each organization, such as public discussion of generic business models, annual reports, publicly available investor relations reports and presentations, as well as wider business media coverage.

3. Strategic HR planning processes, where we have co-worked with the HR strategy teams in a number of workshops and planning events. We were able to record these events, which provided us with an intimate understanding of the issues involved for the organizations and their HR leadership. Through these processes we have also been able to review and interpret internal employee and performance data.

4. A series of network events run for the Group HR Directors involved, and special interest groups covering functional concerns such as talent management, organization design and employee engagement, again recorded, at which the emerging research data and themes have been collectively interpreted.

5. A survey of 78 HR Directors and senior HR practitioners run from June to October 2008, and a follow-up survey involving another 59 organizations in July 2009.

From these data it is clear that the answers to the strategic problems faced by organizations are not easy. The HR function has to address the people issues that result from complex operational challenges and contribute to strategic thinking.

1.2. Strategic competence in turbulent times

A key starting point is to ask what is necessary to ensure that the organization is "strategically competent." Organizations still face what strategists such as Richard D'Avini 15 years ago called a period of hyper-competition.[3] Long before the credit crunch led to destruction of several apparently successful and innovative business models, Gerard Hodgkinson and Paul Sparrow[4] asked "how could organizations with high profile and historically successful track records fall prey to catastrophic chains of events that led to their demise?" To answer this question they pulled together the work of organizational psychologists, strategic management writers, management consultants, and organizational researchers. In laying out the psychology of strategic management, they noted that strategists make four assumptions that are inherently false:

Four false assumptions about strategy

1. Strategic decision makers are inherently rational actors who seek to maximize outcomes, first seeking all available information, then secondly, weighing up the various alternatives in order to select the best course of action.
2. Business environments are objective entities waiting to be discovered through the application of formal analytic procedures.
3. Successful strategies are invariably the product of deliberate planning.
4. The locus of strategy-making invariably resides in the upperechelons of the organization, while implementation is everyone's business.

Strategy is not rational and never has been. Rather, people inside organizations – at all levels of the hierarchy, managers and non-managers alike – have to absorb, process, make sense of, and then disseminate a bewildering flow of information in order to make wise decisions and solve problems. Strategic competence therefore concerns the ability of organizations (or more precisely their members) to acquire, store, recall, interpret, and act upon information of relevance to the longer term survival and well-being of the organization. The key message is that in practice being a strategically competent organization means:[5]

> ... being agile, open to the environment, capable of picking up those weak signals indicative of the need for change, which are then selected, filtered, stored, recalled and interpreted in a fashion that enables the organisation to respond as appropriate ... Knowledge management is thus central to this process. In cases where strategic competence is highly developed, the organisation is able to proactively develop new competencies and stake out new strategic territories. Conversely, where the organisation fails to develop such strategic competence, it responds reactively in an ever-viscous circle, which at best enables it to defend its existing markets, products and/or services.

Organizations are managing in an era of disorder. Many changes are placing unprecedented informational burdens upon those responsible for strategy formulation and implementation. Hence, there is a high level of strategic risk associated with managing under these conditions. Strategic competence involves understanding how individuals, teams, and important stakeholders all develop strategy, resourcing the organization with the capabilities to manage this.

However, as Jeffrey Pfeffer[6] reminds us, in all too many cases, strategic insight fails to materialize because of limitations in the mental models of strategic leaders, either because the organization proves incapable of implementing what they see to be important based on evidence or insights (called the knowing–doing problem) or because they do not act on the basis of good evidence (called the doing–knowing problem). The necessary insights are often unconscious, constrained by managerial beliefs and ideologies, and involve different ways of thinking about and conceptualizing competitive forces and business models that result in new and innovative offerings. For Pfeffer[7] therefore

> ... mental models affect organisational performance and ... are a high leverage place for human resources to focus its organisational interventions.

The ability of HR functions to identify and help others discover the mental models that are in operation, coupled with the capability to change these mindsets, becomes:

> ... among the most critical capabilities an HR professional can have or acquire.[8]

This is undoubtedly true. Much has been made of entrance of the HR Director to the boardroom, but what must now follow? Two things:

1. They need to understand how the organization "strategizes."
2. They need to become skilled at boardroom engagement.

They have to find openings and opportunities to add their unique insights to the strategy and change management process. They need to build the skills that enable rapid diagnosis of competing business models.

1.3. Deciphering the language of strategy

What ties all the chapters in this book together is the drumbeat of business model change. More than ever HR Directors must engage in, and use the language of, strategy in order to demonstrate the value of their function.

Why should HR be talking about business model change?

The term has entered the mainstream thinking, for the following reasons:

1. Surveys of CEOs find that in order to remain competitive, business model innovation is their main strategic priority over the coming years.[9]
2. Strategy academics argue that whilst strategy concerns the long-term creation of value and the process of making strategic choices, analysis of the business model facilitates clearer analysis, testing, and validation of these choices[10] and a finer grain differentiation in strategy.[11] This is because business models describe both the organization's value chain (drawing upon Porter's ideas) and its unique resources or position within this (drawing upon the resource-based view of the firm).
3. Moreover, the economic value of business model innovation is increasing.[12] A range of institutional bodies and consulting firms[13] believe that the way in which innovation is fostered is changing under the influence of globalization, information technology, and resulting competitive processes, leading to a democratization of business model innovation. More decentralized ideas generation and handling inside organizations can be used to integrate elements of the value chain in more flexible, but also often disruptive, ways.

(Continued)

4. Advanced economies therefore face intensifying domestic and economic competition.[14]

5. Central to this competition is the ability to bring together the known constituents or knowledge bases associated with a new business model.

In this opening chapter we must remind ourselves about some of the language and some of the theory that have guided the strategy debate. What does HR need to understand about strategy?

Organizations are using the language of business models to articulate what they consider must be the dominant *performance logic* inherent in their strategy.[15] Compared with the very rich history of exploration of the subject of "strategy," a field monopolized until recently by the seminal works of Michael Porter on *Competitive Strategy*, Henry Mintzberg and colleagues on *Strategy Safari*, and then a stream of writers such as Jay Barney, Gary Hamel who developed the *resource-based view of the firm,* [16] the academic treatment of business models is still relatively new.[17] Strategists have been on a journey of ideas, language, and tools,[18] and the idea of business models pulls together a number of developments within the field. There have been three main developments that we summarize early in this chapter:

1. Competitive positioning perspective.

2. Resource-based view of the firm.

3. Advent of technological developments and how they enabled organizations to radically change their strategic contribution, and use the language of new "business models."

Competitive positioning perspective

This produced the analytical frameworks of a value chain and value systems. Business model logic has co-opted some of these early ideas. Michael Porter's competitive positioning approach to strategy argues that in asking the question "what drives an organization's performance?", the answer lies in an outside-in approach – analyzing the external environment (industry and markets) and then looking internally and identifying the organization's value creating activities in this context. A key idea is the *value chain* – defined as the chain of activities that are necessary in order for a product or service to gain some value. These chains in turn may form part of a broader system that can exist across the whole of a supply chain or distribution network – a *value system*. This includes the value chains of an organization's supplier (and their suppliers), the organization itself, various actors in the distribution channels, and the buyers of the organization's products or services.

Michael Porter's competitive positioning approach to strategy was then overtaken from the early 1990s onward by what became known as the *resource-based view of the firm.*

Resource-based view of the firm

Also driven by the question "what drives an organization's performance?" this approach argues that strategy is better served by an inside-out approach. Relative organizational performance and profitability lies in an understanding of an organization's resources – things that it can input to enable it to carry out its strategy. These resources can be tangible (such as physical, financial, or HR) or intangible (such as intellectual know-how and creativity or speed of technological innovation). Such resources are not valuable in their own right, but if they can be marshaled together to create an attribute that assists competitive advantage (a competence), then they at least enable threshold performance. These resources need to be flexible so that they can be configured and reconfigured in new ways that provide competitive advantage. This flexible configuration can lead to a range of core competencies (also called distinctive capabilities). Competencies are only core if they provide access to a variety of markets, make a significant contribution to perceived customer benefits, and are sustainable and difficult to imitate.

A central tenet of the resource-based view is that the value that is embedded in any strategy increases when the bundle of resources and capabilities that the strategy comprises becomes more difficult to imitate, less transferable, and more complementary.[19]

Therefore, writers like John Kay[20] argue that possessing a distinctive capability (or characteristic) is a necessary, but not a sufficient, criteria for success. The capability needs to be sustainable over time and primarily benefit only the organization that holds it. Three things help build the sustainability of these distinctive capabilities:

Key elements of a distinctive capability

1. An architecture or network – which is the system of relational contracts inside and outside the organization. This includes internal relationships within and between employees, and external relationships with customers, suppliers, and other firms working on related activities;

2. Reputation, important when customers can only judge the quality of a product or service over a long period of time – where reliable relationships result in trust and help organizations enter new markets;

3. Innovation, especially where it is embedded in an organization's internal routines and processes.

For writers such as Gary Hamel and C.K. Prahalad, the challenge then is not to match or *fit* an organization's resources to the external environment, but to "stretch" the organization's strategic ambitions in ways that make it understand how it can leverage even limited resources in fruitful and disruptive ways.[21] Central to this need to "stretch" ambition is the ability to work across organizational boundaries. And what has assisted work across organizational boundaries? Information technology.

So some of the latest developments in strategic thinking have come on the back of technological developments that enable organizations to radically change their strategic contribution by doing interesting things across old boundaries.

The advent of business model thinking

The appearance of the concept of "business model" in the strategy literature can be dated back to the "internet revolution" in the second half of the last decade. At this time, the term was used to represent changes in the value proposition of organizations that had been brought about by new "virtually organized" internet businesses.[22] Organizations found ways to exploit the upstream and downstream information that flows along the value chain, or bypassed existing intermediaries, by creating new business models and other improvements to their value system. The term "business model" applies to the framework that is used to create value (that value may be economic or social) in core aspects of a business. This framework may be described in terms of a range of important characteristics that are considered to add value – be they the purpose of the business, its service offerings and practices, the way that the organizational structure helps focus on key activities, the way that infrastructure is managed, and important business processes or policies on which performance is crucially dependent. Business model therefore describes the value chain, the series of activities this chain entails, and the unique resources or position that this brings to an organization.[23]

The advent of the idea of there being business models – and that this way of thinking about strategy is in any way novel and valuable – is not without criticism. It has been criticized as "an indistinct term which passed into general usage in the New Economy era[24]" and "one of those terms of art that were central to the Internet boom: it glorified all manner of half-baked plans. All it really meant was how you planned to make money." To address such criticisms, we now lay out the elements of a more constructive and deeper set of questions that can be associated with business model thinking.

1.4. Getting the measure of business models

Business models are best thought of as a *business performance logic* – a storyline – that can be used to weave together and demonstrate the importance of a range of core components to the execution of a strategy. By modeling how performance is dependent on the management of all these components, brought together as part of a greater whole, organizations are better placed to derive value from their strategy. Describing business models helps to articulate the key components of effective strategic performance, thereby providing an opportunity to link HR more closely to the challenges faced during strategic execution.

What is a business model?

Strategists such as George Yip distinguish between "dynamic" and "static" elements of strategizing.[25] Routine strategies change market share, cost and quality position, and profitability, whereas transformational strategies change the business model.[26] A business model is a dominant performance logic based on an analysis of the value proposition that the strategy offers, the way that important inputs to the strategy are transformed into outputs, choices are made about vertical, horizontal, and geographical scope, and the "organization" that is necessary to deliver the strategy. Typically this analysis explains two key issues:

1. how the organization creates value: by defining a series of activities (from raw materials through to the final customer) that will yield a new product or service, and explaining how value is added throughout the various activities and

2. how the organization's strategy captures a portion of that value: by establishing how a unique resource, asset, or position within that series of strategic activities can help the organization enjoy a competitive advantage.

Innovation in the business model requires developments in the structure and/or the financial model of the business and so also includes the role of strategic partnerships, shared services, or alternative financing vehicles.

The recent opportunity for disruptive technologies to create new ways of competing has seen the issue of business model change start to dominate the attention of business leaders. Business Model Innovation (BMI) has now become an area of separate strategic attention. Clayton Christensen and colleagues[27] have drawn attention to the nature of disruptive innovation – where a new customer paradigm or technology enables new entrants to capture market share and create new markets. They have used theories of innovation to help explain the role played by business model innovation and distinguished two types of innovative technology:

1. sustaining technologies, which improve existing products or services, and

2. disruptive technologies, which completely change the nature of a market or business.

In terms of Business Model Innovation, sustaining technologies might, for example, improve the quality of CDs, whilst disruptive technologies came up with the iPod and the digital downloading of sound.

Drawing upon such ideas, in 2006 IBM's financial analysts[28] argued that organizations that put more emphasis on business model innovation experienced significantly better operating margin growth (over a 5-year period) than did their peers (measuring the per cent compound annual growth rate in operating margin in excess of competitive peers over a 5-year period). Their survey of CEOs found that they were focusing 30 per cent of their innovative efforts on business model innovation. Forty per cent feared that changes in a competitor's business model would radically change the landscape of their whole industry:[29]

> ... They are implementing major strategic alliances, combining their own expertise with the specialized capabilities of partners. Internally, they are making major structural changes, collapsing organisational boundaries and leveraging shared service centers across the enterprise. They are pursuing new business opportunities, new competencies and new alliances, creating value not just for their own companies but also for their industry as a whole. For these companies, innovation occurs proactively rather than in response to specific events, and it has resulted in business designs that are truly differentiating. These important perspectives on innovation are changing the way companies view their business operation and map their future strategy. They are causing business leaders to rethink long-held business models and envision change from the ground up.

A range of other institutional bodies, such as the OECD, Booz, Boston Consulting Group, and the McKinsey Global Institute, similarly believe that the way in which innovation is fostered changes under the influence of globalization, information technology, and resulting competitive processes. Drawing upon such ideas, a special edition of the *Economist*[30] in 2007 offered some insights into the subject of radical innovation. It is now argued that the economic value of business model innovation is increasing. This issue came to the fore quite a few years before the credit crunch hit the business world. As organizations come out of the recession, we should expect even more fundamental changes taking place in many sectors. Vertically integrated research and development organizations and government-backed policies to enhance corporate research are proving to be too slow and insular, and a new model is emerging, which is dependent upon more decentralized, democratic, and anarchic process of ideas generation and handling inside organizations and business model innovation that integrates elements of the value chain in more flexible, but also often disruptive, ways. A business model draws attention to the way that four key elements interlock in order to create and deliver value and performance:[31]

1. Competition based upon a new customer value proposition inherent in an organization's offerings.
2. Supported by a profit formula (how the organization creates value for itself by managing financial elements such as its revenue model, cost structure, margins, and resource velocity).

3. Underwritten by needed resources (the assets such as people, technology, products, facilities, equipment, and brand that are required to deliver the value proposition to the target customer).

4. Enabled by operational and managerial processes that enhance this value proposition.

Building on the original ideas about disruptive innovation, by late 2008 Mark Johnson of Innosight, Clayton Christensen, and Henning Kagermann of SAP[32] discussed the need for organizations to reinvent their business models. For them, innovation is often seen in terms of a new product or service offering, but business model innovation – which refers to the creation, or reinvention, of a business itself – results in an entirely different type of organization and way of competing.

To summarize, most strategy writers have used the term "business model" to draw attention to different qualities that can best explain strategy and its necessary performance logic. They argue that by using the idea of a "model" it becomes easier to help people in the organization to build an integrated and consistent "picture" of the organization and the way in which its strategy can generate revenues. The model has to tell a story that explains how the organization and its strategy works.[33] As a model, it has important component parts, or central themes, that explain how and why the organization must work as it does.

Understanding the business model: Can you answer these questions?

When we look across the various renditions that have been given of business models, we believe that this story has to specify the following:

1. How does the organization create value?

2. Who does it create value for – who are the real stakeholders?[34]

3. Who are the customers?

4. Where are the costs borne and how are profits made?

5. What becomes important in the content, structure, and governance of business transactions, and how can these be designed in order to create value and exploit business opportunities?[35]

6. What is the architecture of the transactions that the focal organization must engineer with its partners, suppliers, and customers?[36]

7. What structure or architecture is necessary to deliver the value proposition within and across this network that is, for each focal organization, how . . .?

8. How must financial and non-financial resources flow through *each* focal organization?

9. What do these capabilities look like when seen as part of a *value network* or *value web*? That is, what organizational capabilities are necessary to ensure such joined up implementation of the business model and to ensure effective strategic execution?

(Continued)

10. Which important organizational capabilities, workforce competencies, and assets support the underlying strategy?[37]

11. How must these capabilities, competencies, and assets be aligned to the products, service, or information flows?[38]

Note that we use the language of a *value web* rather than a value chain. We think this is much more appropriate. For most organizations the "series of activities" comprising the value chain now extend *beyond* the internal configuration of core capabilities, and out across a broad range of external partnerships or other key relationships. Effective business model execution means thinking about and managing not just the organization's own strategic capabilities, but also those others (e.g., outsourced or allianced operations[39]).

Rather than thinking about adding value through a traditional two-dimensional value chain – one that comprises the horizontal flow of value through successive points of value delivery – more and more business models recognize the importance of a third dimension – which is the existence of multiple stakeholders and external partners at each stage – and the need to think about building complex capabilities that capitalize upon, and are built through, more collaborative space.

1.5. Engaging the boardroom

We need to turn the problem of the possible inability of other key players in the organization to recognize or contribute to the strategy of the business on its head. How do CEOs and CFOs understand the people aspects of their strategy and how can HR enable this understanding? Top teams have often spent months learning about the realities of a new business model, but then expect their businesses to execute the new model in short-order.

HR Directors need to be able to unpick the strategic learning process and use this to educate both the workforce and the board about the realities involved. This raises two important questions:

1. What does the capability of being able to discuss new strategies and business models look like?

2. What sort of knowledge does talent really need to be able to do this?

We have argued that knowledge of business models – and the theories of action that are implicit in such a business model – serves to both inform and limit what is proposed for the business. This knowledge also determines how well senior managers (high talent) define and scan the environment, analyze data, consider alternatives, and decide upon the most appropriate organizational forms.

To signal the importance of top team relationships, we draw attention to recent insights into the reality of top team dialogues. John Storey and Graeme Salaman have studied what happens in top teams as they develop strategy. At senior levels of the organization, external talent is often brought in to inject a new knowledge system into the team's thinking. This knowledge system in practice is[40]

> ... a constellation of diagnoses, values, guiding principles, and solutions which are unfettered by the knowledge constraints of the previous regime.

In the search to confirm that the right candidate has been chosen, peers scramble to find confirmatory evidence of this sound judgment.

To examine the centrality of such knowledge to the judgment that they are "talented," they looked at the "knowledge claims" made by directors at the strategic apex of organizations – the claims they make about what their organization needs to do, what it should be like, to do these things, and why. These knowledge claims – or business knowledge – involve knowledge about the organization's purpose, products and/or services, environment, customers and competitors, structure, processes, and its people. Such insights into the business model – which may be shared among the senior team or around which there may be competing variants – emerge from[41]

> the ways in which these knowledge elements are related [to each other] ... [there is a meta-narrative articulated by Chief Executives that is] ... linked markets, structures, customers, values and organisation design.

HR Directors therefore do not just have to make sense of complex strategic changes. They also have to see their role as one of "giving sense" to other members of the top team. In practice most business models remain contested for a considerable time. Despite a common ability of chief executives to provide a narrative, knowledge of the strategy of the organization varies considerably across members of the executive teams. There are differing and incomplete accounts of the business model. Knowing *about* the organization, in terms of the interpretations given to various forms of information, performance goals, and appropriate metrics, and knowing *how* the design the organization delivered this were central to the execution of business models, but was always contested territory. The implication of this is that HR Directors need two understandings:

1. The different renditions of the business model and
2. The politics, alliances, and conflicts around the model, and which "accounts" are in the ascendancy or are waning.

This means knowing how to behave, prioritize, and act strategically, and also knowing what other talent needs to know about (having sufficient knowledge to be able to discharge the role of acting strategically).

The amount of knowledge that is needed about others' domains is always strongly contested. There is often considerable variation in the depth of knowledge about the business model within executive teams. Moreover, the currency of knowledge about various components of the business model is short-lived, as new environmental conditions mean that various components take on more or less importance.

In the ebb and flow of human interactions and real time talking that in practice represent the process of strategizing, the process of top team dialogue has long been known to require participant strategists to

> ... negotiate over and establish meanings, express cognitions, articulate their perceptions of the environment, and from this basis legitimate their individual and collective judgements ... knowledge, know-how and expertise must be expressed in some way ... and made to count ... It is through speaking these forms of knowledge, the competitive landscape and possibilities for one's own organisation are made sense of and realized.[42]

The characteristics of effective strategy talk

Six characteristics of effective "strategy talk" – this process of projecting a viable sense of the "organization" into the future – have been identified.[43] Two types of skill – and knowing how and when to use these skills – become central:

1. Rhetorical skills include the ability to speak appropriate forms of (business model) knowledge, and this required an ability to project a sense of "knowing how to" question and query – for example, as in a courtroom drama, knowing how to gloss, let pass, or question – and also a sense of "knowing of" key elements of the business model. Talented managers know how to deploy metaphors and put history to work.

2. Relational skills included the ability to mitigate and avoid social collisions (called observing the moral order of what is right and wrong and good and bad). Making such judgments of course requires considerable socialization into the nature of previous dialogue, the ability to display appropriate emotion, and challenging the way that fellow strategists interpret the business world, as "strategy talk" often attacks their identities.

To summarize, HR Directors need to "manage the knowledge of talent." Their ability to do this, or not, has important implications for the role of their HR functions.

1.6. Thinking more broadly about value

They also need to think more broadly about their value. For organizations that undergo business model change, the implications for *Leading HR* are often fundamental. As the previous section has made clear, the *relationship between* the various components of any one business model has become ever-more complex, and the *dependency of this strategic performance upon effective implementation and people management* has become all the more crucial. A central task for HR

Directors is to identify how they as a leader, and how their function's own delivery model, structure, and the people processes it manages, add value during periods of business model change.

In order for organizations to make their models work, they have to understand the potentially deep implications they have for people management. People management experts have to make sure that those engineering the new business models are working on assumptions that can reasonably be executed.

Even if their own organization's models are not (yet) changing, HR Directors need to prepare their workforce to compete with competitors whose models have changed. Facing competitors from different sectors, their own organizations may still face deep changes in systems, work practices, and the mindset of managers and employees alike.

There is another problem. All functions use the phrase "adding value" with a degree of abandon for themselves, or chastisement for other functions. The truth is, value is looked at and thought about in narrow terms. Value may well have become, in the words of Dave Ulrich and Wayne Brockbank, "the bellwether for HR." In their book *The HR Value Proposition* they pointed out the function's value remains very much in the eye of the receivers not the givers of HR services.[44] We need to understand that the word "value" in this case does not *necessarily* relate to any intrinsic economic value, but is more a product of *peer perceptions* – the things that peer functions would expect to see being done by the function.

However, business model change is the great leveler. HR has to go beyond just *being seen* to add value. It must actually do it, and in this regard, line managers are not always the best judges. Why do we say this? Not just to be provocative. The truth is that line managers too may not be adding value, or may not have understood how value is created, especially in the context of a new business model. Moreover, deep strategic and operational insight from within the HR function is just the starting point. Given the uniqueness of this knowledge and the need often to operate across partners, bespoke HR structures may be the best way of meeting business needs.

So although both practitioners and the academic literature use the term *value creation* with abandon, in practice this term too is still a little-understood concept. In reviewing work that has been carried out on the concept, Dave Lepak, Ken Smith, and Susan Taylor[45] concluded that there is still much work to be done:

> . . . value creation is a central concept in the management and organisation literature . . . yet there is little consensus on what value creation is or how it can be achieved . . . while one would be hard pressed to find a management scholar who would disagree that value creation is important, one also would find it equally difficult to find agreement among such scholars regarding what value creation is, the process by which value is created, and the mechanisms that allow the creator of value to capture that value.

Beyond theoretical discussion, and the provision of some descriptive case studies, there has been little examination of the linkage between business models and HR.

Figure 1.1 draws attention to some of the language that we shall use throughout this book – language that enables HR Directors to demonstrate HR's

Figure 1.1: The Three Dimensions of HR Value

Ensuring organization has ability to build and acquire talent, develop the value proposition inherent in the business model (BM). Requires: understanding new capabilities central to the BM; manage immediate and sustained talent challenges; and develop performance-driven HR processes (innovation, service, efficiency, or effectiveness)

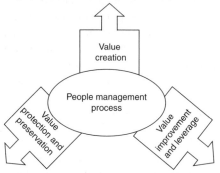

Ensuring value created does not get lost. Requires: design and maintenance of effective governance processes; constructive surfacing of risks inherent in BM and appropriate mitigation strategies; strong reputation across range of stakeholders; and ability to retain best capabilities

Enhancing BM as it develops; learning how best to execute strategy. Requires: HR function involved in transferring knowledge; know how to optimize policies and practices; manage learning from change and execution process; and multiple structural channels to ensure engagement of the business with these issues

© Paul Sparrow, 2009

contribution to the business and its functioning, or more specifically how it contributes to value inside the organization. We believe that the HR's value contribution is evidenced in three ways.

Articulating how HR contributes to the creation, improvement, and leveraging of value through the reconfiguration of business model change in our view represents the central challenge to today's HR executives.

To understand what becomes important in *Leading HR*, therefore, we need to examine the sorts of capabilities that come to the fore in being able to actually deliver on strategic change. The current academic consensus is that the implementation or execution of strategy is as important as, if not more important than, the formulation of strategy. Mark Huselid and Brian Becker[46] acknowledge that

> ... the challenge is to operationalise the process of strategy implementation within Strategic HRM theory.

They cite the work of Richard Priem and John Butler to argue that what is now needed is an examination of "the specific mechanisms purported to generate competitive advantage."[47] This is a challenge we pick up throughout this book.

1.7. Structure of the book

Our first challenge was to work with HR Directors and to lay out what, for them, should be the agenda for performance-Led HR. From 2006 to 2007 we worked with our HR Directors to define what is implied by the concept of performance-led HR. We identified seven areas that we jointly believe define the current HR agenda (see Figure 1.2):

1. Strategic competence and business model change
2. Boardroom engagement
3. Performance drivers and Organization Design
4. The engagement–performance link
5. Changing the way that talent is managed
6. Evaluating and benchmarking the ways in which people improve the capital of an organization
7. HR trajectories: coping with the changing technology and ways in which HR services can be resourced

Together the themes introduced in this chapter help define what, at the level of organizations, performance-led HR requires. To be effective, organizations need to master a range of areas. This book is intended to enhance our understanding of what these areas must be.

Much of the book is turned over to the HR Directors that we have worked with on this project. We have been keen as academics not just to impose our ideas about *Leading HR* onto their agenda. A key priority has been to co-work and

Figure 1.2: Performance-led HR

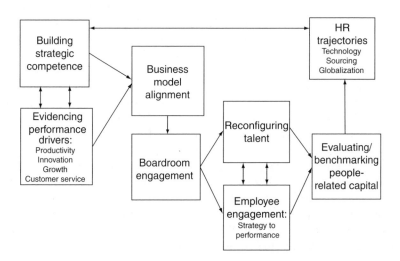

co-write with leading practitioners of HR. We draw upon experiences at organizations such as Vodafone, McDonald's, Nestlé, British Aerospace Systems, Co-operative Financial Services, and NG Bailey; each chapter is based on what the HR Directors of these organizations see as their primary strategic issue.

We have organized the book into 13 chapters to capture this learning. This opening chapter has laid out the agenda for *Leading HR*. Chapter 2 examines just how pertinent the issue of business model change is for HR drawing upon our qualitative work with HR professionals. It also raises questions about HR structures and reviews the current experience that organizations face with regard to their delivery models. HR has to reverse its thought process. The field of HR has concentrated on trying to identify practices that might lead to performance, using an organizational model of transformational, transactional, and business partnering HR as its starting point. Such a solution is likely too simple in the face of the strategic complexity that we outlined throughout this chapter.

Jumping to off-the-shelf structures on the assumption that they will fit the challenge of business model change can be dangerous. HR needs to adopt an outside-in, not an inside-out, approach to structure and avoid hard-wiring in generic models. There no one-size-fits-all structure or line of best fit be used to combine business strategy, model and HR, as the daily challenges faced by organizations are highly contingent on the contexts in which they operate.

These issues are picked up in Chapters 3, 4, and 5. Chapter 3 uses experiences at Nestlé to explore how thinking about HR delivery systems continues to develop. Chapter 4 addresses the issue of HR agendas in the context of business model change based upon some of our case study work and shows the different political and business challenges faced. An example of business model change is presented in Chapter 5 using experiences at NG Bailey.

These chapters make it clear that people management needs to start by looking at the important performance outcomes that its customers expect and design people management inside the organization in ways that deliver this. Only then might specific policies and practices be evidenced as being important. The performance outcomes that matter are innovation and growth in the business, world-class productivity and efficiency, and customer service levels that deliver sustained profitability and sustained brand value.

It is also the building of organization reputation and the mitigation of risk that drive the attention of senior managers. So in addition to discussion of business models and complex HR transformations, we need to develop an understanding of HR leadership as it relates to enabling business model change. Chapter 6 uses the metaphor of a Golden Triangle to explain how HR Directors have to serve many stakeholders and bring together competing interests. It is only through their leadership that they can bring these issues to the attention of the highest level of an organization. The chapter addresses the issue of strategic relationships for the HR Director, in particular the relationship between themselves, the CEO, and the CFO.

Chapter 7 then picks up the thorny question about the assessment of senior HR talent, using experiences at BAE Systems. Reconfiguring the management of talent is a crucial process. How we assess talent – what we focus on – also depends on how we view performance. There are several people-related forms of capital that contribute to performance – human capital, social and political capital, intellectual capital, customer capital, and so forth. Systems have to be designed in ways that recognize and manage all these forms of capital. Talent provides the leadership through which employees can be engaged, and engaged employees provide the opportunity for talent to blossom. Another important aspect of performance-led HR clearly has to concern the notion of talent – which can be defined in broad or narrow terms. It is often the business partners and others who have to map the talent of the organization, identify its contribution to key emergent strategic levers, and then hold talented people accountable for deliverables that serve both long-term and short-term performance across the business.

Two final injections of knowledge are then provided to help build further insight into the nature of strategic capability. Chapter 8 argues that organization design has become a lynchpin capability. The role for HR is to understand how best to match the individual capabilities needed to lead businesses through turbulent times, with the most appropriate organization designs that can then protect this capability. You cannot separate out the need to have competent leadership that has the ability to demonstrate thought leadership, from the need to also build the sorts of organizational designs that facilitate this competence.

Chapter 9 addresses the complex issues of linking employee engagement to organizational performance. In addition to keeping the HR function engaged with such complex business transformations, the workforce too needs engaging. Historically, the two key HR contributions would have been called competence and commitment, but in the complex business environment of today the terminology – and the nature of the HR intervention – has shifted. One of the most challenging issues today is that of employee engagement, and the question of whether or not there is robust evidence for the often-assumed link between engagement, service, and profit. Just about everybody measures engagement and the concept is seen as a universally good thing. But how does engagement drive workforce productivity and what tools and techniques can we use to identify its impact, if any? Do the returns match the investment in engagement? What is the psychology behind engagement processes?

The book then moves on to address a series of key HR capabilities that have to be built in order to establish a *Leading HR* function. Chapters 10–12 focus on a range of strategies necessary to handle the following issues: linking ethics, employee engagement, and brand (drawing upon experiences at Co-operative Financial Services); moving from the management of corporate reputation through a model of trust-based HR (drawing upon experiences at McDonald's); and creating an HR architecture for sustainable employee engagement (drawing upon experiences at Vodafone). These chapters bring together the actions and perspectives of the key players involved in the HR strategy. Chapter 13 pulls together the key messages from the book about *Leading HR*.

The book helps unravel how these various issues should best be managed inside organizations. The chapters tell a consistent narrative, and have been written sequenced as such. The story is not a simple one, but there is a consistent thread through it. This thread has to be followed to the end, and is an important one to grasp for those interested in the future of HR.

To help reveal this thread, each chapter summarizes the key themes as follows. To break the narrative down into more easily digestible "headlines," *each* of the themes is represented in *three* ways, that is, as a

1. series of headline issues that invite the reader to reflect on their own situation and attitude to that particular area of HR work;

2. set of strategic imperatives that represent the theme in a few sentences – why we believe the theme to be important, and what issue it raises about the HR agenda; and

3. number of "must-win" battles for HR, which represent our own conclusion about the theme of the chapter.

NOTES

1 Sparrow, P.R., Hesketh, A., Hird, M., Marsh, C. and Balain, S. (2008) *Reversing the Arrow: Using Business Model Change to Tie HR into Strategy.* Centre for Performance-Led HR White Paper 08/01. Lancaster University Management School.

2 John Sullivan famously asked this question of Enron in 2002, along with many articles in the popular press such as Gladwell, M. (2002). The talent myth. *The Times*, 20 August, pp. 2–4.

3 D'Avini, R.A.I. (1994) *Hypercompetition.* New York: Free Press.

4 Hodgkinson, G. and Sparrow, P.R. (2002) *The Competent Organisation: A Psychological Analysis of the Strategic Management Process.* Buckingham: Open University Press.

5 Ibid., p. 3.

6 Pfeffer, J. (2005) Changing mental models: HR's most important task. *Human Resource Management*, 44 (2), 123–128.

7 Ibid., p. 124.

8 Ibid., p. 125.

9 Pohle, G. and Chapman, M. (2006) IBM's global CEO Report 2006: Business model innovation matters. *Strategy and Leadership*, 34 (5): 34–40.

10 Shafer, S.M., Smith, H.J. and Linder, J.C. (2005) The power of business models. *Business Horizons*, 48: 199–207.

11 Schweizer, L. (2005) Concept and evolution of business models. *Journal of General Management*, 31 (2): 37–56.

12 *The Economist* (2007) Something new under the sun: A special report on innovation. 13 October. *The Economist*, 385 (8550): 7–8.

13 This view has been expressed by the OECD, Booz, Boston Consulting Group, and the McKinsey Global Institute.

14 *The Economist* (2007).

15 Johnson, G., Melin, L. and Whittington, R. (2003) Micro strategy and strategizing: Towards an activity-based view. *Journal of Management Studies*, 40 (1): 3–23.

16 See: Porter, M.E. (1980) *Competitive Strategy: Techniques for Analyzing Industries and Competitors.* New York: The Free Press; Porter, M.E. (1985) *Competitive Advantage: Creating and Sustaining Superior Performance.* New York: The Free Press; Mintzberg, H., Ahlstrand, B. and Lampel, J. (1998) *Strategy Safari.* Harlow: Prentice Hall; Barney, J. (1991) Firm resources and sustained competitive advantage. *Journal of Management,* 17 (1): 99–120; Prahalad, C.K. and Hamel, G. (1990) The core competence of the organisation. *Harvard Business Review,* 68 (3): 79–91.

17 See: Magretta, J. (2002) Why business models matter. *Harvard Business Review,* 80 (5): 86–93; Schweizer, L. (2005) Concept and evolution of business models. *Journal of General Management,* 31 (2): 37–56.

18 Henry, A. (2007) *Understanding Strategic Management.* Oxford: Oxford University Press.

19 Schweizer, L. (2005).

20 Kay, J. (1993) *Foundations of Corporate Success.* Oxford: Oxford University Press.

21 Hamel, G. and Prahalad, C.K. (1993) Strategy as stretch and leverage. *Harvard Business Review,* 71 (2): 75–84.

22 See: Venkatraman, N. and Henderson, J.C. (1998) Real strategies for virtual organizing. *Sloan Management Review,* 40 (1): 33–48; Teece, D.J. (1998) Capturing value from knowledge assets: The new economy, markets for know-how, and intangible assets. *California Management Review,* 40 (3): 55–79; Teece, D.J. (2000) *Managing Intellectual Capital: Organisational, Strategic, and Policy Dimensions.* Oxford: Oxford University Press; and Hamel, G. (2000) *Leading the Revolution.* Boston: Harvard Business School Press.

23 Chesbrough, H.W. (2007) Why companies should have open business models. *Sloan Management Review,* 48 (2): 22–28.

24 Froud, J., Johal, S., Leaver, A., Phillips, R. and Williams, K. (2009) Stressed by choice: A business model analysis of the BBC. *British Journal of Management,* 20: 252–264, p. 254.

25 Yip, G.S. (2004) Using strategy to change your business model. *Business Strategy Review,* 15 (2): 17–24.

26 Ibid.

27 Christensen, C.M. (1997) *The Innovator's Dilemma: When New Technologies Cause Great Firms to Fail.* Boston, MA: Harvard Business School Press; Christensen, C.M., Roth, E.A. and Anthony, S.D. (2004) *Seeing What Is Next: Using Theories of Innovation too Predict Industry Change.* Boston, MA: Harvard Business School Press.

28 IBM Global Services (2006) *Business Model Innovation: The New Route to Competitive Advantage.* Somers, NY: IBM plc.

29 Ibid., p. 6.

30 *The Economist* (2007).

31 Johnson, M.W., Christensen, C.M. and Kagermann, H. (2008) Reinventing your business model. *Harvard Business Review,* December, 51–59.

32 Ibid.

33 Magretta, J. (2002).

34 Morris, M., Schindehutte, M., Richardson, J. and Allen, J. (2006).

35 Amit, R. and Zott, C. (2001) Value creation in e-business. *Strategic Management Journal*, 22: 493–520.

36 Zott, C. and Amit, R. (2007) Business model design and the performance of entrepreneurial firms. *Organisation Science*, 18 (2): 181.

37 Hamel, G. (2000).

38 Timmers, P. (1998) Business models for electronic markets. *Electronic Markets*, 8 (2): 3–8.

39 Voelpel, S., Leibold, M., Tekie, E. and von Krogh, G. (2005) Escaping the red queen effect in competitive strategy: Sense-testing business models. *European Management Journal*, 23 (1): 37–49.

40 Storey, J. and Salaman, G. (2005). The knowledge work of general managers. *Journal of General Management*, 31 (2): 57–73, p. 70.

41 Ibid., p. 60.

42 Samra-Fredericks, D. (2003). Strategising as lived experience and strategists' everyday efforts to shape strategic direction. *Journal of Management Studies*, 40 (1): 141–174, p. 143.

43 Storey and Salaman (2005).

44 Ulrich, D. and Brockbank, W. (2005) *The HR Value Proposition*. Boston, MA: Harvard Business School Press.

45 Lepak, D.P., Smith, K.G. and Taylor, M.S. (2007) Value creation and value capture: A multilevel perspective. *Academy of Management Review*, 32 (1): 180–194, p. 180.

46 Becker, B.E. and Huselid, M.A. (2006), p. 901.

47 Priem, R.L. and Butler, J.E. (2001) Is the resource-based "view" a useful perspective for strategic management research?. *Academy of Management Review*, 26 (1): 22–40, p. 34.

CHAPTER 2

HR Structures: Are They Working?

MARTIN HIRD, PAUL SPARROW, AND CRAIG MARSH

2.1. Introduction

In this chapter we examine the nature of HR structures and delivery models. Throughout the book it is argued that HR should start with the organization's business model and reverse engineer what this means for the most appropriate structure, rather than start with structure and shoe-horn it into business strategy. However, in order to set the case up for such an argument, paradoxically, we have to start with a discussion of the challenges surrounding structure before moving on to business strategy and business models in Chapter 4. So, with regard to HR structures, what is the headline issue, the strategic imperative, and the must-win battle?

HR structures

Headline issue:

There exists the strong possibility that some HR leaders have made an over-simplistic interpretation of their delivery models and the power of structure alone to achieve strategic influence. Have those responsible for *Leading HR* learned how to operate their delivery model and embed it in an appropriate structure? Are their structures efficient enough to give them a clear line of sight to deal with the question of added-value? If internal players perceive that structures create too much "background noise," will the route to end-user (customer-perceived) added value be blocked?

Strategic imperative:

HR's strategic role begins with designing this unique HR architecture and then emphasizing and reinforcing the implementation of the organization's strategy through it relentlessly.

HR needs to resolve whether the specifics of the structure are inappropriate to the organization's need and in need of refining.

Have other motivations (such as cost cutting and work simplification) hijacked or distorted otherwise well-intentioned HR-structure change projects?

Has the quality of HR professionals been found wanting, in terms of the demands the model makes upon them?

HR Structures: (Continued)

Is the surrounding culture of the organization that has to receive the model non-accepting of change?

Must-win battle:

The real skill is in aligning and balancing how the three main legs of the HR delivery model (or more recent 5-Box models) are integrated with each other, understanding how this logic operates beyond the formal structure, and that the function needs a very good business-minded HR team to design a structure that truly reflects the needs of the business model and the line managers within that model.

We argue that

The key messages that emerge from this chapter

1) Existing HR thinking – dominated recently by Ulrich's views on delivery models – has helped the function think about the structures (how HR should organize its processes) and role changes associated with a separation out into transactional work, HR business partners, and centers of expertise/excellence. It has also helped change HR from a process-specific function into a business with its own Profit and Loss and concomitant transparency and ROI visibility.

2) However, it is not easy to locate the origin of the now-famous "three-legged stool" of HR structure. There has been a substantial degree of interpretation of Ulrich's original ideas into the "structures" now commonly implemented by HR units.

3) The trend in HR publications in the last 3 years or so, backed up by our own research, is that an Ulrich 3-Box model does not always work. The challenge of optimally synchronizing the three parts becomes a complex management issue.

4) This is not a criticism of the work of Ulrich. It is more useful to explore what is going on. Rather, the concern is with regard to capability – a lack of business acumen within HR, the upskilling potential of the HR team, its level of cultural insight, and relational skills.

5) We bring the issues down to three problems in execution. These concern the existence still of signs of structural deficiency, not enough attention to the need to embed the structure in surrounding networks, and a lack of insight often into the definition of what a center of excellence should really be.

6) A number of issues have remained consistent over time in relation to HR business partners – difficulties that are not eased through the luxury of learning. By far the most difficult issue with HR business partners is the question of capability, followed by managing expectations.

7) Centers of expertise or excellence still face problems of resource alignment, instability in demand for expertise, and communication problems with other elements of the HR

delivery model. The quality of expertise remains a perennial issue, as does maintaining an appropriate blend of knowledge in the centers between generalist skills and specific business model insight.

8) Within HR service centers, the issue of provider performance (reliability, skills levels, insight into business culture, and quality of communication) has become more prevalent. User behavior, quality assurance, and service responsiveness also continue to present problems.

9) The HR Director has to understand how the HR Delivery Model is underpinned by effective relationships, networks, and influence – both within and outside of the HR function. How will the balance of relationships between the three main components of the HR structure be optimized and carefully maintained?

Mark Huselid, Brian Becker, and Dave Ulrich in their classic book *The HR Scorecard*[1] use the label of an "HR architecture" to explain how HR has to be delivered. They define this architecture as

> ... the systems, practices, competencies, and employee performance behaviours that reflect the development and management of the firm's strategic human capital.[2]

As such, this architecture is seen as a unique combination of the HR function's structure and delivery model, the HR practices and system, and the strategic employee behaviors that these create. It is argued that HR's strategic role begins with designing this unique HR architecture and then emphasizing and reinforcing the implementation of the organization's strategy through it relentlessly. The infrastructure, system, and organization of this HR architecture need to be aligned consistently – and it is this alignment which raises the importance they argue of a holistic set of metrics.

The architectural metaphor

This has been used by several US writers including Brian Becker, Barry Gerhart, Mark Huselid, Dave Lepak, Scott Snell, and Pat Wright to highlight the locus of *value creation* in Strategic HRM. There is an organizational system that is reflected in the HR architecture, and it is the whole system that creates value. Questions have been asked as to which part of the system is most valuable. Is it the resulting workforce skills and competencies, the levels of employee commitment and engagement that it produces, or the nature of employee performance? Mark Huselid and Brian Becker argue that it is the HR system that is the most important strategic asset. This is seen as a source of value creation in the subsequent outcomes from the whole of the HR architecture. The system is also harder to imitate, especially in terms of how it is aligned with the organization's strategy (see the resource-based view of the firm in Chapter 1).

However, the metaphor of HR architecture is often misused. For example, in the United Kingdom, a recent report by the CIPD[3] uses the term "HR architecture" solely to refer to the HR delivery model and the adoption of Dave Ulrich's 3-Box Model (discussed in this chapter and the next). As we shall argue in this chapter, many then go on to reduce the outline of appropriate delivery channels for HR services still further into the structural solution that tends to be associated with it.

2.2. A brief history of ideas

There is an intriguing paradox when we consider the debates about how HR should best structure itself to deliver organizational value. On the one hand, it is unlikely that there is a function that has been more dominated by the theories of one individual, such is the influence of Dave Ulrich on HR departments over the last 15 years. On the other hand, the trend in HR publications in the last 3 years or so – backed up, it seems, by research, including our own – is that "it doesn't always work." Although it has been argued by Ulrich himself that the key to success in HR is managing paradoxes,[4] our feeling is that – given the continued impetus toward implementing the Ulrich 3-Box Model – this particular paradox needs further exploration.

It is approaching a truism to say that Ulrich has added substantial value to the function since the publication in 1997 of his (first) seminal book *Human Resource Champions*. Ulrich himself has gone on record recently to state that the structures being implemented by HR based on his work are not actually "his idea" at all, but an interpretation of his writing, including the much-vaunted "three box model" (or "three-legged stool" as another well-known tag). Rather, we intend to assess the level of comfort with existing structures and attempts to reconfigure HR operations. We believe, however, that Ulrich's work now needs to be augmented by a better understanding of the management of structural implementation. We need to understand how effective HR functions have made this model work, and where issues are still being faced, what appears to explain them. Our approach can be summarized by asking "what is going on, why is it happening, and what must organizations learn from this?"

Curiously, for such a dominant concept in the HR function, it is not easy to locate the origin of the now-famous "three-legged stool" of HR structure. The earliest reference that we have discovered originates – not surprisingly, perhaps – from an HR consultancy firm, Mercer, dating from 1999 – 2 years after the publication of HR Champions. The article in *HR Magazine* was describing the evolution of HR departments away from functions to a "team-based model." The article claimed that about 80 per cent of businesses today have a mix of the traditional and three-legged stool models.[5]

The basics of the Ulrich model that it – and most other practitioner discussion – laid out is shown in Figure 2.1. These principles have now become a general mantra. At the model's heart lies a set of HR professionals, embedded within line businesses and working on processes and outcomes central to competitive success. They are supported by both efficient processes to handle the

Figure 2.1: The Ulrich 3-Box model

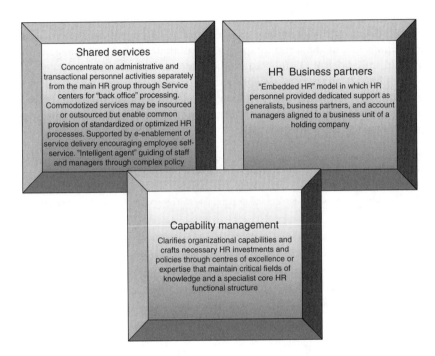

Shared services

Concentrate on administrative and transactional personnel activities separately from the main HR group through Service centers for "back office" processing. Commodotized services may be insourced or outsourced but enable common provision of standardized or optimized HR processes. Supported by e-enablement of service delivery encouraging employee self-service. "Intelligent agent" guiding of staff and managers through complex policy

HR Business partners

"Embedded HR" model in which HR personnel provided dedicated support as generalists, business partners, and account managers aligned to a business unit of a holding company

Capability management

Clarifies organizational capabilities and crafts necessary HR investments and policies through centres of excellence or expertise that maintain critical fields of knowledge and a specialist core HR functional structure

more transactional aspects of HR work. More strategically orientated expert HR knowledge is handled by functional expertise or Center of Excellence (COE) structures.

This way of segmenting work into three broad groupings of activity is based on a formula that can be, and has been, applied to several other service functions beyond HR at a macro level (IT and finance being obvious examples).

In practice, however, we shall argue that the challenge of optimally synchronizing the three parts becomes a complex management issue. Although Ulrich has moved beyond this 3-Box model, in practice most HR functions have not and are still trying to execute the base model. Some organizations therefore seem to be more effective than others at transforming their HR structures and making them work effectively.

Why is this? We argue that when practitioners have to match the model to the more micro-level decisions associated with the peculiarities and idiosyncratic nature of their particular business (a "the devil is in the detail" argument), it is essential that they apply the model with sufficient clarity allied to effective processes and a high-quality HR team. If implementation has been difficult or problematic – and we argue in this chapter this appears to be the case – then there are a number of deeper questions that should now be asked. Implementation of a particular type of structure in HR is no exception. We argue later in the chapter that HR Directors need to be sure that their implemented structure

1. avoids any symptoms of "structural deficiency,"
2. shows "structural embeddedness."

In order to draw attention to these questions, we first lay out a range of provocative observations that might currently apply. Some of these critical views suggest potential limitations of HR functions, others draw attention to the impact of difficult contexts on the execution of structural change, yet others suggest that there have been too simple interpretations about how structures work and that there are some important and too-easily ignored issues of implicit operating logics, power, influence, and embeddedness.

Possible causes of dissonance in HR delivery models: Is it that . . .

1. The specifics of the design are inappropriate to the organization's need and require refining?

2. The architect's plans have simply been misread and misunderstood?

3. Other motivations (such as cost cutting and work simplification) have hijacked or distorted otherwise well-intentioned HR-structure change projects?

4. The quality of the human resource (HR professionals!) has been found wanting, in terms of the demands the model makes upon them?

5. The surrounding culture of the organization that has to receive the model is non-accepting of change?

6. Client/line managers may not be receptive to a strategic business partner philosophy?

7. Linked to the previous point, client/line managers may not be ready and prepared to make the adaptation to their own responsibilities, in terms of people, that are frequently a requisite part of implementing HR structure change?

We return to these potential alternatives at the end of the chapter. But why must we still ask these questions about current HR structures?

It is common in contemporary organizations, and specifically in HR functions, to accept received wisdom about how things should be done as though that wisdom has been handed down to the recipients on tablets of stone. These tablets, commonly known as "best practice," are reinforced by management texts and consultancy material, and often receive minimal critical reflection regarding their validity and origins. Little time may be spent on considering alternative possibilities. Busy managers, under pressure, look for the "quick fix" that can have an instant impact, especially in difficult economic circumstances. HR, as a function, seems more prone to this than most, possibly due to a "chip on the shoulder" about their role and value to organizations and the relatively short window of time open to them to prove this case.

We believe this to be a risk, as it results in poor value-added solutions, which in turn damages long-term competitive advantage (after all, returning to the theoretical discussion about unique resources that act as competitive resources, where is the "edge" in an organization's HR delivery systems if everyone else is doing the same thing?).

The counterargument to this from Ulrich would be as follows: the structure and the delivery model are merely enablers. It is what the delivery model enables HR to do as perceived by customers that adds the value.

In discussions with us,[6] he expresses the view that HR can and should deliver value, as much or more in tough times as in good. HR delivering value is not about what HR needs to do to be credible, but about what line managers want from HR. HR work, when done well, can deliver value to employees, customers, investors, and communities. He also believes that HR being organized like a professional services firm is not a new organization design, but is new in its application to HR. This organization design does not make sense in all settings, and it should be aligned to the way the business is organized. Having the design right and doing it are two very different things. With this view we have no significant points of difference.

But what we do believe needs to be asked is this: what if the challenges of implementation prove to be more complex than anticipated? What if, in an attempt not to appear too inward-looking, HR functions ignore some difficult issues and then find that they do not go away? What if the need to attend to these issues sucks away all the energy that was intended to be spent on adding value?

This is why we begin the chapter with a brief survey of the origins of some of the most common current practices in structuring HR units. We do this in the belief that a demonstration of the history of an idea can, to an extent, demystify it, help us understand it more profoundly, and show that alternatives are possible. Once following this line of thought, it becomes clear that the practice itself may not be the real problem.

The phrase "from doing to delivering" – now almost a mantra in terms of perceptions of Ulrich's early work – best sums up his contribution. First introduced widely in 1997 in the *HR Champions* book, he has used it consistently and regularly since. As recently as 2008 he is still quoted as saying "For HR professionals to contribute in the future they must add value now. This means focusing less on what HR does and more on what HR delivers and to whom."[7]

This notion was the "big idea" in the mid-1990s when thought leadership in HR focused upon two interlinked issues:

1. "Can we abolish the HR function?" And the response to this question:

2. "HR needs to be more strategic."

The "doing to delivering" argument

This can be summarized as follows: HR units have, to this point, concentrated too much on being expert in particular areas – recruitment, staffing, reward, communication, organization development, employee relations, and so on – in other words, activities. What HR needed to focus on instead were the results of HR activities, the valued outcomes that

> **The "doing to delivering" argument: (Continued)**
>
> improved the business bottom line. There were four general categories of these "deliverables" defined by Ulrich:
>
> 1. strategy execution,
> 2. administrative efficiency,
> 3. employee contribution, and
> 4. capacity for change.

How did these "value" outcomes for HR map onto a new type of structure? In the original book, Ulrich applied the concept of "business partner" to all four areas, which became the four "roles" of HR. So, the administrative expert role would be a business partner, for example, because they "save their business money through the more efficient design and delivery of HR systems."[8] He also states that

> ...HR professionals have mistakenly defined business partnership as taking place exclusively in the strategic arena, not recognising the importance of with, and for, employee contribution.[9]

In the discussion of the role of "strategic partner," the concept of "business partner" is never mentioned. In his seminal book *Human Resource Champions*, Ulrich did *not* attempt to define how HR ought to structure itself to deliver the four value outcomes; this was clearly not his intention, and until recently, never has been. Instead, he restricted himself to describing, with the use of examples, how value *could be delivered* by HR.

Ideas get co-opted. To illustrate the extent of this, here is a quotation from the CIPD website on "what is HR Business Partnering" (revised in October 2008):

> ...The concept of business partnering emerged in the mid 1990s. It was one of a number of key HR roles proposed by Dave Ulrich necessary for HR to transform itself into a "value adding" function. In his initial work, *Human Resource Champions*, Ulrich referred to the role as that of "Strategic Partner".[10]

This is at best misleading; at worst, simply not true. There has, therefore, clearly been a substantial degree of interpretation of Ulrich's original ideas into the "structures" now commonly implemented by HR units.

HR delivery systems, and in particular the "three box model" – or "Ulrich's model" by inaccurate association – have come under fire in the popular HR press. Despite very significant levels of adoption of the model, as shown above, criticism has been along two dimensions:

1. We risk fragmenting or distancing HR from the line.
2. Some key elements of the model are not delivering the value expected of them.

In relation to the first charge, first leveled back in 2003, Lynda Gratton wrote:[11]

> ...during the past decade we have fragmented the roles and responsibilities of the function. We have outsourced the lower value, operational work, and we are

beginning to develop the staff profiling work that will enable us to act as "employee champions". We are also putting the "change agent" roles back into the streams of business to work closely with their line manager partners. Meanwhile the "business partners" are either going into the businesses or clustered around "best practice" centres, which may be located in different places ... this fragmentation of the HR function is causing all sorts of unintended problems. Senior managers look at the fragments and are not clear how the function as a whole adds value

Moreover, it seems clear that there are difficulties being experienced in implementing an Ulrich model. Ulrich and Brockbank note that this research suggests that partial success (and they feel even such a statement can be overstated) is mostly attributed to "the implementation rather than the fault of the model per se"[12] and that a survey that finds that (only) 26 per cent of HR managers reported that HR business partnering was not proving successful in their organizations means that "headlines suggesting HR business partnering is failing based on these findings is inaccurate and does the HR field no great service." We would concur with this observation, but we are not quite so sanguine about the consequence of implementation difficulties. The implementation problem might not remain a static and background phenomenon – it depends on whether such proportions are likely to increase or not.

The partial success arguments leveled against the Ulrich HR delivery model

A summary of the findings of recent more critical reports on HR Delivery Models concludes that the following are issues which commonly lead to partial success:

1. an "off-the-shelf" introduction of a new HR structure without careful thought as to how the model fits the organizations' requirements;

2. a lack of care in dealing with the boundary issues between elements of the HR structure which can easily become fragmented;

3. a lack of attention to the new skill sets needed by business partners to ensure they can play at the strategic level;

4. a lack of understanding on the part of line managers as to the value of a new HR structure;

5. a lack of skill on the part of line managers to make the required shift to greater responsibility for people issues entailed by the new model; and

6. what is referred to as the "polo" problem:[13] a lack of provision of the execution of HR services, as the business partner shifts to strategic work, and the center of expertise to an advisory role.

It seems both likely and possible, therefore, that the interpretation of Ulrich's original ideas was developed by consultancies marketing new structural possibilities to HR departments, with those consultancies looking to package their offerings/solutions into something easily implemented on the ground, and the client HR departments looking for a quick fix to show that they were reacting to "the move to strategy." Internal reorganization of the function and the attraction of a major cost reduction in administrative overheads are the two ways of showing responsiveness. They are also comparatively easier to sell to hard-pressed Boards than actually, or necessarily, delivering a better and more strategic HR service. This is especially true where the latter involves the line changing their attitude to HR, which is a much more difficult proposition. As one recent commentator has expressed it:

> Shared services, centres of expertise and business partners are too often erroneously referred to as "structure". They are actually delivery channels and they should occur only as a consequence of changes in the HR . . . value proposition.[14]

2.3. HR structures: Finding the devil in the detail

So are HR functions missing a trick if they just focus on executing the structural changes associated with an "Ulrich" model? We believe so. To support this view we move onto an analysis of our data based upon a survey of 128 HR Directors and senior HR practitioners in the United Kingdom, representing a wide range of organizations, with the data gathered from June to October 2008 and again in June 2009. The survey picks up many of the concepts associated with business model change outlined in Chapter 1. The question to consider is this: Do the symptoms that the study reveals constitute sufficient "background noise" – a sufficient level of distraction – to be classed as evidencing structural deficiency, as defined earlier in the chapter?

There was, as one might expect, a great deal of change going on, but in general, respondents indicated a relatively low level of understanding of the organization's business model among HR staff.

In 2008, 60 per cent of organizations were rethinking their value proposition, financial models, structures, and capabilities. Only 19 per cent had no change in the organizational capabilities that were needed. However, only 25 per cent of HR Directors believed that more than 3/5ths of their HR function had a deep understanding of the organization's strategy and business model. Similarly, only 21 per cent believed that more than 3/5ths of their HR function understood the line issues that were faced when making the components of the business fit together in the business model.

Key findings from the 2008 survey research:

1. 53 per cent of HR functions understand the organizational capabilities the business model requires.
2. 65 per cent have experienced internal HR transformations to a large extent.

3. 89 per cent feel (agree/strongly agree) that their HR structures need further refinement to truly add value.

4. Only 30 per cent believe their HR structures are flexible enough to meet any strategic challenge.

5. 41 per cent believe that they now have to deliver "joined up" HR across organizational boundaries.

6. Only 25 per cent believe that HR has helped develop learning about how best to execute strategy.

A number of reasons were forwarded for why recent developments in HR delivery models may have only had partial success.[15] Part of the problem undoubtedly concerns the level of churn in strategy and in business models (see Table 2.1). In 2008, 21 per cent of HR managers believed that their value proposition, financial model, organization structure, processes, and core capabilities were *all* in a state of continuous evolution. By 2009 this figure had risen to 31 per cent.

Table 2.1: Percentage of organizations experiencing significant or complete change in various elements of their business model

Element of Business Model Change	Percentage of organizations experiencing significant or complete change in 2008	Percentage of organizations experiencing significant or complete change in the economic downturn in 2009
The sorts of demands that customers make for value	61.5	63.3
Who your customers actually are, or how you segment them	25.7	16.6
Your value proposition for customers	42.9	36.6
Where costs are being incurred in your business/organization	38.2	73.3
How profits get generated	38.9	37.9
The pace at which new products or services have to be generated	52.6	48.2
The organizational capabilities featured in your strategic planning processes	48.1	58.6
Who the "corporate heroes" are (a shift in the jobs, roles, or skill groups now seen as critical to performance)?	35.5	40

Table 2.1: (Continued)

Element of Business Model Change	Percentage of organizations experiencing significant or complete change in 2008	Percentage of organizations experiencing significant or complete change in the economic downturn in 2009
The systems that you use to manage (business/organizational) performance	46.1	33.4
The organizational culture needed to deliver the business model	51.2	63.3

They are in varying stages of transforming their HR structures, but regardless of the stage, some key themes emerge. The issues faced with each "box" are shown below in Tables 2.2 (HR business partners), 2.3 (Centers of Expertise/Excellence), and 2.4 (Service Centers). Each table gives

1. the type of issue raised by the respondents;
2. the percentage of organizations raising that issue in (a) the 2008 survey, (b) the 2009 survey, and (c) combined over the 2 years;
3. some quotations from the survey illustrating the issue.

Table 2.2: Implementation issues with business partners

Business partner implementation issues	2008	2009	08/09
1. Capability: Upskilling, business acumen, cultural insight, and relational skills	*36%*	*31%*	*34%*

"Getting HRBPs to think 'business' first and 'HR' second"
"HRBPs are still operating reactively focused on today's problems not predicting and addressing tomorrow's challenges"
"Lack of skills required by the individuals placed in the roles from previous transactional positions within the team"
"BPs by title don't necessarily truly know how to operate at a strategic/change orientated level"

2. Expectations: Selling the proposition, education of the line, and line capability	*27%*	*24%*	*26%*

"Some real progress made to integrate HRBP as a true 'partner' with the business but still some areas who fail to recognise the benefits of this working model"
"line managers still want admin support and short term HR advice above all else. The most highly regarded HRBPs are those that provide this service effectively. What does this look like? – React immediately to the line manager's wishes, do most of the line manager's people management work (particularly paperwork) for him/her and ideally hold any difficult conversations with individuals on behalf of the line manager"
"Remote and Matrix operations require clear responsibility and good continuous communication. We need to improve both"

3. Resource alignment: Aligning to the business, role overload, and support to BPs	*14%*	*18%*	*15%*

"Has created a BP silo mentality within the HR function"
"Ensure consistency across all the business"
"Ensuring HRBPs have the right level of support to do their jobs effectively (e.g. systems, data, admin)"
"Too big a day job to do the business partner strategic & change aspect of the role"

4. Agenda alignment and regulation: Corporate versus business unit alignment, line manager decision-making mechanisms, and consistency of HR delivery	*11%*	*10%*	*10%*

"Due to the size of the largest part of the business the BPs are generally implementers of national initiatives/strategy rather than empowered to develop and implement strategic people plans that are particular to their unit"
"HRBP's required to operate at differing levels of complexity based upon the area of the business to which they may be aligned"
"Challenge to join up local initiatives with corporate ones – potential misalignment"
"Provision of HR advice and services across multi site environment"

5. Role drift: Reactive, operational, and residue of transactional work	*5%*	*15%*	*8%*

"Day to day caseload has not been separated from strategic BP role"
"How to stop HR BP's from 'going native' and aligning to local priorities"
"Strategic model for the BP role has been slow to materialise – too much low level involvement in basic HR queries"

6. Boundary Management: BP relationships with, and sequencing the introduction of service centers and COEs	*7%*	*2%*	*5%*

"Getting HRBPs to reach back into corporate HR or work with their counterparts – replication of effort"
"Who and how the central functions liaise with the specialist/centres of excellence areas"

7. Costs	*1%*	*2%*	*1%*

"Financial considerations by directors – cost of HR support comes off their bottom line"

Table 2.2 is based on 165 qualitative comments. A number of issues have remained consistent over time. This in itself is an important finding – it suggests enduring difficulties that are not eased through the luxury of learning. By far the most difficult issue with HR business partners is the question of capability, followed by managing expectations. Both these issues have become (only) slightly less prevalent in the last year. Problems of aligning resources and role overload have increased a little in this last year, as indeed too has the problem of role drift.

Table 2.3, examining implementation issues associated with Centers of Expertise/Excellence, is based on 86 qualitative comments. The last year has seen some strong changes in prevalence of implementation issues. Down in importance come problems of governance arrangements, role specification, and quality assurance, but up come problems of resource alignment, instability in demand for expertise, and communication with other elements of the HR delivery

Table 2.3: Implementation issues with COEs

Center of expertise/excellence implementation issues	2008	2009	08/09
1. Role Specification: Proposition and governance arrangements	*20%*	*13%*	*18%*

"Business to see that this is for the global benefit of the company and not their own silo"
"How you keep the centre of excellence areas close to the customers (commissioning the work and evaluating the service)"
"Accepting the centre of expertise holds the budget for the activity and that their area is not entitled to a certain percentage"
"I don't want to create an ivory tower again"
"To align the business strategy and the HR value proposition"

2. Availability of Expertise: Skill depth, business acumen	*17%*	*17%*	*17%*

"Lack of business acumen & insights"
"We are a small Dept and can't have the luxury that this is just your expertise. We need to cover other jobs and also be able to cover for sickness/leave"
"People capability – availability of deep experts"

3. Resource alignment: Costs associated with instability of expertise demand, when to use it, engaging with the services	*12%*	*27%*	*17%*

"Instability of demand when resources are internal"
"Getting people to use them rather than remote business partners or actioning themselves"

4. Quality assurance: Quality of services across business units and countries	*22%*	*3%*	*16%*

"Ensuring the same excellence is upheld when translated to other countries"
"Balancing global standards with local needs"
"Amalgamation of process between operating divisions"
"Ensuring centre can deliver to (high) expectations of business of a 'Centre of Excellence' "

5. Role drift: Local-central boundaries, COE versus local HRBP authorities	*10%*	*7%*	*9%*

"Interface between Experts and business partners is sometimes unclear"
"Over reliance of business partners on central expertise (e.g. ER skills and knowledge)"
"Some resistance to giving up local initiatives to be done by central team e.g. recruitment"
"Balancing the resources needed for " corporate" working versus specific functional needs"
"There is always tension between one standard practice and bespoke requests for every different business area"

6. Innovativeness: Level of proactivity and exploitation of knowledge	*8%*	*7%*	*8%*

"Creating a flexible model fit for an organisation of c.1000"
"Exploiting knowledge sharing across the organisation"

7. Communication: With other elements of the HR delivery model	*5%*	*10%*	*7%*
"Communication between other HR functions"			
8. Expertise blend: Maintenance of generalist HR and business model knowledge	*5%*	*7%*	*6%*
"Over reliance on staff who are deemed to be the 'experts'" "Tension between group wide centres of excellence and the need for business unit specific experts"			
9. Division of Labor: Within small teams	*2%*	*0%*	*1%*
"Division of labour expertise"			

model. The quality of expertise remains a perennial issue, as does maintaining an appropriate blend of knowledge in the centers between generalist skills and specific business model insight, and ensuring effective exploitation of the Centers' knowledge.

Table 2.4, examining implementation issues associated with Service Centers, is based on 122 qualitative comments. Some of the findings are quite stark. The issue of provider performance (reliability, skills levels, insight into business culture, and quality of communication) has shot up in prevalence – 50 per cent of reported implementation issues now concern this. User behavior, quality assurance, and service responsiveness continue to present problems. The issue of attractiveness to staff has become a little more important, whilst problems associated with the technology and systems performance or the optimization of HR processes have become less prevalent.

Table 2.4: Implementation issues with service centers

Service center implementation issues	2008	2009	08/09
1. Provider performance: reliability, skills levels, insight into business culture, and quality of communications	*27%*	*50%*	*34%*
"Constant errors due to lack of attention to detail" "Ownership/accountability vs following process" "Knowledge transfer in the relocation of service centres from one country to another" "Getting service centre staff to be fully conversant with a wide breadth of HR issues"			
2. Expectations: Points of entry, loss of face-to-face contact, and depersonalization of service	*15%*	*8%*	*12%*
"The standardisation required removes any move for the personal touch often favoured by line management" "The business needs to recognise the importance of managers managing people effectively and not divest itself of accountability"			

Table 2.4: (Continued)

Service center implementation issues	2008	2009	08/09
3. User behavior: Self service take up, narrow advice lines	*11%*	*8%*	*10%*
"Getting managers to use Service centre process, versus contacting somebody they know in the service centre via local network"			
4. Quality assurance: Service levels and fragmentation of service across business units and regions	*7%*	*13%*	*9%*
"Service centre provision fragmented across business units" "Uncertainty about level of service at regional locations" "Tracking and monitoring services required by our internal customers" "Getting excellence all the time"			
5. Staff attractiveness: Staff turnover and boring careers	*6%*	*13%*	*8%*
"HR team have a reluctance to take on only transactional work"			
6. Responsiveness: Needs met and speed of response	*6%*	*8%*	*7%*
"Loss of responsiveness to new/urgent issues (which looks like lack of commitment)" "Sometimes limited flexibility to act quickly & creatively"			
7. Technology and systems performance	*9%*	*3%*	*7%*
"To work successfully it is reliant on a good HRIS system"			
8. Optimization or Standardization of HR process redesign	*9%*	*0%*	*6%*
"Balancing control & standardisation with the need to also flex to the internal customer needs. This often clashes" "Alignment of existing policies and new systems"			
9. Return on Investment: Scale, costs versus efficiency, and operational efficiency	*9%*	*0%*	*6%*
"Time taken to embed and settle in 'reduced cost' better efficiency model" "How to identify 'the basics' and then prioritise areas for improvement (operational efficiency)" "What, and how far to go – making economies of scale versus HR and line people development"			
10. Service mix: Delivery across multiple media channels	*1%*	*0%*	*1%*
"Challenge of providing huge array of services, consistently and well to large and diverse customer base, via variety of media"			
11. Data analytics: Exploitation of data	*1%*	*0%*	*1%*
"Using the vast amount of data and Management Information we can now generate/have access to in an intelligent way to proactively add value back into the organisation"			

2.4. The three flaws of implementation

These data suggest that some important questions therefore need to be asked about this focus on, and fascination with, HR structure:

1. Have HR functions learned how best to operate received wisdom about the best delivery model and to design its associated structures effectively?
2. Are existing structures working smoothly, and if not, why not? If there are deficiencies in the structure, can these be ignored or will they hamper HR in delivering real value?
3. To achieve end-user value (shaping HR services around the sorts of practices and processes that assist customer value), how much "background noise" can be tolerated internally? If internal users (line managers) perceive difficulties as a result of new structures, will this impact their perception of real added-value?

To think about these questions, we need to introduce a little theory and remind ourselves briefly what the experts on organization design, the operation of structures, and the strategic management of capabilities through centers of excellence have learned is important.

The first flaw in implementation concerns the level of dissonance within the structure. When structure can be seen from an information processing and knowledge sharing perspective (see Chapter 8), two litmus tests can be applied: Does it avoid symptoms of deficiency? And is it sufficiently embedded?

Symptoms of structural deficiency

Writers such as Richard Daft and John Childs[16] have long analyzed organization theory as it applies to structure and design. Even the best structures and designs can develop disruptive symptoms. Structure is made up of vertical and horizontal linkages with different capacities for carrying information. When thinking about structural alignment, the most important decision made by managers concerns getting the right balance between the goals of efficiency and stability (called vertical control, and driven by the need to specialize and get control over scarce resources) and of learning, innovation, and flexibility (called horizontal co-ordination, and important in achieving a differentiated and rapid response to customer needs). When organizational structure is out of alignment, three symptoms of structural deficiency appear:

1. Decision-making is seen to be delayed or lacking in quality (overload may result from too many problems being funneled at them, information is not shared via the right people, and linkages may be inadequate).
2. Innovation and problem sensing and scanning is felt to be hampered (elements of the structure are not considered to be identifying with the same priorities, nor scanning the same problems, nor arriving at the same analysis of the problem).

Symptoms of structural deficiency: (Continued)

3. Conflicts are evidenced (the interests of key elements of the structure hamper line of sight toward overriding goals).

The desired model provides the structure, but people within the structure provide the behavior. Execution of structure is more important than the logic of the structure.

A second concept that is useful for understanding how effectively a structure works can be borrowed from work on effective knowledge creation and sharing. This is the idea of structural and relational embeddedness.

Structural and relational embeddedness

Network researchers and sociologists, such as Mark Granovetter, argue that the performance of a structure – its effectiveness – is dependent on the presence of value-creating behaviors in the organizational network in which the structure is embedded.[17] So structural embeddedness is a function of how many participants in the structure interact with one another, how likely future interactions are among these participants, and how likely participants are to talk about these interactions. In short, one should judge a structure by a range of social mechanisms that are necessary to make the structure work well. These include restricted access (parties know with whom to exchange and whom to avoid), macroculture (a common set of values, norms, and beliefs that are first created and then institutionalized), collective sanctions, and reputation. All these mechanisms serve to coordinate and safeguard the exchanges that are needed to make the structure work. This structural embeddedness is in turn very dependent on people relational embeddedness – the quality of interactions (information and knowledge sharing) that take place.

A third flaw of implementation may be that almost every HR function that you look at seems to have the same old "Centers of Excellence" – Talent management, rewards and compensation, and organization development? It is rare to find the HR Center of Excellence built around innovation, consumer insight, productivity, or some other fundamental capability. Every organization seems to have taken the existing "peak" of its HR functional expertise – existing high-level expertise – and hived it off, or simply relabeled it, as a Center, claiming that this somehow therefore has a transformational and strategic mandate.

All our data so far – our ongoing research interviews into HR strategy, the internal workshops run with HR teams implementing new delivery models, the quantitative survey data linking elements of HR structure with perceived value, and the qualitative data examining the implementation issues faced over time with each of the main "boxes" of an Ulrich model – suggest that those responsible for *Leading HR* have clearly not yet resolved the best delivery systems and structures for HR. Why should this be?

2.5. The issues created for HR

At the beginning of this chapter we presented a range of challenging questions that might be asked of HR's structure, the first of which was "is the specifics of the design inappropriate to the organisation's need"? Chapter 1 argued that one of the key requirements that HR must meet if the function wants to play a major role in the process of business model adaptation and change is to ensure that the HR structure delivers effective service to all employees. It was noted that overall we are witnessing some advocacy for thinking through carefully whether an introduction of the 3-Box Model structure would enable HR to lead and support the business model. Does it fit what HR aspires to? We would argue that yes it does in most instances, but

1. the real skill is in aligning and balancing how the three main legs of the "stool" are integrated with each other,

2. this logic is often beyond the formal structure,

3. you need a very good business-minded HR team designing a structure that truly reflects the needs of the business model and the line managers within that model, and

4. this ability to optimally integrate is about the HR senior team being truly "fit for purpose."

The second challenge that we posed was have the architect's, plans simply been misread and misunderstood? There exists the strong possibility that some HR leaders have made an oversimplistic interpretation of the implications of "HR Champions" and not thought through in enough depth what are the many implications of moving to a 3-Box Model including the balance of responsibilities, the integration issues referred to above, the quality of staff required for the in-house or outsource possibilities, and any global or international issues.

The third challenge is have HR structures been hijacked by cost-cutting or work simplification? Suffice to say that we are aware of situations where shortsightedness has impeded the successful implementation of HR delivery change programs. During a period of recession, for instance, HR leaders need to carefully estimate the costs of any restructure and make judgments about the availability of investment funding for the duration of the project.

The fourth challenge that we posed concerns the question of HR team capability. As revealed by the research data in this chapter, there is a strong consensus that major concerns exist with regard to HR capability and the successful implementation of HR delivery systems. The concerns with regard to capability tend to focus upon lack of business acumen, the upskilling potential of the HR team, cultural insight, and relational skills.

Chapter 6 will focus upon two interrelated issues at play here, namely, the mindset and the power position of the HR leader. Exploring this mindset factor, first we believe that to successfully introduce and operate a 3-Box Model, particularly in terms of business aware, strategically minded business partners, HR leaders will need to replenish their cadre of business partners and center of excellence members with some existing HR team members departing and "new blood" being recruited. We believe some HR leaders find such a "clinical" process difficult and therefore "mend and make do." To overcome this reluctance the HR leader will need to possess a strong drive to really improve quality – what we term an "Excellence Mindset." Possessing the mindset may not be enough, however, as replenishing will require budget. Thus if the HR leader is part of the Golden Triangle[18] outlined in Chapter 6 then it is more likely that they will be able to lever the power and influence to champion any temporary budget increase.

The fifth and sixth challenges posed the question of whether there is an unsuitable organizational culture and unreceptive client/line managers. Put very simply, our research indicates that the 3-Box model does not suit all cultures. In some cultures the concept of the strategic Business Partner would be beyond the conception of even the most powerful line managers. This may be where HR is far from Golden Triangle membership and, like it or not, is seen as the "hire, fire, and train" function. Very technically based companies may be resistant to a customer service perspective and find it difficult to relate to Ulrich's perception of value.

The seventh challenge that we posed raises the issue of line indifference and resistance to HR restructuring. In terms of delivery, HR would appear to be in quite a difficult position at present and in the near-future within organizations. In order to respond strategically to the recession HR clearly needs a well-oiled strategically informed and high influence delivery model. Our research indicates that it is clear that going into the recession many HR models were in need of refinement. The recession may well make the implementation problems more problematic as energy is directed at recession solving problems and not on the necessary relationships and networking with client/line managers that tie a 3-Box Model together and make it work effectively. Also if line managers sensed that, in the recession and immediate post-recession climate, HR saw its delivery model as a strategic priority, then they may write off HR as a serious partner. HR Directors will need to put their energy into correcting and re-balancing the model by stealth!

2.6. Conclusions

Research over the last 20 years (to which Dave Ulrich in particular has been a major contributor) has helped HR Directors

1. think about the structures (generally based around how HR organizes its processes) and role changes associated with a separation out into transactional work, HR business partners, and centers of excellence;
2. change HR from a process-specific function into a business with its own Profit and Loss and concomitant transparency and ROI visibility.

Ulrich's ideas clearly have given much impetus to the HR function from the late 1990s. They have propelled it forward and helped it look at its contribution to value and the bottom line. However, by thinking more deeply about the changing value of knowledge inherent in business model change, and about the capabilities that HR Directors need to align the HR contribution to this, we argue that we now need to move beyond this perspective.

In *Human Resource Champions* Ulrich does not mention the issue of business models in relation to HRM. He mentions strategic business units (SBUs) as the focus of attention twice – once in the context of a chemical company and once in a pharmaceutical company. An SBU is an entity within an organization that is given responsibility to serve a particular part of the business area and is allowed to develop its own mission, objectives, and strategy. The term "unit" relates to a part of the business that has a defined external market that enables a separate strategic plan to be developed and so often relates to large organizational structures such as a whole division.

Ulrich argues that SBUs should be used as the level at which HR business partners should be organized as "... the initial point of contact for each business unit's line managers" and also interfaced with the central centers of excellence.[19] Using Johnson and Johnson as an example, he notes that SBUs often

> ... have independent philosophies and operating histories as well as unique customers, products and cultures.[20]

We believe that although these SBUs may be pursuing slightly different strategies and potentially operate to a different business model, these operations can be seen as "components" of the broader performance logic that exists once all such models are brought together under the "architectural" (organization strategy level) business model.

However, aligning HR to the higher level business model is by default a complex task, as the alignment has to deliver a degree of coordination across what might be conflicting "component" interests.

Not surprisingly, then, this chapter has signaled the crucial importance – in terms of the long-term success of HR delivery systems – that the system is linked to effective Relationships, Networks, and Influence – both within and outside of the HR function. The balance of relationships between the three main components of the HR structure needs to be optimized and maintained carefully. This is certainly the case in terms of Business Partner/Expert relationships. These positive or otherwise relationships will often be based on good personality "fits," so HR Directors need to be alert when influential jobholders depart their function as the positive balance may erode.

There is also a warning for HR Directors. They must avoid or navigate successfully what we term a number of Fatal Flaws. One fatal flaw that emerges, when we look at our data on the implementation problems faced, is that we believe it is possible that there is a double capability problem that is making implementation currently very difficult:

1. not only is the capability of the Business Partner in question,
2. the capability of the line to use the Business Partner appropriately can be questioned.

The line behavior problem is not just one of education – it might be a fatal flaw in the model in that they will always need to have low-level transactional solutions, but solutions provided by an individual HR person and not a service center.

A second fatal flaw might be that the key to success is not having the "boxes" per se, but having a clear logic as to how the boxes must be joined together and how they are used interdependently. This "way of working" is very dependent not just on the formal structure, but on the networks of connections and relationships that key players inside and "on top of" the boxes have. Historically these networks (often held by a handful of key players) help glue the system together, handle the problems of power and influence, and help solve the difficult issues that sit between boxes.

It is important to note that a key issue for HR Directors in to "optimise" each of the three boxes in the model, as they tweak the roles and structure, rebalance it and re-educate the users and operators accordingly. They also need to be able to respond flexibiblity to events as they happen – for example talent shortages – and re-assign responsibilities across the model. Finally, to the extent that there is a new generation of line managers who are willing to drive the people agenda, and an "air traffic controller" sitting on top of the model handling the optimisation activities, then they may be more or less willing or able to use external consultants to run their Centres of Expertise and devise strategy. Similarly, if they have entered early on into service level agreements and outsourcing arrangements that restrict this ability to learn how to optimise the model, then they may experience problems of execution. Corporate stewardship of the 3-Box model can be hampered by these sorts of considerations.

Fatal flaws are design faults that are accidents waiting to happen – a subtle set of events can disrupt the networks and power and knowledge that have made the model work in the past. The credit crunch might have proved to be this accident – attention was distracted (understandably) from managing the health of the HR delivery model, to managing the consequences of the recession. A possible outcome of such distracting pressures is the emergence of a "sick" 3-Box model system. The problem is one of reputation – once the model gets sick, the line will lose belief in it and it might take years to repair the reputation hit.

As a final observation, however, we would observe that all these design faults can be fine-tuned and hopefully corrected before they wreak real damage. *Leading HR* involves surfacing the key networks and power relationships that currently make the delivery model work and surfacing the "design intelligence" of the key players that currently (and in the future) help to tie the boxes together and keep the system healthy.

The next chapter reviews the experience of Nestlé in evolving its HR delivery models. Chapters 4, 6, 8, and 9 then describe the key activities and capabilities that are necessary for *Leading HR*. In introducing the chapters it is important to stress:

1. First and foremost, the activities outlined in each chapter may be viewed as a totality that, if all are present, should provide for a high level of proactivity within that HR function. There is a logic that links each set of capabilities to the next, and this logic has dictated the order in which each chapter is presented

2. However, few HR functions, at the present time, would have "mastery" of all the capabilities outlined.

NOTES

1   Becker, B.E., Huselid, M.A. and Ulrich, D. (2001) *The HR Scorecard: Linking People, Strategy, and Performance*. Boston, MA: Harvard Business School Press.

2   Becker, B.E. and Huselid, M.A. (2006) Strategic human resources management: Where do we go from here?, *Journal of Management*, 32: 898–925.

3   CIPD (2006) *The Changing HR Function: The Key Questions*. London: CIPD.

4   Ulrich, D. (2008) The three HR paradoxes, *Human Resources*, January, p. 5.

5   Joinson, C. (1999) Changing shapes – Trends in Human Resource Reorganisations, *HR Magazine*, March 1999.

6   Personal correspondence between Paul Sparrow and Dave Ulrich. 16th October 2009.

7   Joinson (1999) p. 5.

8   Ulrich, D. (1997) *Human Resource Champions: The Next Agenda for Adding Value and delivering Results*. Boston, MA: Harvard Business School Press. p. 38.

9   Ibid., p. 126.

10 See for example: http://www.cipd.co.uk/subjects/corpstrtgy/general/hrbusprtnr.htm Accessed on 15 December 2009.

11 Gratton, L. (2003) The humpty dumpty effect: A view of a fragmented HR function, *People Management*, 9 (9): 18.

12 Ulrich and Brockbank (2008) p. 6.

13 Reilly, P. (2006) HR transformation – Pitfalls of the Ulrich model, *People Management*, 23 November 2006, p. 36.

14 Higgins, N.J. (2007) Thought leadership: Real HR transformation, *Journal of Applied Human Capital Management*, 1 (3): 19.

15 Hird, M., Marsh, C. and Sparrow, P.R. (2009) *HR Delivery Systems: Re-engineered or Over-engineered*. Centre for Performance-led HR White Paper 09/05. Lancaster, UK: Lancaster University Management School.

16 See: Daft, R. (2001) *Organization Theory and Design. 7th Edition*. Ohio: South Western Publishing; and Child, J. (1984) *Organization*. New York: Harper Row.

17 See: Granovettor, M.S. (1985) Economic action and social structure: The problem of embeddedness, *American Journal of Sociology*, 91 (3): 481–510; and Uzzi, B. (1996) The sources and consequences of embeddedness for the economic performance of organizations: The network effect, *American Sociological Review*, 61 (4): 674–98.

18 Hesketh, A. and Hird, M. (2009) The golden triangle: How relationships between leaders can leverage more value from people, *Human Resources Business Review*, 2 (1): 24–37

19 Ulrich, D. (1997) p. 210.

20 Ibid., p. 84.

CHAPTER 3

Nestlé: Reflections on the HR Structure Debate

MARTIN HIRD AND MATT STRIPE

3.1. Introduction

The opening chapters have raised the issue of business model change and noted its implications for the structure of HR and the choice of delivery model. A key issue therefore is the business utility of the delivery model that HR chooses.

The business utility of the 3-Box model

Headline issue:

How do you organize your HR function and delivery service to employees? What does the nature of this delivery look like? Does the context of business model change alter the business utility of Ulrich's 3-Box model?

Strategic imperative:

The current dominating influence of the Ulrich 3-Box Model upon HR structures is amply demonstrated by the frequency with which the topic occurred. Both HR and operational managers demonstrate familiarity with the characteristics of the model and what it could imply for the HR contribution.

However, we are witnessing some advocacy for thinking through more carefully whether the introduction of the 3-Box Model structure would enable HR to lead and support the business model. Does it fit what HR aspires to achieve?

Must-win battle:

HR Directors need to ensure that the Ulrich model – even if it is the right high-level structure for HR – follows the analytical process and does not precede it.

It is clear that HR functions have become extremely focused on the Ulrich 3-Box model of structuring the HR department, even though this model is not the only way to address the headline issue noted above. We argue that

The key messages that emerge from this chapter

1) It cannot be taken for granted that there is enough of an experience-base to know how to work the Ulrich model. In practice, this model itself models very complex mechanisms. Making these mechanisms operate together like clockwork has been something achieved by some, yet has proved challenging to others.

2) Maintaining a true course through history requires considerable forethought. Far from being planned, most changes in HR structures are organic. Ideas get developed within small communities of practitioners, the network of "on-side" practitioners grows, business forces bring renewed integration pressures, consulting propositions evolve, and the key proponents themselves move in their careers. The frameworks to coordinate structures are often not widely understood.

3) It has long been recognized that the quality of business partners is a key success criterion for HR Delivery Models, and therefore so is the role of assessment processes – a fair proportion of existing professionals are inevitably found wanting and cannot make the journey.

4) Account management skills and an attention to the "what" and "when," as opposed to the "how" of HR, become a differentiating characteristic. Much of the benefit comes of course not from the structure itself, but from the quality of supporting infrastructure such as service level agreements, e-enablement arrangements, and the protocols that ensure coordination between each part of the structure.

5) The strategic priorities within HR Delivery Models have themselves evolved over time – prescribed models continue to change. The need for tight operational oversight was overlooked in early iterations of the delivery model.

6) There is still a need for "optimization" of HR Delivery Models, and this issue requires careful thought in terms of *Leading HR*, not least because duplication could unnecessarily increase costs within the HR function as well as leading to ongoing conflict. There is still an underlying belief that new HR Structures will and do lead to cost economies, but questions remain about whether these HR Structures enable HR professionals to play an effective corporate role in managing the complex problems that will emerge from an era of global recession and beyond.

7) The 3-Box Model is not a globally accepted HR Structure concept, although it continues to find more global attention and relevance. Global complexities in business structures often mean that the HR organization in operation can have a series of three-box models *within* a "macro" three-box model. Practical decisions about the nature and organization of geographically diverse resources based on size, complexity and geographic location units and sites, and the level of local HR capability require bespoke solutions.

8) The Shared Services box should be viewed as broader than just an HR problem. Many functions in global corporations will centralize (either outsourcing or keeping in-house) but using a more flexible range of locations.

The key messages that emerge from this chapter: (Continued)

9) Different capabilities across the global dimension will mean that business partners may be designed as a series of tiered roles driven off a common competence model. In order to act in a truly strategic way, there may need to be a tier of "junior" business partners to support the lead HR players. Centers of excellence may well become more differentiated, based around pragmatic thinking about local capability.

10) The 3-Box model emerged inexorably within HR, driven by, for instance, the emergence of comprehensive HR IT systems via providers. Ulrich's writing provided a clear insight into the different roles that HR can play, with a particular emphasis on that role being strategic in nature

On September 11, 2008, my taxi – as the lead author of this chapter – dropped me in front of Nestlé's imposing headquarters building in Vevey, Switzerland. My mind turned to the various experiences I had shared with my host, Matt Stripe, currently Assistant Vice President for Human Resources Nestlé SA. Matt and I had first worked together at Matra-BAe Dynamics in 1996. The Company was then a recent creation from the first major structural joint venture that British Aerospace had embarked upon. Matra-BAe Dynamics or MBD as it became known was, upon its creation, the largest missile defence company in Europe. Matra itself was part of the Lagadère Organisation which held interests in television, print media, motor vehicles, and defense. BAE Dynamics had an operational headquarters building at Stevenage in Hertfordshire, whilst Matra's operational headquarters was at Velizy just outside Paris. Matt held a series of HR positions at MBD between 1990 and 2001. In 2001 he and I also worked together within the Programs Division of what had become BAE SYSTEMS (following the merger with Marconi Defence). In 2002 I left BAE SYSTEMS and joined Tag-McLaren and then in 2003 was employed by Royal Mail. However throughout these changes Matt and I stayed in close contact and retained our shared fascination in HR Structures and their continuing evolution. In 2003 Matt left BAE SYSTEMS to join Nestlé's Confectionery business (then Rowntrees) in York and gained promotion rapidly to become HR Director of the UK Confectionery Division. In 2008 Matt had been appointed HR Assistant Vice President for Strategic Business Units and was based at the Company's headquarters in Vevey.

So what was the purpose of our meeting in September 2008? Given our mutual interest in HR Structures, we wanted to explore and evaluate how those structures had evolved over the last 10 years or so. Two days of discussion and exploration followed. By virtue of our joint experiences, this chapter is partially a case study and a case history, but it also documents how our thinking has evolved in terms of where HR Structures may develop in the future.

In the context of HR Structures, it is also informative and indeed intellectually stimulating when one considers the truly global nature of Nestlé. It is the largest food corporation in the world by a very large margin; it employs 280,000 people and operates in 84 countries with 456 factories. Sales in 2008 were 109.9 billion Swiss francs yielding a profit of 10.6 billion. The headquarters in Vevey employ and accommodate over 80 different nationalities. Structures at Nestlé are therefore necessarily complex to manage its global leadership position. Consequently, HR Structures, in terms of their architecture, require much thought and a good level of intellectual horse-power to get them right!

In this chapter we focus to a great extent on the emergence of the "3-Box Model" and its application as a focus for HR Structures. We will discuss, based on our experiences, the strong linkage between the 3-Box Model and Professor David Ulrich. We believe that the model is in many ways an inevitable design pattern for HR and that the model was present in some companies from the late 1980s/early 1990s onward. The model, then, predated the publication of Ulrich's seminal book *Human Resource Champions*.[1]

We might expect there is enough of an experience-base to know how to work the Ulrich model – but as Matt and I reviewed our experiences it became clear that this cannot be taken for granted. In practice, this three-part model itself models very complex mechanisms.[2] It seems that making these mechanisms operate together like clockwork has been something achieved by some, yet has proved challenging to others. Research presented in Chapter 2 questions the ease with which the Ulrich 3-Box model can be implemented.

In this chapter we add substance to the debates about HR Delivery Models and Structures introduced in Chapter 2. We draw upon our insights into practice at a number of organizations we have worked at, and with. The chapter consists of three sections:

1. The case history of our experiences of structural change/architecture in HR drawing upon some shared, some individual, observations at MBD, British Aerospace/BAE SYSTEMS, Nestlé, and Royal Mail.

2. A review of where HR Structures currently find themselves and the issues that need to be confronted.

3. Reflections on how structures have evolved over time, including the conclusions and recommendations that emerged from our discussions.

3.2. Early experiences of HR structure change

In recounting history, it is instructive to consider just how planned, or organic, changes in HR structures really are. Ideas get developed within small communities of practitioners, the network of "on-side" practitioners grows, business forces such as mergers bring renewed integration pressures, consulting propositions in the BPO market evolve, and the key proponents themselves move in their careers across divisions and organizations. Maintaining a true course through history requires considerable forethought.

As we talked at Vevey, Matt Stripe recalled the history of how thinking about HR structures developed across his network. He explained when he first became aware of the imperatives driving HR Structural Change:

... I think around 1997, when there were fears about the inflating costs of HR, I started to become a bit more aware of what HR's role was currently and likely to be in the future. My bias, at that point, was software engineering, as I originally come into HR as a software engineer, and so I was more interested in the systems part of it at that time. I got quite interested in the values of the Intranet, the use of Shared Services and how HR could make its contribution in those areas. So in 1997 we started thinking about reorganising HR at MBD UK. I can remember designing an Intranet quite quickly.

He continued:

... At that time the Internet or Intranet didn't really exist within the organisation I knew. The Internet was still pretty new, and those who were interested in technology were starting to use software like Microsoft Front Page ... There were shared drives that were starting to be used as a mechanism for sharing information. The platform just wasn't there. I had free rein, at the time, to put some software in. We just moved very quickly – I remember doing it every weekend at home – designed the first Intranet, which we communicated to the MBD HR team at one of our Bi-Annual Mini Conferences. So that was the kicking off of MBD's Shared Service box.

So, in 1997 the main focus of MBD's HR Structures was upon HR teams, colocated with their operational clients. The lead members of those teams focused their attention on individual members of MBD's Management Committee (six in total), and the HR team leaders attended directorate senior team meetings as full members, equivalent in status to the senior managers responsible for finance, commercial/procurement, project management, and so forth. They were in many ways embryonic business partners. Indeed, their unbroken reporting line was to their client, and their dotted line to the MBD UK HR Director. The HR teams also, however, carried all transactional/process responsibilities – they had their own clerks and administrators. This increasingly appeared to be uneconomic – the ratio of HR staff to general employee was not particularly spartan!

As a consequence, throughout 1997 and early 1998, the HR teams focused increasingly upon more strategic and policy activities, with their clients and transactional HR activity being moved to a central "hub." If one were to summarize the HR structural trends by late 1997, the scenario was one of HR advisors being colocated with their clients, increasingly centralized HR transactional work, which relied to an increasing extent upon IT support and also was located physically close to the transactional hub. There were also a small number of relatively senior specialists with responsibility for learning and development, rewards, pensions, and industrial relations.

However, these changes were quite organic. There was an overall notion of a framework to guide the changes but that framework was not widely understood.

Perspectives were going to change in the near future! In early 1998, at one of the Bi-Annual HR Conferences, referred to earlier, the key guest speaker was Adrian Walker, then a senior HR figure with the highly successful Sun Microsystems. In his keynote address he introduced the senior MBD UK HR Team to the work of David Ulrich, the book *Human Resource Champions*, and the notion of what was to become called the "3-Box Model." The content of what Adrian presented was extremely relevant to where MBD UK HR was heading. His input gave all the senior HR team a framework to use in taking HR Structures forward. *Human Resource Champions* surely had a surge of sales in the Hertfordshire area!

Events moved rapidly during 1998. Matt Stripe describes that change process:

> . . . With Ulrich, we had something to hang our ideas upon. We took a look at the central hub and decided that we had to drive forward at a quicker pace. One of the first changes we made was to establish a software team who could put the technology in place to actually make the Shared Server work properly!

> Then there was the re-establishment of what would now be called Expert Services, because at that time MBD UK, under its previous HR Director, had taken large parts of rewards and compensation, recruitment and learning and development, and put them into the generalist teams. We re-established not only the Shared Services piece – and got that working – but then re-established real, central Expert Services in the same areas.

As MBD UK restructured and reoriented its HR proposition there was, of course, the need to consult with French joint venture partners at Matra. Matra HR operations were very much site-based, with a major emphasis upon employee–union relations and health and safety. They were less interested in the notion of a transactional center. They also took a more conservative and skeptical stance toward the notion of senior and powerful "Experts." In summary, an increasingly clear 3-Box Model "emerged" at MBD UK, but there was little movement across the Channel in terms of a new HR Structure emerging in France.

3.3. British Aerospace Group involvement

What happened next? By late 1998 MBD UK's 50 per cent owner and "cultural" parent, British Aerospace, became aware of the changes in HR Structure being implemented at MBD. Matt Stripe describes the interest:

> Well, we started to get a little exposure around that time (1998) because MBD UK was small in terms of the British Aerospace context (3,500 employees) and because we were in a joint venture and weren't bound by the same sort of restrictions of 100% owned BAE divisions. So we had a bit more freedom. We were able to put the model in place and most of MBD UK's policies became self-developed rather than being direct BAE policies.

In fact, in 1998 MBD UK was part of one of the four "Groups" that constituted British Aerospace globally, namely, the Land and Sea Systems Group. The HR Director for the Group was Tony McCarthy (he is currently Group HR Director at British Airways having previously also been at Royal Mail), who was intrigued by MBD's structures, and visited Stevenage to sample the impact of the changes that had been made there.

Tony McCarthy was impressed by what he saw at MBD UK and asked the HR Director for MBD UK and Matt Stripe to present their developments at the Land

and Sea Systems Senior HR meeting. At that meeting the structural approach of MBD UK was well received. Shortly afterward, the MBD approach was presented to the Corporate Senior HR meeting chaired by Terry Morgan, then the Group HR Director for British Aerospace. Morgan was enthused by both the MBD approach and the accompanying outline of Ulrich's ideas as expounded in *Human Resource Champions*. He initiated a commitment by the British Aerospace Senior HR Team to explore, very positively, the feasibility of British Aerospace HR moving to a 3-Box Model. Chris Dickson, Corporate Employment Policies Director, was tasked with undertaking the feasibility study.

The year 1999 was to be a momentous year in British Aerospace's development, and these corporate developments were going to impinge upon the HR structural developments. The significance of the year was to revolve around the announcement in the autumn of 1999 of a merger between British Aerospace and Marconi Defence creating what would be the second largest defense company in the world. The resulting company was to be titled BAE SYSTEMS.

Within HR there was another significant development. Chris Dickson was reporting back that there were going to be major issues regarding the installation of a common HR structure. These issues were mainly related to the differing range of legacy IT systems that existed across the various divisions of British Aerospace. However, during 1999, Terry Morgan had been approached by Xchanging, one of the earliest BPO organizations, founded and led by David Andrews. When Morgan discussed the issue of legacy IT systems with Andrews it was claimed by Xchanging that they could overcome the issue and create a common "People Portal" for British Aerospace, using their IT expertise.

The Xchanging proposal in essence consisted of British Aerospace and Xchanging creating an outsourced 50/50 joint venture that would be responsible for all so called transactional HR activity. Discussions with Xchanging continued throughout the merger machinations and an agreement was signed between BAE SYSTEMS and Xchanging to create the joint venture which was to be named "Togethr." Togethr commenced formal operations in 2001.

Over 300 former British Aerospace and Marconi Defence HR staff moved out of their parent companies and joined the new operation. Corporate internal experts were confirmed and appointed in areas such as learning and development, reward, corporate and social responsibility, and employee relations.

To ensure that the remaining business partners were sufficiently prepared and developed for their role, a tender was announced for a major Business Partner development program linked to a Business Partner assessment process that was provided by external HR consultants. It was stipulated that the business schools and consultancies who responded with a tender proposal had to be able to demonstrate a significant presence and experience in both the United Kingdom and the United States. The reason for this was that the new BAE SYSTEMS had over 20,000 employees based in the United States.

The contract for the program was given to the Global Consulting Group from the University of Michigan, whose proposal was led by Professor Wayne Brockbank and project managed by Matt Stripe. The program commenced by focusing on understanding the business strategy, then linking HR and business strategy and culture and management. It provided processes and tools for diagnosing and creating organizational capability, as well as organizational design and consulting skills and change management. The program also required the business partners to undergo an assessment prior to being given a place on the program to ascertain their current capability. This assessment identified a number of business partners who would not make the journey and therefore those individuals were placed in other roles or outside the organization. The Program was judged to be extremely successful both in presenting HR business partners with a vision and in equipping them with the skills, knowledge, and competences for their new role.

Thus, in a period from 1999 to 2002, British Aerospace/BAE SYSTEMS was transformed in organizational terms, including the completion of a historic arrangement with Xchanging. Matt and I reviewed that exciting, but in many ways daunting, period that we shared and considered some of the key learning that had emerged from the HR transformation centered upon the creation of Togethr. For us, the key lessons were the following:

1. It was crucial that in a structure such as that at BAE SYSTEMS it needed to be clearly understood by all that *business partners focus upon the "What" and the "When" whereas Togethr focus on the "How."* As an aside, we still believe this distinction of account management is a crucial piece of understanding that a Business Partner needs to have. We still sometimes witness business partners wasting time and energy meddling in how the process is being done instead of trusting the shared service to do it effectively.

2. The creation of an effective "People Portal" was a major force in gaining the support of operational/client management professionals to the changes in structure. Initially operational managers at BAE SYSTEMS had deep reservations about the majority of their HR teams moving into transactional centers. The accessibility and scope of the People Portal undoubtedly eased those doubts and reservations.

3. The financially prescribed service agreements that underpinned the new HR Structure drove a much stronger cost awareness within the residual HR business partners at BAE SYSTEMS, and it was this which served to increase their internal credibility with their clients.

At this point it is important to signal our awareness that in recent times – now a decade since the initial changes were made – the in-house HR resource at BAE Systems has increased quite substantially, to provide more operational support for, the initially lean, HR Business Partner structure. This move accords with recent observations by David Ulrich that HR structures may require five legs to the "stool," including an HR operational execution resource, to give that support to more strategically oriented HR generalists. BAE Systems seem to have recognized this requirement. It was not part of the discussion though back in 2002.

3.4. New experiences at Nestlé Confectionery UK

In July 2004 Matt Stripe joined Nestlé as Head of HR for their Confectionery manufacturing facility in York (formerly the main site for Nestlé Rowntree). As we mentioned earlier, Nestlé is the largest food company in the world, employs 280,000 people, and is based in 84 countries. So now the context was a truly global corporation. Matt found Nestlé Confectionery very different to BAE SYSTEMS in terms of HR culture. He describes his first impressions:

> ... It was a complete shock when I arrived at Nestlé Confectionery, in the sense that coming from the BAE model that we've just described [had meant] a very clinical 3-Box Model, where you had Shared Services being delivered and managed in a very tight budgetary manner. There were also clear and crisp service level agreements with a comprehensively understood divide of roles and responsibilities. The new BAE Structure had been embryonic, but HR at the company was a powerful function and frankly had strong standards of excellence. Nestlé had some good HR mechanisms in place, but it was very different to BAE [in the other regards].

Nestlé UK's operation focused principally on two elements: confectionery (representing 60 per cent of turnover) and beverages. Nestlé also had a number of sister organizations, such as Purina and Nestlé Waters, operating in the market. However, these companies had a different reporting structure and therefore were not coordinated through Nestlé UK. Nestlé is an organization in which growth has been partially built on acquisition, for example, the acquisition of Rowntrees and Mackintosh in confectionery. In terms of culture, Nestlé has a strong commitment to its people and is a long-term employer with, in essence, a "cradle to grave" employment philosophy.

This culture was reflected in the HR team that Matt Stripe joined. On the whole, the members of that team had joined into a classic "personnel" environment, but it is important to record that there had been changes to that approach, and a Shared Service model (one of the three legs of the 3-Box model) had been introduced around 2002. Matt Stripe describes his initial perspective on the situation thus:

> ... My initial observations of the whole model were that Shared Service, in other words the administrative arm and their centres of excellence, were relatively well put together. But their efficiency and effectiveness could be improved. Shared Service had a generous level of resourcing and not a particularly strong IT structure, but it was evolving in the right direction. I had stronger reservations in terms of the generalist HR population. There were a lot of them and many had been used to undertaking tactical and transactional activity. They were struggling with the idea of a Shared Service handling that. So, there was a lot of duplication of effort.

From his arrival at Nestlé UK in July 2004 to his move to Vevey in August 2008, Matt occupied three roles in the United Kingdom. Initially, he was appointed as

Head of HR for the York Plant. Then in 2004 he was promoted to Deputy Director HR for Nestlé Confectionery UK, which involved responsibility for five locations. Then in 2006 he became the Division HR Director and led the restructure of manufacturing capability, addressing the archaic working practices that had existed, in order to ensure the Division was fit for the future. However, there was a continuity of focus during this 4-year period that always seemed to revolve around structural changes to UK Confectionery HR. The changes that were made are summarized below.

The structural changes in UK Confectionery HR

Business Partners

1. At a senior level there were two other external appointments, in addition to Matt's appointment, that were made in 2004.

2. At York, which was the largest site and undoubtedly the hub of Nestlé Confectionery UK Operations, the number of business partners was reduced from 18 down to 5. The remaining 5 were made accountable for larger areas and clearer support lines, which were constructed in terms of the effective usage of Shared Services.

Shared service

1. To achieve economies of scale, a process review/redesign was commissioned and staffing numbers were reduced by approximately 35 per cent.

Experts

1. Expert functions tendered to be located at the Croydon HQ of Nestlé UK and therefore must be viewed from within this broader perspective, rather than just Nestlé Confectionery.

2. Learning and Development developed as an expert function, and out of this a Talent function emerged.

3. It was decided that organization development and design responsibilities should be vested with business partners, and not with learning and development, and a development program to raise capability was put in place.

Clearly, all these elements of HR architecture are still being reviewed at Nestlé UK, under the leadership of the UK HR Director Steven Battalia. Steven Battalia and Matt Stripe worked closely on the issues together. However, for Matt Stripe, a move out of the United Kingdom beckoned and in August 2008 he moved to Nestlé headquarters in Vevey, Switzerland, where he was confronted with the complexity of now needing to help Corporate HR Director Jean Marc Duvoisin optimize HR Structures across a major global corporation.

3.5. The Nestlé global HR experience

From an organizational design perspective, Nestlé is a matrix organization. It splits the globe into three zones with respective reporting hierarchies: Zone AOA – Africa Oceania and Asia; Zone Americas – North and South America; and Zone Europe – Western, Central, and Eastern Europe. Whilst the majority of its businesses are organized within this structure, it also has a number of businesses with global mandates and structures, such as Nestlé Water and Nestlé Nutrition.

Moving to the Nestlé HR organization, at a macro level, it looks like a classic three-box model. However, in order to take account the complexity of the business structure, and the complexity added by operating within the global footprint of 84 countries, the HR organization in operation has a series of three-box models *within* a "macro" three-box model! The structure is explained below:

The three boxes at Nestlé

Shared services or centers of scale

Some of Nestlé shared services operate globally within a structure called Nestlé Business Services (NBS). Payroll would be a good example of this. Other services operate at a Zone level or local (market) level, such as personnel administration.

Centers of Expertise

The Centers tend to be organized at a local or regional level, but they are coordinated globally.

Operational HR

HR business partners are organized locally, but they are coordinated throughout the hierarchy, and so are coordinated either zonally or globally, dependant on the organization.

Figure 3.1: Nestlé's macro HR organizational model

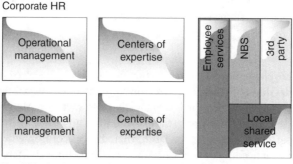

Confused? Well, whilst this model may sound complex, but it is based on some very specific design principles to ensure that the model can be implemented in a flexible manner, dependent upon each Market's size, complexity, and structure. Operating this design maintains a lean and efficient HR organization (Figure 3.1.)

What are the key design principles? They are as follows:

1. To be consistent and simple, where there is no competitive advantage in being different and complex.

2. People management must be a managerial responsibility.

3. The maximum amount of information must be available at lowest possible level.

4. Local HR Strategy sits with Operational HR Managers, and is to be developed in conjunction with the relevant elements of Corporate Strategy and Market/Business HR.

5. Business/Operational Units Heads and Factory/DC Managers do not necessarily need to have a dedicated HR Manager. The decision on the nature and organization of these resources should be taken according to the size, complexity, and geographic location of the concerned Units and Sites.

6. Employee Services and HR Centers of Expertise are centralized and provide service to all Businesses operating in a Market – unless by exception it makes sense for them to be localized.

7. Where NBS organization operates, it is independent from any particular business in the Market, and must offer competitive advantage with regard to alternative providers.

Underpinning these global design principles, there are global development programs that ensure a consistent level of HR capability. Clearly this is an evolving model, and Matt Stripe remains clearly enthused about his role in helping to develop it. As we discuss the HR operating model, and the global design principles, the future challenges become evident.

3.6. The HR structure debate by 2009: Acting locally

We discussed where we believe many HR Structures were in 2009. Whilst one needs to accept that it is important to avoid, if possible, over generalization, one can assume, with a reasonable level of confidence, that Anglo-American Organizations have followed, to a greater or lesser degree, the notion of the 3-Box Model, and have linked this to the writings and "teaching" of David Ulrich and the Michigan Group. This "linkage" has almost become accepted as a firm reality. We believe that this tenet is true, to an extent, but later in the chapter we will discuss the notion that the origins of the 3-Box Model actually predate Ulrich's work. In our thinking, we were already aware that Ulrich recently has emphasized the possibilities of a structure based upon five legs – not three legs – to the HR "stool."

Where we need to be cautious is that in terms of drawing conclusions about HR Structures in 2009, can we presume that the 3-Box Model is a globally accepted HR Structure concept? Our experiences of working within some continental European companies and also when discussing HR Structures on international programs lead us to a more cautious stance in terms of declaring the 3-Box Model as a universal form of HR architecture.

Research has shown, however, that despite significant questions about the global introduction of a 3-Box model, the relevance of this development to international HRM is considerable.[3] Shared service thinking – and the associated technologies being used to enhance delivery – represents a force for a fundamental realignment of the HR function on a global basis and of course it carries implications for the level of centralization–decentralization and devolvement evidenced across countries, regions, and corporate headquarters. Moreover, it changes the economics of HR service provision and introduces competing dynamics for both the standardization of HR processes and the potential for mass customization. Few international HR functions will be able to ignore this development.

Practice however rarely matches theory. To date there does not appear to be a common international path to the internationalization of shared service models.[4] Central organization can also imply that a small subset of HR experts hold sway over HR system design and if they are not internationally minded, then their perceptions of (country level) customer need may themselves be stereotyped. HR professionals from one country to another have very different levels of professionalization. The depth of HR talent capable of taking on an HR business partner role varies markedly. The attractiveness of the idea varies across countries, as does the role of line managers and their ability to help employee self-management. Finally, legislative constraints around data protection and management, and cultural differences in the relationship between line managers and employees, and employees and HR, have all impacted the ease with which an Ulrich model can be implemented.

The activities and responsibilities that end up being devolved both to the local line managers and to the local HR staff have varied considerably. Some organizations have chosen to create regional centers as part of a single international organization structure, some have changed their country-based systems to regional centers but allowed the managers to stay in their original offices, others have used service centers to support global business streams rather than organize them at a regional level on a geographical basis.

Scale is an important consideration. Many international organizations do not have sufficient numbers of HR professionals in particular geographies, and so the policy is hard to justify. There are not enough intermediaries to cut out from the process to justify the investment. Moreover, not all countries are supportive of the service center concept. In part this is because there is still a lot to learn about the operation of global service centers as evidenced by the professional networks that have been set up. Rather than confront countries around the world with an over-standardized solution – which is fraught with political and cultural problems – MNCs are persuading various businesses and country operations to support the concept of global service centers and then managing a step-by-step migration toward them. The strategy has tended to be to establish the principle of e-HR first, and then to reorganize the supporting infrastructure that is needed to enable this, such as the service centers.

Specifically, Matt Stripe's experience with global HR Structures at Nestlé has introduced an issue into our thinking about the 3-Box Model and how it accommodates global complexity.

Chapter 2 laid out the main evidence that CPHR has gathered about difficulties in implementing an Ulrich model. Our own discussions of the findings of such research have led to lively and illuminating debates. The data from the CPHR study in Chapter 2 dove-tail, to a great extent, with the findings presented by Joe Hennessy, Director of Research at Roffey Park. Roffey Park initiated a research project in 2008 titled "The Organisational Context for Effective Business Partnering." This research had concluded that "the verdict is still out on the role of HR business partners." Figure 3.2 shows the proportion of respondents reporting success or not in implementing business partners.

One of the key follow-up "threads" that Roffey Park was pursuing was the influence of the actual implementation process and contextual factors upon the longer term success of a Business Partner structure in the organizations surveyed.

Figure 3.2: Success levels of business partnering

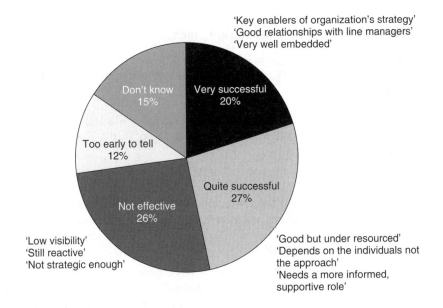

'Key enablers of organization's strategy'
'Good relationships with line managers'
'Very well embedded'

Don't know 15%

Very successful 20%

Too early to tell 12%

Not effective 26%

Quite successful 27%

'Low visibility'
'Still reactive'
'Not strategic enough'

'Good but under resourced'
'Depends on the individuals not the approach'
'Needs a more informed, supportive role'

We believe that this research helps shed some light on crucial issues of Business Partner implementation.

The situation with regard to HR structures in 2009

1. Certainly, in terms of the United Kingdom, a large number of HR functions are wedded to a form of the 3-Box Model.

2. Shared Service functions have been established in many HR structures – some of these have been outsourced to providers such as Xchanging, Accenture, Capita, and so forth, but others have been retained within house as, for instance, in Royal Mail.

3. Both HR Directors and client managers perceive implementation issues and problems in terms of establishing new HR Structures, and many issues remain in terms of the quality of service, individual competence in areas such as business understanding and strategic capability, and the ability of both HR departments and the business at large to change and adjust to new structures.

4. There does still seem to be an underlying belief that new HR Structures will and do lead to cost economies.

5. The key question that remains at present is will these HR Structures enable HR professionals to play an effective corporate role in managing the complex problems that will emerge in most companies during the current era of global recession (or possibly depression)?

3.7. Reflections on the HR structuring process

Toward the end of our time together at Vevey, we turned our discussion toward reflections on the nature of HR Structures past, present, and future. Four issues come to the fore:

1. The implementation of HR delivery models in global businesses and the need to understand fine-grain differentiations in the role of each of the three boxes in global operations.

2. A more critical examination of many of the assumptions that surround advice in the area. We use the question of the origins of the 3-box model by way of example, and argue that 3-Boxes were emerging inexorably in HR driven by the prior emergence of comprehensive HR IT systems. Unravelling the true causes behind HR Delivery Systems will lead to better quality decision making around the options that exist.

3. The notion of the optimum HR model. In essence the core of the debate concerns, when operating a 3- or 4-Box model, does duplication of responsibility exist between business partners and Experts, where, and does this matter? We argue that the evidence is that it does matter.

4. Central to the performance of HR structures is the question of Business Partner capability. However, there are two interrelated issues at play here, namely, the mindset and the power position of the HR leader. Both have to be addressed.

3.7.1. The 3-Box model and its implementation in global businesses

During our discussion, Matt Stripe offered his views on each of the 3-boxes. In relation to Shared Services, he argued:

> ... I think the Shared Services box needs to be viewed at the present time as broader than an HR problem. Lots of functions in global corporations including procurement, IT, finance and HR have looked to centralise the administrative and process element of their activities. That centralisation has been either outsourced or kept in-house, but always with the aim of being faster and cheaper. I think we are there now at Nestlé. Therefore, I think we will centralize, to the extent of having all employees paid by one provider in maybe one or two locations. But you could move the location around, depending on costs at any time – so from Poland to India say.

In relation to business partners, he believes that the global dimension means that there must be a series of tiered roles within the role, driven off a common competence model:

> ... You then come to the more interesting piece in terms of HR, which is your so-called Business Partner Structure. I think when you are large and global, you will have tiers of Business Partner boxes. You will have business partners who sit in the HQ functions who will, in truth, perform a different sort of role in many ways, to the Business Partner who sits in a division that has got five or six factories attached to it will, to an extent, have different skills – similar but different [to another context]. But I do think for those individuals you will have a common competence model and a common profile/job description.

Finally, for Centers of Excellence,

> ... Now in terms of Experts or Centres of Excellence I think Nestlé, in the short-term, will follow a pragmatic logic of centralizing, unless it makes sense not to do so and, if it makes sense to be local, then things stay local.

> Recruitment, for me is a great example where you would do it at different tiers. Graduate recruitment you could probably do globally, however even with graduates, different working permit arrangements across the world might make it difficult [to centralize]. However, local school recruitment will be operationalized locally, coordinated by the Shared Service operation. A lot of training and development would similarly have a local focus.

When one considers HR Structures in truly global corporations, then the notion of differentiation allied to some quite subtle but pragmatic thinking comes into play.

There is also likely going to need to be effective "interplay" between Expert Centers of Excellence and Shared Services. For instance, the Talent Vice President/Director is likely to be the key player with regard to top talent resourcing, but Shared Services may well provide the lead in terms of lower paid employees, working closely with local business partners and Operational Managers.

3.7.2. The origins of 3-Box HR structures

It seems to us that there has always been a lack of clarity regarding the emergence of 3-Box Model HR Structures and the ideas postulated by Dave Ulrich in *Human Resource Champions*. This, by the way, is not the responsibility of Professor Ulrich, who refers in the book to his observations of good HR practice at companies such as Hewlett Packard and makes no claim to have invented the 3-Box Model. Indeed, *Human Resource Champions* focuses upon HR roles in building a competitive organization and labels those roles metaphorically as Strategic Partner, Administrative Expert, Employee Champion, and Change Agent.

Yet time after time HR practitioners refer to "Ulrich's 3-Box Model" and bestow upon Professor Ulrich and the 1996 book the legacy of being the launch pad for the 3-Box Model. To us this is a puzzle, a conundrum.

Why a puzzle? Basically, because we believe that HR Structures that closely conform to the characteristics of the 3-Box Model existed before 1996. One of the authors was employed in 1990 in a large division (25,000 plus employees) of a large corporation (100,000 plus employees) when a newly appointed HR Director for the division introduced a new HR Structure, linked to a 30 per cent reduction in the then "personnel" employee numbers. That structure involved a break first of all with the tradition and culture of the bulk of the HR team being housed in the established Personnel Blocks or the Training Department building, and a move to a structure with three components:

1. HR Advisors – colocated with their operational line clients. These HR Advisors were managed by heads of HR and were derived from a mix of new external recruits and those existing HR team members who had survived an internal assessment process.
2. Divisional Experts, nearly all externally recruited in areas such as resourcing, learning and development, employee communications, reward, and employment policies.
3. A substantially enhanced HR IT capability, based upon a new system, with a team focused upon managing the core "HR Processes."

Clearly, this company was not unique in developing a new HR architecture. It will certainly be the case that other organizations, at that same time, started moving their HR Structures to a very similar pattern as described above.

Why, we might ask, does the true genesis of 3-Box thinking matter?[5] Well, first it leads us to conclude that an important component of understanding change in HR Structures is to recognize the true drivers of this change. Second, it makes it clearer what Ulrich's real contribution has been. Our mutual experiences remind us that 3-Boxes were emerging inexorably within HR, driven by, for instance, the emergence of comprehensive HR IT systems via providers such as PeopleSoft (PeopleSoft version 1 was released in the late 1980s) and that these forces predate the publication of *Human Resource Champions*. The spread of an "HR" philosophy as against a "Personnel" approach, which again emerged in the late 1980s, was almost certainly a driver toward client colocated HR Advisors, as seen, for instance, in the Personnel Operations Managers (POMs) pioneered in Rover, during this period.

What is important to recognize, in our view, is the real contribution that David Ulrich has made to HR practice. His writing has continually provided a clear insight into the different roles that HR can play, with a particular emphasis on that role being strategic in nature. This was important to a function that can often be labeled as internally focussed and prone to gimmickry. As Matt Stripe observes:

> ... HR is one of those functions that spends an awful lot of time looking in, rather than looking out, almost justifying its own existence, looking for a platform. Ulrich created a scenario that a lot of HR people wanted to follow, which was around a strategic contribution that people, the function could play and the journey that it could go on. I think that is what HR people have signed on to.

Matt also believes that

> ... Most organisations that introduced the 3 Box model recognized quite quickly that there might be a two-tiered set of business partners. It's interesting that the second tier is now being recognized i.e. that in order to act in a truly strategic way, there may need to be a tier of "junior" business partners to support the lead HR players.

Of course, since 2000, on his lecture tours Ulrich has acknowledged the possibility of requiring four or even five legs to the HR "stool." This moves us into a final consideration of what the optimum model might be.

3.7.3. The optimum model

An important discussion regarding the future of HR structures is the notion of the optimum HR model. In essence, the core of the debate concerns the following question: when operating a 3- or 4-Box model, does duplication of responsibility exist between business partners and Experts, where, and does this matter? This duplication may be particularly marked in areas such as Organization Development/Design (see Chapter 8) and Talent Management (Figure 3.3).

Is the "ideal-type" model as follows? Organizations run with a top-quality Business Partner who is able to coach his/her colleagues in the senior team, as well as playing a full role in business decision-making, possessing particular skills (such as employee relations if operating in a heavily operational environment), but

Figure 3.3: The optimum HR delivery model

The Optimum model?

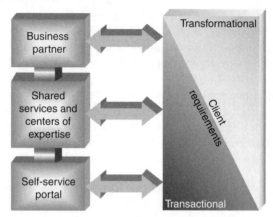

© Matt Stripe, 2009

utilizing within the team other heavyweight centrally based experts in areas such as Organization Design and Development or Talent, as and when required?

However if the business partners, in a particular organization, are, as advocated by Ulrich, in possession of a level of "mastery" in, for instance, Organization Design and Development, is it more rational to omit a central OD expert unit and, if one extends this thread of logic, appoint lower key HR professionals into central expert roles? We considered the probability that some emerging HR structures may, in fact, have been influenced by "personality" factors. When changing to a 3-Box structure, some organizations with powerful HR Experts in place may have shaped Business Partner and Expert responsibilities to fit with that particular legacy.

We feel that the "optimization" issue requires careful thought by HR leaders, not least because duplication could unnecessarily increase costs within the HR function as well as leading to ongoing conflict. We also suspect that the duplication issue may be most pointed in the area of Organization Design and Development, due to the reality that mastery of OD is a crucial element in the Business Partner tool-kit (see Chapter 8 for the reasons behind this argument). Matt Stripe confirms this complexity:

> . . . I've never been convinced that you can have a team of central Organisation Design specialists. If the role of the HRD is to operate in a "Golden Triangle" with the Managing Director and the Finance Director, acting as a key counsel to both, and, playing a strategic role, in, for instance, business model change, then they must lead in OD. That's possibly their major individual contribution to the business strategy.

Figure 3.4: Where HR delivery models can go wrong

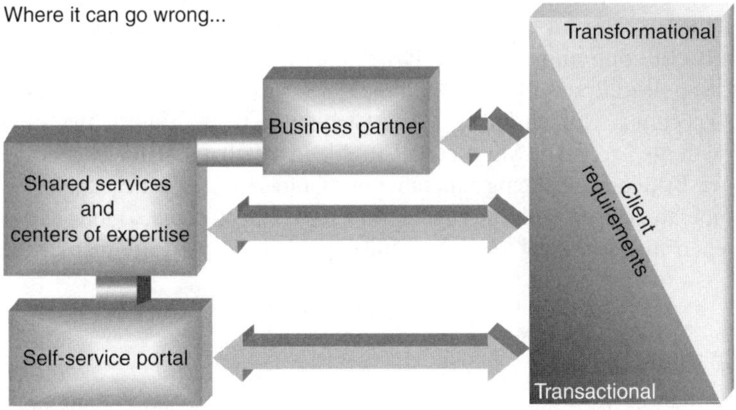

Where it can go wrong...

Transformational

Business partner

Shared services
and
centers of expertise

Client requirements

Self-service portal

Transactional

© Matt Stripe, 2009

3.7.4. Issues of power and mindset

We are both empathetic to, and intrigued by, the negative feedback regarding the level of performance derived from the introduction of new HR structures as exemplified by the findings of the CPHR and Roffey Park data, outlined earlier in the chapter. We endorse the research findings. There does seem to exist a substantial level of dissatisfaction with the realities of the 3-Box model in many organizations. By far the most common issue that was cited, as in the CPHR research, was focused upon the "capability" of business partners. Issues within this cluster included business acumen, upskilling potential, cultural insight, and relational skills.

If one follows the logic thread from this capability issue then the inevitable conclusion is that in terms of Business Partner quality, many organizations are deficient in terms of their HR staffing. Why is this an issue?

We conclude that there are two interrelated issues at play here, namely, the mindset and the power position of the HR leader.

Let us explore the mindset issue first. Evidence would suggest that to successfully introduce and operate a 3-Box model, particularly in terms of the possession of business-aware, strategically minded business partners, HR leaders will need to replenish their cadre of potential business partners, with some existing HR team members departing the organization alongside the recruitment of quality external "new blood." We believe that some HR leaders find such a "clinical" process difficult and therefore "mend and make do" with the existing team, some of whom will be incapable of making the switch to the Business Partner role.

This reluctance will be overcome if the HR leader has a strong drive or mindset to achieve excellence – what we call the HR Director "Excellence Mindset." This mindset is dominated by a need to create individual and team excellence in all activities in which the HR leader has responsibility. That mindset will provide the impetus for what may be perceived as brutal actions to ensure that the HR structure is optimally staffed.

However, the reality is that providing this pattern of leadership will be greatly aided if the HR Director has sufficient power within the organization to implement this optimum structure. Possessing the mindset may not be enough unless the political/power position of the HR leader is also strong. If that HR leader is part of a "Golden Triangle" (see Chapter 6), then it is likely that the HR leader with the Excellence Mindset will be able to install a potentially effective HR structure. By definition, being a member of a Golden Triangle means that the HR leader operates closely with the CEO and Finance Director and, as long as a strong argument is made, is likely to get their full support for a new HR organization.

3.8. Conclusion

This chapter has described a journey that commenced in the mid-1990s and runs through to the present day. During that period we have experienced a range of HR structures in a range of situations and contexts. In earlier sections of the chapter we have outlined what our key reflections are in terms of that journey, and what we have learned from the experiences. It remains to outline what major conclusions should be drawn. It seems to us that those conclusions are as follows:

1. Appropriate HR structures that will optimize the ability of the HR function to support effectively required business strategies are actually contingent upon a range of factors. These will include alignment with the requirements of the organization's business model, organization size, degree and complexity of globality, and the cultural history of HR role, power, and influence.

2. There is empirical evidence that the so called 3-Box Model is now evolving and flexing. Questions are being asked regarding the success that it brings to HR activity. It is possible that rigid adherence to, and uncritical questioning of, "3-Box" can bring its own problems.

3. Finally, truly global corporations, such as Nestlé, must view HR structures from a pluralistic perspective whereby a range of architecture will evolve depending upon market and business circumstances and drivers.

This evolution of structure will remain a constant factor in the lives of HR functions and will ever remain a great source of interest.

NOTES

1 Ulrich, D. (1997) *Human Resource Champions: The Next Agenda for Adding Value and Delivering Results.* Harvard: Harvard Business School Press.

2 Hird, M., Marsh, C. and Sparrow, P.R. (2009) *HR Delivery Systems: Re-engineered or Over-engineered?* CPHR White Paper 09/05. August 2009.

3 Sparrow, P.R., Brewster, C. and Harris, H. (2004) *Globalising Human Resource Management*. London: Routledge.

4 Ibid.

5 The genesis of the 3-Box model is analysed in more detail in Hird, M., Marsh, C. and Sparrow, P.R. (2009) *HR Delivery Systems: Re-engineered or Over-engineered?* CPHR White Paper 09/05. July 2009.

CHAPTER 4

Using Business Model Change to tie HR into Strategy: Reversing the Arrow

PAUL SPARROW, ANTHONY HESKETH, MARTIN HIRD, CRAIG MARSH, AND SHASHI BALAIN

4.1. Introduction

This chapter examines the issues involved for those *Leading HR* in linking HR to business model change. It

1. unravels the reality behind business model change based on a range of interviews with senior line and HR professionals;

2. outlines and explains the business context for a number of organizations;

3. uses these data to develop a taxonomy that are situated in practice. This taxonomy lays out four different 'political' spaces that HR has to operate in; and

4. identifies four separate transitions that those *Leading HR* have to cope with and keep strategically aligned.

Chapter 1 drew upon strategic management literature to argue that business models may be seen as a static map or snapshot that represents both an organization's value chain and how that chain is configured. This configuration is referred to as an *architecture*. This architecture is in turn underpinned by a range of organizational capabilities. These capabilities typically now extend across traditional organization boundaries as organizations find new ways in which they can create value by fitting their existing architecture into a broader value system or value web. The use of the word "web" is important. It signals that value typically extends beyond the traditional two dimensional value chain (that comprises several points of value delivery) into one that covers value creation across a third dimension – the existence of multiple stakeholders and the need for complex capabilities that capitalize on new and more collaborative forms of strategic delivery.

Chapter 2, which drew upon some of our survey work, showed that a high proportion of HR Directors currently face the challenge of significant business model change, but do so at a time when they are still refining their existing HR delivery models. *Leading HR* is therefore becoming a more complex affair. As business models change, then by definition, so too do the demands for the sorts of capabilities that HR must itself possess or attempt to develop. But when the business is reinventing itself, the last thing it wants to hear from those *Leading HR* is discussion of a new structure for HR that will make it more strategic!

We begin with some opening observations about the nature of HR for the Business.

HR for the Business

Headline issue:

If one considers HR activity as a value chain, at what point on the chain does one commence the HR contribution? Does the HR function start from HR structure, best practices and performance management, or from the opposite perspective that is a clear and thoughtful evaluation of internal client needs?

Strategic imperative:

People are of intangible value. One manifestation of the chief executive officer (CEO) 'getting' the people proposition is that HR has to 'get' the business proposition in return. Only then can it release the people value that is inherent in the business. In this regard HR acts as value brokers. Business model change provides a perfect opportunity for HR to provide this value brokerage.

Must-win battle:

"Reversing the arrow" means developing a clear, business-oriented explanatory framework for the centrality of HR. The HR Director needs to be driven by an analysis of the nature of business model change, only then shaping the organization structure and HR processes, not as often is the case, the other way round. Measurement of performance becomes the end of the process, not the beginning.

The challenge for *Leading HR*, then, is to cope with alterations to strategy, business model, and the change management approach and to understand how they fit together. We argue that

The key messages that emerge from this chapter

1) HR work at strategic level entails a deep understanding of the organization's business model, in particular the opportunity, its value web presents for HR to add value to the change.

2) The transformational nature of business model change entails the primacy of an organization design (OD) agenda in HR at the highest level for it to be effective. However, what is meant by the term "organization design" is changing (see Chapter 8).

3) HR "Strategy" ceases to exist in the ideal situation; there is business strategy, and this will be associated with an HR process. The two become synonymous with HR nested

The key messages that emerge from this chapter: (Continued)

within the business strategy. There is only a separate HR strategy when HR is not playing at the highest level.

4) For HR, added-value derives from an intuitive relationship with the line, an understanding of the organization's strategy and business model, and a creative business-led explanation of how HR process integrates with this (a process we call "reversing the arrow"). Such insight is necessary to counterbalance a recent trend in HR to install generic processes and structures with little regard to business model.

5) In this chapter we present a more refined analysis of business model change – analysis based on the scale, stage, and political scope of change. This leads to a better understanding of the true nature of HR work and reveals the multiple transformations that HR has to manage. We show that HR have a remarkable opportunity to influence strategy, and they can do this at two levels.

6) At the highest level, this influence might be achieved through facilitating Board-level discussions about the organizations' value proposition and key operating principles. Chapter 6 will develop this theme through discussion of the importance of an HR Director's political and relationship skills in being able to build the necessary credibility, in what is called the Golden Triangle.

7) At the second level, once important choices about the business model are being debated and designed, HR is often called upon to offer advice about the organization design issues. Chapter 8 will develop this theme by arguing that in order to be able to meet the demands that CEOs are increasing putting upon them, HR Directors need to build an advanced organization design capability inside their function.

8) This advanced capability is called "Architectural Design" – not because we want to introduce another set of jargon into the HR lexicon – but rather to signal that this new combination of skills is based in organization design thinking, but when applied to the challenge of business model change is also introducing a set of strategic considerations that demand more complex thinking than has previously been the case in much organization design work.

One way of thinking about the level of challenge faced by HR in a process of business model change is to consider the significance and depth of knowledge change associated with the new model. Rebecca Henderson and Kim Clark[1] made a distinction between two different types of knowledge that have to be combined:

1. component knowledge (knowledge of the parts rather than the whole); and
2. architectural knowledge (the shared understanding of the interconnection of all components, or how things fit together).

This work has been developed by Sung-Choon Kang, Shad Morris, and Scott Snell[2] to argue that knowledge may be disconnected, or common. Two HR architectures are needed:

1. Knowledge of common components, which is applied to sub-routines or operations that overlap so that new possibilities may be explored (i.e., the organization and its key talent needs deep enough knowledge of an internal or external partners' expertise to assimilate, interpret, apply, and recognize the value in it),

2. Knowledge of common architecture, which relates to firm-wide routines that coordinate and combine the various components (i.e., the organization and its key talent needs knowledge of the bigger picture and of the conflicts contained within it, and hence a greater ability to tweak and exploit the business model).

The ability to bring together the known constituents or knowledge bases associated with a new business model is "mission critical" (organizational learning experts call this "architectural capability").

The type of knowledge shifts involved in business model change

HR Directors can help the organization understand whether business model change might involve changes to only one, or to a combination of both, of the following:

Component knowledge (also called Operational knowledge): It refers to an understanding of the nuts and bolts of the operations of the business. It is based on knowledge of the parts – or components of the business – rather than the whole. This knowledge of common components can be applied to the sub-routines or operations that overlap in the new business model. HR Directors have to understand whether – and how – their organization can develop deep enough knowledge of all the various partner's (such as internal functions or external business partners) expertise so that it can assimilate, interpret, apply, and recognize the value in this knowledge. Only with deep component capability can new possibilities be explored.

Architectural knowledge: It requires the shared understanding of how the new strategy and business models require interconnections between all of the operational (component) knowledge. In short, how things fit together. Knowledge of common architecture relates to the organization-wide routines (or indeed cross-organization and cross-partner routines) that have to be coordinated and combined, so that the various components can deliver their value. It is knowledge of the bigger picture. It requires the HR Director to be sure that the organization has thought through the strategy and business model and has understood the (potential) conflicts contained within this picture. This type of capability gives the organization a much better chance to tweak and exploit the business model.

Business model change alters the strategic value that is attached to particular types of knowledge. It also changes the way that different types of knowledge have to relate to each other. Of course, knowledge represents the starting point, but once this knowledge has become internalized into an organization and is supported by all of the supporting systems, structures, and processes, a deeper capability has been created.

However, we do not know the answer to the following question: what are the activities that HR should engage in and be prepared to deploy when faced by demands to support business model movement and change successfully and build these new capabilities?

To answer this, we have questioned both operational and HR executives about the key characteristics associated with a range of business models deployed inside their organization and used this investigation to clarify the characteristics and requirements of that model. Only through seeing business model change through the eyes of the line can the true contribution of HR be discussed.

The HR agendas outlined in this chapter are based upon the combined insights of senior line managers – such as Chief Executives, Business Directors, and Capability and Transformation Directors – *and* HR Directors. We interviewed 30 executives from eight different organizations, and draw upon a subset of this interview data and secondary analysis of the situation in this chapter. It is important to capture the diverse sectoral realities faced by HR Directors. The case studies presented later in the book, based upon other interview data, involve a number of these organizations – the analysis of their business model change context here helps to contextualize the various *Leading HR* practices that we examine later.

Before we begin the analysis, let us briefly remind ourselves about some realities.

The reality of HR's position in the context of business model change

1. Thinking inside most organizations is at varying degrees of sophistication in terms of the level of insight into a new business model.

2. Regardless of the necessities for HR change dictated by business model change, the relationship between the HR function and the business reflects different levels of strategic embeddedness that often predate the changes taking place.

3. The degree of control that HR Directors, or indeed their CEOs, have over the business model might be subject to other external influences.

4. The pace at which new business models are operationalized (and the need for associated HR transformations) has to be balanced against the need to ensure safe "steady-state" operations and an "HR as usual" level of service.

So we must understand the different contexts – or political spaces – that HR Directors typically find themselves operating in. To do this we develop a framework that summarizes the challenges for HR in four different spaces:

1. "Incremental changes" in the business model change;

2. Externally driven business model change – "The Changing *Rules of the Game*";

3. Internally driven business model change – "*Changing* the rules of the game (for others)"; and

4. Continuous business model change – "Persistent Fluidity."

The issue of HR Delivery models was discussed in Chapters 2 and 3. As you read the different challenges faced by HR in this chapter, consider whether a one-size-fits-all way of structuring HR will remain viable.

4.2. Incremental changes in business model change

In the first political space in our taxonomy, the strategic landscape is known and, despite the potential still for significant HR transformation, is comparatively stable or evolving slowly. The business model is being refined and extended, but the key concepts and core capabilities that underlie the business model remain the same. We use McDonald's and Rowntree Nestlé to illustrate this space.

McDonald's UK is Britain's biggest restaurant chain with 1,200 outlets and 17,000 farm suppliers. Families account for about a third of total sales in the United Kingdom, a higher proportion than in the United States. About 60 per cent of staff at McDonald's are under the age of 22, and behind-the-counter staff stay with McDonald's for an average of two-and-a-half years. It recruits staff for its restaurants on the basis of attitude rather than experience or qualification. The HR strategy is based on a holistic approach to training and development that is designed to unlock the potential of employees by giving them transferable skills that they value.

McDonald's: Shifting the balance toward franchisees

McDonald's established the "fast food" system of providing quick service and uniform quality to customers. It earns revenue as an investor in properties, a franchiser of restaurants, and an operator of restaurants. In addition to charging franchise fees and marketing fees, calculated as a percentage of sales, it collects rent, calculated on the basis of sales. It does not make direct sales of food or materials to franchisees, but instead organizes the supply of food and materials to restaurants through approved third-party logistics operators. As consumers increasingly become interested in the quality, sourcing, and ethics of the food and drink they buy, this enables it to align rapidly behaviors in the supply chain. The standardization of product and pricing has been a large factor in the success of McDonald's, with attention paid to replicability and operational detail. There is a key focus on menu choice, food quality, value, and convenience.

Decentralization is fundamental to the business model. At the corporate level McDonald's provides a global framework of common goals, policies, and guidelines rooted to its core values, but geographic business units have freedom to develop programs and performance measures appropriate to local conditions.

McDonald's: Shifting the balance toward franchisees: (Continued)

A dramatic financial turnaround in 2003 was driven by a two-pronged strategy in the United States: focusing on increasing sales at existing locations by renovating stores by expanding menu options and store hours; and expanding aggressively internationally, opting to franchise rather than operate its new locations, providing new income with little overhead.

In the early 2000s the UK business also stalled but the response was different. Whereas in the United States, 15 per cent of restaurants are owned and operated by McDonald's Corporation directly (with 85 per cent operated through franchise or joint venture agreements) until recently in the United Kingdom it was the opposite – only 30 per cent of restaurants were franchised.

In 2004 independent research from the Work Foundation showed that McDonald's franchisee-owned restaurants locked in more economic benefit and returned more value to the local community compared to the company-owned counterparts. McDonald's relaxed controls over rigid brand uniformity (moving to a situation where the brand was seen as best run by local business people, supporting local communities), and the United Kingdom also moved to a greater proportion of franchise-operated restaurants. The business model continues to evolve. In 2009 McDonald's UK researched how the market for informal eating out (less than £15 per head) is changing. The market is worth over £40 billion. Steve Easterbrook, the Chief Executive said, "... people are slightly concerned about the squeeze on discretionary income discretionary spend ... I think there will definitely be some structural changes ... people will not return to the excess of before and in the terms of frequency they eat out and how much they are willing to spend when they go out ... it's going to be a market share fight over supplying the market place."

At McDonald's the HR focus is on continuous improvement of the engagement – performance link by (for example) setting up HR metrics to measure the link, clarifying HR's value proposition to employees, capitalizing on a good social mobility position, and implementing coaching and development to improve restaurant-level HR climate. The shifts certainly impact the HR function – as Chapter 11 will show it has to go through a process of educating employees and franchisees alike about the value of HR in the context of the service-profit chain – and in selling the HR value proposition to a different set of stakeholders (franchisors) much of the tacit understanding about the value of HR that exists inside the organization has to be reaffirmed to new stakeholders. However, the business turnaround based on a shift in the balance of operating company-franchise ownership is not associated with significant change in the business model.

There may still be a busy HR agenda and significant transformation programs may be taking place. We use the example of Rowntree Nestlé to show how the challenge of *Leading HR* in the Incremental space can be to look at an *existing* business model, but through new lenses.

Rowntree Nestlé: Reinvigorating the existing business model

Nestlé operates across a range of business models, with different models for globally driven premium businesses, regionally managed (zonal), very local, stand-alone, or service-driven businesses. It relies on the GLOBE system to allow businesses to operate their own optimal structure whilst benefiting from best practice adoption and continuous improvement in components of the business model such as food quality, pricing, supply chain management, and marketing. Nestlé UK is an important component of Nestlé's multinational operations. Nestlé Rowntree was formed after the 1988 acquisition in 1988. It is the United Kingdom's third largest confectionery company after Cadbury's and Mars. The brands include Kit Kat (the United Kingdom's top selling confectionery product and 11th overall consumer brand), Milky Bar, Aero, Smarties, Quality Street, and After Eight.

Senior management was overhauled in late 2003 to refocus the business, and then again in 2005 when the sector share was eroded after a series of unsuccessful spin-off products. The performance of the Kit Kat brand had provided one of the incentives for Nestlé to acquire Rowntree. By 2004 the UK confectionery market was worth nearly £4 billion (the biggest in Europe), but growth was hard to come by and competition was fierce. Sales of the leading brand Kit Kat first met saturation point and then fell by 5 per cent in a year. In December 2003 analysts reported that the incoming Managing Director saw Nestlé Rowntree as a business in crisis. The strategic intent was to get "more people to buy more products more often at higher prices to make more money for ourselves and our retail customers." Attention was given to the relevance of the brand. Nestlé Rowntree targeted workplace snacking, but retaining Kit Kat's former association with relaxation. The launch of the first brand extension of Kit Kat Chunky in 1999 was followed by limited-edition flavor variants and spin-offs such as Kit Kat Kubes. Expenditure on trade marketing was reduced along with levels of supermarket discounting. The strategy met with mixed success. The Managing Director left less than 2 years later.

Despite heavy investment in brand proliferation sales had fallen. Whilst consumers had bought more, variants cannibalized sales of the core brand. There was a lack of customer focus or attention to retailers and continued issues with product quality. The solution of the new Managing Director was a restoration plan based on a business improvement strategy. Poor forecasting had created problems with demand planning. Key processes had to be fixed. Attention and investment was shifted away from sales into brand management, measurement of stock-in-trade, sustainable new product development, and product quality. A number of management processes around business modeling capability were altered. The decision to shut down the antiquated five-storey Victorian building at its plant in York was announced in 2006, some production was moved elsewhere in Europe, and £20m was invested in the York plant to improve production facilities. By August 2007 Nestlé's financial reporting noted that there had been a "notable performance improvement" at its UK Nestlé Rowntree confectionery business.

It is easy to assume then that just because there is a significant business improvement or process redesign program, this automatically entails business model change. As made clear in Chapter 1, it does not.

Why is the distinction important? *Leading HR* in this political space still involves advancing a case for the added-value of HR where this case may not be well understood. The HR agenda pursued may still be innovative where the level of other business improvement activity allows for it. Business model change need not always be the driver for what still can be fundamental HR change. The level of activity in HR may be frenetic and change tough and challenging. The organization may be making investments in different components of the model (though not changing its basic architecture), and HR still has to understand the implications of the operational transformations. There may be shifts in strategic attention – perhaps to maintain or restore the health of the existing business model – and to assist this HR needs deep operational insight.

But – and it is an important but – innovations in strategy occur around the margin. The key performance challenges reflect the continuous need to manage underlying operational efficiencies and market/ customer perceptions. However, the recipe needed to deliver optimal performance – and the core organizational capabilities that underpin this recipe both in the business and in HR – remain the same. The key challenge for HR is to advance the value proposition through better internal exploitation of the core performance logic of the current business model. The incremental business model change space is more manageable and less threatening to HR than the other three political spaces that we lay out (Table 4.1).

Table 4.1: Incremental business model change: Key characteristics of the political space and implications for *Leading HR*

Key characteristics of the political space		Implications for *Leading HR*	
1.	Stable or slowly evolving competitive landscape – innovations in strategy occurring around the margin	1.	Management of transformations in narrow domains, such as operational efficiencies and market perceptions
2.	Performance recipes and core organizational capabilities needed to manage remain the same	2.	Deep operational insight needed into these components to better understand the implications of operational transformations
3.	Relatively stable and predictable demands for value from customer	3.	HR often needs to restress this value and articulate it to a range of new audiences, but requisite talent is readily available internally and externally
4.	Business model is relatively well known and already implemented	4.	Continuous improvement of HR practices is needed to ensure reinforcement of the capabilities relevant to model
		5.	Value is created through the better exploitation of a performance logic always inherent in the current business model

4.3. Externally driven business model change: The changing *Rules of the game*

Why less threatening? Consider the second position on our taxonomy. Here a fundamental shift has taken place in the way that customers, or other key stakeholders (government, or regulators), perceive the value of the organization's product or service.

As the traditional capabilities of the organization rapidly become outdated, there is a threat to survival. Although the organization *should* be reacting to this shift with a transformation of its business model, the nature and speed of potential transformation depend on how quickly the organizations' leaders perceive the threat, *or* are able and free to react to it. In many instances, despite elements of radical change, much of the real HR agenda has to be held in abeyance for several years as alternative futures are considered, or external (often political) influences chop and change.

This is why we call *Leading HR* in this space "The Changing Rules of the Game." The *rules of the game* keep shifting, but the HR function, as with the organization as a whole, are not the ones really driving the changing part of the agenda.

Royal Mail: Repositioning against new business model competition

Royal Mail Group Ltd. is the parent company of Royal Mail, Post Office, and Parcelforce Worldwide. It is a good example of the unique pressures some Public sector organizations face in today's fast changing business environment. On the one hand are a series of social responsibilities, business values, and ethos embedded in centuries old history that must be adhered to: an argument that "post matters" to the UK economy, the requirement to offer a universal service at common price which means that costs cannot be removed from the business in line with volumes; and a social cohesion role with regard to small businesses, social customers, and communities. On the other hand are business pressures that deregulation of postal services brings. In the exchanges during the independent review of the UK postal services sector from December 2007 to May 2008, both the reviewers and Royal Mail agreed that the old business model "was untenable."[3] The challenge is to devise a business model that provides incentives for Royal Mail to modernize operations and stabilize finances. Royal Mail argues that it needs more access to equity and also that the regulatory regime is based on erroneous assumptions about the decline in post volumes, level of price controls and returns, controls over its retail and wholesale businesses, product development and withdrawal, and artificial incentives to new entrants and disincentives for Royal Mail to remove costs. The pace at which new entrants (such as TNT) captured share in the upstream delivery business has been faster than anticipated. Changing technology, the decline of postal services as a share of the communications market, and e-substitution continue to decrease the size of the market.

The vision of Royal Mail remains unchanged: "To be the best and most trusted mail company in the world" but it has changed its strategy. "Modernization" – defined as making the culture more customer focused and focusing on complex and sometimes conflicting

Royal Mail: (Continued)

performance demands for innovation in products and services (transforming the value of advertising mail, providing new sender and receiver options, offering sustainability through recycling, and finding additional sources of revenue through ventures into new financial products markets) – is the main agenda. But this is to be driven by continued and more radical improvements in productivity and efficiency to the value of £1.5 billion, with plans to restructure the Post Office and mail center networks, introduce new technology, and standardize and simplify work practices.[4] By July 2009, government plans to sell a 30 per cent minority stake in Royal Mail to a private company to form a partnership were delayed again, despite claims that its finances were "reaching crisis point." It has a pensions deficit said to be near to £8 billion.

At Royal Mail, the HR strategy has to date been to get to a "steady-state" position – stabilizing the industrial relations climate following investment in new technology, implementing major cost reductions, and moving the HR department to a modern operating model. HR in the nuclear industry is in a similar position. For example, at Sellafield Ltd., one of the United Kingdom's major operating sites, the uncertainty of the Government's position on the future of the Nuclear industry – only recently resolved – meant that for several years the organization knew only that the business model was to change, without knowing precisely which variant might prevail. The HR team had to focus on maintaining the capabilities needed to ensure continuous safe operations, whilst also assisting the organization to develop new capabilities that might underpin any future option, such as cross-functional structures, and new ways of working as the organization shifted from a cost-plus to fixed-price contract system.

What then does *Leading HR* look like in this political space? It often involves having to sell one business model after another, and along with other directorates, weighing up the likely consequences of each option, or finding temporary holding positions. These temporary holding positions often involve very radical changes in HR – huge business transformations – as the businesses fight just to stay alive. But, the transformations currently being experienced are just the beginning, and the learning that results from the transformations may still have little relevance for the future yet to be faced. HR has to look, Janus-like, in two directions:

1. establishing some stable space in the transition, through "best practice" HR processes
2. keeping an eye on the strategic goal, where more fundamental changes to the HR architecture will be needed once the end-state business model is clarified.

It is easy for HR to appear to be "on the back foot." It may not yet be clear what the future business model is; HR will therefore be reacting to operational challenges imposed by a shifting and uncertain landscape and – in the

Table 4.2: Externally driven business model change: Key characteristics of the political space and implications for *Leading HR*

Key characteristics of the political space		Implications for *Leading HR*	
1.	External change in the competitive landscape means that the organization value proposition is no longer valuable	1.	HR reacts to short-term strategic challenges and uncertainty
2.	Shift has taken place in the way that customers, or other key stakeholders (government, or regulators), perceive the value of products or service	2.	Often involved in very radical changes in HR with the fight being just to stay alive
3.	Threat to the survival of the organization, as its traditional capabilities rapidly become outdated	3.	HR has to help maintain the capabilities needed to ensure continuous low-risk operations, whilst also assisting the development of new capabilities that might underpin any future option
4.	Leaders may or may not perceive the threat, but may claim an inability and level of freedom to react to it.	4.	HR needs to keep business model change on the agenda because the more valuable HR agenda may be held in abeyance for several years as alternative futures are considered
5.	New capabilities needed	5.	Keep an eye on the strategic goal, where more fundamental changes to the HR architecture will be needed once the end-state business model is clarified
6.	Organization *may or may not be* responding with Business Model Change	6.	Seek temporary holding positions to establish some stable space in the transition, through "best practice" HR
		7.	Recognize that the learning from current transformations may still have little relevance for the future yet to be faced

worst case – implementing HR strategy which is rapidly becoming outdated or irrelevant, and therefore losing its value to the business (Table 4.2).

4.4. Internally driven business model change – *Changing* the rules of the game

In the third position on our taxonomy, the change may be in response to a shift in the competitive landscape, but the organizations' leaders have reacted quickly to drive business model-led transformational change through the organization, often before competitors have reacted, or before others see the necessity of the change. We examine the consequence of business model change for the approach to talent management in BAE Systems in Chapter 7. We explain below why it can be seen as an example of internally driven business model change.

British Aerospace Systems: Leading the way toward through-life capability management

BAE Systems is the 4th largest defense company in the world, behind the US firms of Lockheed Martin, Boeing, and Northrop Grumman, with annual sales of over £15 billion and 97,500 employees. It is engaged in the development, delivery, and support of advanced defense and aerospace systems in the air, on land, and at sea and has customers and partners in over 100 countries. In the defense industry many constituents may be suppliers, customers, and partners but also competitors; firms can act as both suppliers and contractors, and a significant range of processes may be outsourced. In the old business model, based around large contract procurement, concern grew that there was a risk that the United Kingdom could end up having no onshore defense capability and that open competition might actually decrease the ability of UK firms to compete globally. Procurement decisions were sporadic, so if an organization lost capability it might be 5 years before the next contract, by which time the skills could be lost to other sectors. BAE was able to use its work with certain sectors – for example, on logistics issues with defense equipment suppliers – to argue that there could be a more intelligent service model.[5]

As an integrated suite of equipment was developed, after which it became possible to make the final switch to an availability contract business model. BAE Systems would take on the management of a customer's assets, and reduce their cost of procurement by the hour. The new business model – for which there were some parallels in lean management within the automotive industry and the aircraft engine design sector – was based around the contracting for availability of military assets, and involved shared ownership and shared risk taking over these assets. Central issues were asset and inventory cost management, which could best be solved through better supply chain management, linked to procurement and the predictability of costs. This thought process enabled a clearer value proposition to be articulated for government. The model required a shift in attention to Through Life Costs – the resources needed to run equipment throughout its life cycle – and this depends on the complexity involved in its design.

Reflecting this thought process, the Defense Industrial Strategy (DIS), published in December 2005, recognized that many of the Armed Services' platforms will likely have long service lives, requiring extensive support and upgrades, and set out those industrial capabilities for which the United Kingdom needs to maintain both appropriate sovereignty over this capability. The most expensive aspect of military platforms is rarely the acquisition cost but is the ongoing support and maintenance contracts. Through Life begins from concept design, assessment and demonstration, through manufacture and migration to initial service, in-service support, and transition out of service.

A number of agreements followed the DIS. The Secretary of State of the time explained that "... In short, we are telling industry what we think we will need, what will be strategic to the UK, where we will be spending tax payers' money, and how we will engage with the market." BAE Systems applied the model principally to military air platforms such as Tornado and Typhoon, land systems, and some naval programs such as Type 45 frigates and Astute class submarines, but as it builds its capability to operate the business model and demonstrate sustainable profitability, it will be applied more deeply and to wider parts of the business in Air, Land, and Sea. From an HRM perspective the model also requires that a strong service capability be developed on top of the existing production, engineering, and project management culture. The model also shifts the relative importance given to different people, knowledge, skills, and experience.

At BAE Systems, the through-life capability business model is allowing them to take a lead position in a highly competitive landscape. Those organizations that understand both the key capabilities that get thrown up by the model – such as integrated business systems modeling or partnership arrangements – but can also demonstrate secure execution of these capabilities can capture significant value in existing markets and apply this learning to the development of new markets. BAE Systems' HR leadership has already reacted to the demands of changing the rules of the game by outsourcing of most of its HR function.

Put simply, the changes taking place in the business model shift the likes of a BAE away from being an engineering company that manufactures military equipment, toward an organization that provides services that assist the war-fighting capability of its customers. Such a shift has immense implications for the performance logic inside the organization, the nature of executive talent (see Chapter 7), the way employees must be managed, and with what they would be expected to engage with (see Chapter 9).

The changes above have been paralleled in lean management within the automotive industry and the aircraft engine design sector. Another example is the utilities and water services sector. Here, business models have been driven by consolidation and privatization, but high returns on assets invested have to be bought through attention to customer service and the quality of the product. The more innovative business models in the sector are designed to achieve the best balance between financial and operational results, achieved in the main by restructuring to increase the line-of-sight to, and managerial responsiveness of, supporting operational processes and technologies. However, this is still based on a "whole-life" asset management approach that encompasses specification, design, and commissioning of infrastructure and facilities, and end-to-end processes from distribution and operational delivery to the issuing of bills and payment processing. These depend on selling volumes of water to pay for necessary capital, operating, and maintenance costs. As conservation demands and environmental pressures mount, seeking rent from the sale of volumes of water will produce contradictory drivers. Consumers and businesses will become driven more by the provision of quality water services rather than just the supply of essential volumes of water. Continued innovation in business models in the sector is expected.

Leading HR brings new demands in this political space. Whereas being in the "Changing *rules of the game*" space requires problem solving skills on behalf of the HR Director, being in the "*Changing* the rules of the game" space requires problem generation skills. HR has to build a deep understanding of the debates that have taken place around business model change, and acting as the champion of that strategy by diagnosing in advance what the organizational problems will be. HR has the opportunity to be on the "front foot." Not only does the HR agenda have

Table 4.3: Internally driven business model change: Key characteristics of the political space and implications for *Leading HR*

Key characteristics of the political space	Implications for *Leading HR*
1. Organizations' leaders are *proactive* in driving transformational (business model) change	1. Although the CEO is often the catalyst for a rethinking of strategy and business model, HR can co-create strategy (along with all other directorates) by diagnosing the changing demand on resources and consequences for both operational performance and longer term performance metrics
2. New (and often little understood) capabilities needed	2. HR needs an understanding of the debates that have taken place around business model change and the thought process used to enable a clearer value proposition
3. Redesign of the organization to increase the line-of-sight to, and managerial responsiveness of, supporting structures, operational processes, and technologies	3. Display of constructive problem generation skills – acting as the champion of the strategy by diagnosing in advance what the organizational problems will be
4. Creation of new value-added service activities	4. Strong service capability to be underpinned by an Architectural Design capability and innovative HR structures
5. Reshaping the business portfolio to focus on new skills and activity streams – shifts in the relative importance given to different people, knowledge, skills, and experience	

the potential to be central to the success of business model change, to an extent the HR agenda may be synonymous with it, but business model change also entails redesigning the organization's value web, and developing new strategic (or "architectural") capabilities. These issues are firmly in the domain of HR expertise (Table 4.3).

4.5. Continuous business model change – persistent fluidity

In the fourth and final position on our taxonomy, the competitive environment is in a state of continuous and rapid evolution. We examine HR at Vodafone in more detail in Chapter 11. However, at Vodafone the challenge can be categorized as future-proofing talent in a world of continuous business model change. We admit to some caution in categorizing Vodafone in the continuous business model change space and suspect that the need to do so reflects the fact that the high level of technological and product market change creates the need for a generalized and persistent level of fluidity in strategy, and an inability for any organization in this space to make a technological bet – or to take a position on key talent – that will remain unchallenged.

Vodafone: Future-proofing talent

Vodafone Group Plc is the world's leading telecommunication company with a significant presence in Europe, the Middle East, Africa, Asia Pacific, and the United States. It has experienced remarkable growth having become the world's leading mobile telecommunications company within 25 years. In the financial year ending 2008/09, the company reported revenue of £41.0 billion, a 15.6 per cent increase over the previous financial year. Its proportionate customer base stood at 303 million, again an increase of c. 25 per cent over the previous year. During this rapid rise is has moved from being a conglomerate of acquisitions toward the formation of a singular identity – that of "One Vodafone." It has three segments of customers: Enterprise, wholesale, and individual consumers. It operates in four product areas: mobile voice, mobile data, specialist products (where they sell live to customers), and mobile solutions (bespoke solutions for organizational clients). The previous business model focused on capturing market share in the mobile voice product area, but increasingly the industry is moving toward convergence where the phone can do everything.

Vodafone's business model is highly susceptible to four forces: changes in technology; new entrants in the competition (such a providers of fixed-line services, or providers of other services such as VoIP); changes in regulations; and an increasingly aware, discerning, and demanding customer with lots of options. In response, it is concentrating on developing expertise in selling complex IT solutions to targeting high revenue-generating Enterprise customers. It also identifies the need to stay ahead of its competitors in technological innovations. Convergence of voice and data providing true mobility for its customers is Vodafone's major objective.

The Group has been extending its business model to generate revenue from mobile advertising by partnering with advertising specialists in individual markets. As part of the total communications strategy, it is also offering its business customers solutions intended to meet a wider variety of their communications needs. This involves the development of new ways of enabling business customers to "mobilize" and increase the efficiency of their workforce. Such solutions open up new revenue streams for Vodafone. As with the example of BAE Systems, by providing an end-to-end solution and integrating these into a customer's infrastructure and subsequently managing the service, innovations in the business model also change the boundaries between organizations. In terms of innovating and delivering on customer's total communication needs, Vodafone has focused on four key areas: increasing data revenue by continuing to develop product and services to integrate the mobile and PC environment; increasing presence in fixed broadband business; converting fixed line users to mobile through fixed location pricing plans offering customers fixed prices when they call from within or around their home or office; and increasing revenues generated through mobile advertising and concentrating on technological innovations that help them do so. Though its core operating model remains the same – sell mobile products and solutions – Vodafone customizes its strategy according to the market it is operating in.

Table 4.4: Fluid business model change: Key characteristics of the political space and implications for *Leading HR*

Key characteristics of the political space	Implications for *Leading HR*
1. Continuous change in competitive landscape, entailing continual evolution of key components of the business model evolution for example, channels to market, product technologies with potential to converge sectors	1. HR can be at center of change: HR agenda may be synonymous with the business strategy
	2. HR can contribute to the redesign of the organization's value web, and the development of new strategic (or "architectural") capabilities
	3. HR is seen as a strategic partner sharing and leading strategic evolution within the business
	4. Demonstration that HR can capture significant value in existing markets and apply this learning to the development of new markets
	5. Understand both the key capabilities that get thrown up by all future-bet models, and demonstrate secure execution of these capabilities

Organizations in this space cannot afford the luxury of crystallizing one business model for any length of time, due to the volatility of the market place, and at the risk of being left behind by competitors. Continuous evolution of key components of the business model is central to competitive advantage and ultimate success within the market place. The ultimate HR challenge when in this political space is to future-proof talent (Table 4.4).

4.6. Managing strategic reciprocity

The typology captured in Tables 4.1–4.4 is intended to be illustrative and not prescriptive. Business model innovation though always requiring transformational change may still be considered as more or less radical. Any organization positioned in the taxonomy may, or may well in future, evolve through the different stages shown. It also represents the current state of what we call "strategic reciprocity" in the organizations studied.

An important task is to understand the HR architecture that is associated within each of the four political spaces, and how HR can transition itself both through and across each space. Little work has been undertaken on the possible ways in which such an HR architecture interchanges with the existing business strategy and business models to add value. This interchange between strategy, business model, and HR architecture we refer to as *strategic reciprocity*.

Strategic reciprocity

This is more than the alignment of HR (and its architecture) within what Boris Becker, Mark Huselid, and Dave Ulrich call "the larger system of a firm's strategy implementation."[6] Strategic reciprocity captures the current *state* of HR in relation to the interchange that takes place during emergent strategy and business model change.

Crucially, reciprocity does not suggest that HR strategy is determined by an overarching business strategy. Rather, it is complimentary to it. For example, whilst overarching business strategies and models may move through significant change, the underpinning business models and state of HR may be able to meet the people management aspects of such strategic changes whilst simultaneously remaining itself unchanged. It has been designed in such a way that it can adapt its capabilities to meet new ends.

Conversely, whilst organizations may find themselves in a period of strategic consolidation with little overarching business model change, HR functions may be experiencing internal transformations involving the radical overhaul of their structures, capabilities, service orientation, and, critically from our perspective, their underpinning business models and their correlation to overarching business strategies.

How are these critical capabilities developed? They are often a consequence of bringing together or understanding the interdependencies of systems.[7] Looking across the examples in this chapter, we argue that

1. these capabilities – although embedded in and dependent upon people-related issues – are novel and deeply operational: they might relate to the supply chain, distribution and logistics, product and service innovations, consumer insight, and knowledge or information flows;

2. the business model may be delivered through an organization's own architecture, and/or through a network of partners whose own business model helps create, market, and ultimately deliver value. Understanding a business model therefore requires both deep strategic *and* operational insight; and

3. for HR, influencing thinking around the business model is more important and impactful than being aware of strategy and having a seat at the top table.

Strategic capability, then, is about being situated in the *operational hot seat* in such a way as to ensure the alignment and execution of HR so that it drives the business models underpinning organizational strategy.

4.7. Deconstructing the HR transformation

What is involved, then, in aligning and executing HR effectively in the context of business model change? Understanding the political space that the HR function sits in with regard to business model change is of course just the starting point. Our research shows that *Leading HR* involves the HR Director in four separate transitions – each of which tests their leadership skills. When you break the various HR transformations taking place down and dismantle them into their core elements – what academics like to call deconstructing – it becomes clear that multiple agendas have to be aligned.

Before we explain each of these, we provide a quick anecdote that reflects the attitude of many HR Directors. When having their HR agenda "deconstructed" by an academic presenter at a conference, an HR Director leaned over to one of the authors and whispered in his ear "I don't mind them deconstructing my HR, as long as they know how to put it back together again!" They were making a serious point. They were alluding to the complex set of leadership skills – not just technical and analytical skills – that an HR Director needs to navigate their function through the complex transformations that it becomes responsible for managing. What does this leadership involve?

1. Understanding the true extent of business model change that is being faced, and the political space that the HR function is in.
2. Being clear about – and to ensure the alignment between – the multiple transformations that the function has to manage.

Figure 4.1: Managing complex transformations

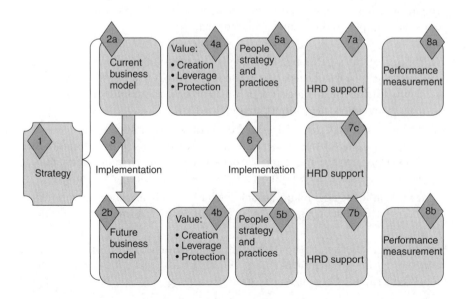

We summarize these transformations in Figure 4.1. When using this framework with an HR team at one leading organization, one of the team commented that the diagram looks like a plane with two engines. They quipped that the challenge for the HR Director was knowing when to power up and power down each engine in such a way that the plane keeps flying! Eventually, one of the engines stops firing, by which time the HR Director had better have got the other one working well!

Think about the different "stories" that HR Directors have to tell the organization during complex business transformations.

Keeping the plane flying whilst the engines are changed

Transition 1: An HR Director has the existing business model. Hopefully they have already demonstrated their worth by showing how HR adds value, leverages value, and protects and preserves value in this situation (see Chapter 1). They will have optimized their HR practices against this, and as an HR Director, provided support to their function and designed a delivery model that best enables this. They will have become comfortable that the performance measurement that the business applies to their business is appropriate. Or perhaps they may still be working through this agenda!

Transition 2: But there is a new business model – the HR Director might be in a particular political space (see Table 4.1), but nonetheless they face the complex task of unraveling the strategic change and understanding the new business value chain and the organizational capabilities that have to be built. Likely as not this represents a radical change for their own function's value proposition. So they have to re-analyze how their function adds value, leverages value, and protects and preserves value in the new model. They have to decide which HR practices are now defunct or have become a luxury (best practice policies rarely generalize across all business contexts). They have to provide support to the top team as they think through this business model (the issue of top-team relationships is discussed in Chapter 6). And they have to negotiate the new performance metrics and cost structures.

Transition 3: But there is a third transition – at least if the business values the HR function. The whole organization is moving to a new business model and there are the inevitable business transformation projects – often large and complex – that the embedded HR business partners need to support and that likely need central oversight given the resources they might consume, or the generic issues (such as culture or performance management) that they address. The HR Director has to support a set of Business Implementation transitions.

Transition 4: And finally there is the fourth transition. All of this invariably impacts on an HR Director's own business. As they manage the capabilities of their own function to support the business as it transitions from the old world to the new, they are providing personal leadership to their function. They are making judgments about the HR delivery model and its robustness, they are assessing the capability of their own team to handle the new roles, or are looking to new talent to take on complex jobs. They are looking to see if they can find a friendly "air traffic controller" who will manage the day-to-day of their new HR operations whilst they deal with the politics of transitions 1, 2, and 3.

An HR Director has to prove their worth against all four transitions. They are only as good as their last project, and these four transitions have to be kept on track and in alignment.

4.8. Key HR activities and capabilities

The key elements of HR strategy and practice that need to be "mastered" by HR Directors and their teams in order to contribute effectively to business model change – be it fluid or incremental – are outlined throughout this book.

The balance of HR competence that a particular function needs to possess is dependent upon the position in our business model change taxonomy and the political space that they inhabit. So, for instance, an organization operating within the Fluid space may require a more comprehensive organization design resource than one operating within the incremental change space.

In terms of *Leading HR*, there are a number of areas that an HR Director needs to have mastered, if they are to engage effectively with the line in order to add value during periods of business model change. We see these themes as areas of HR capability that an HR Director, and their HR function, should possess as proprietorial knowledge; what is at stake is no less than the survival of the function. Get them right, however, and we believe they point to a transformation of the way HR work is thought about, and done, in the twenty-first century.

HR must be fully responsive to the strategy and business model of the business. HR is not a rule for itself. It is not "HR for HR," but HR (as broadly defined across the competing stakeholders whom HR has to satisfy) for the business.

We refer to this trend as "reversing the arrow." Structuring HR for the business reflects a key perspective on the part of the HR Director and the HR function, where HR provides relevant contributions to the business in terms of the business model. One of the HR Directors interviewed gives perhaps the clearest statement of what we mean by *Reversing the Arrow*. Talking generally about recent trends in HR:

> . . . I think we've done it back to front, I think we've defined the model before we know what the organisation is. To what degree is responsibility transferred to the line? And where is the best commercial value for that? Because I think in HR we have a view that says it's the HR model that dictates it and not coming at it not just from our internal customer, but our external customer. If our values are about value to the customer, sustainability, keeping people safe, what therefore is the HR model that supports that? . . . I keep saying Ulrich's never been an HR Director, so what would he know!?

If we consider the question in terms of an HR "value chain" then the opportunity described by this HR Director is to deliver an HR agenda in which the direction of the arrow is from a clear definition of the clients' needs, with a deep understanding of the HR elements of business strategy, and with an "intuitive" relationship as a prerequisite, through to the organization's HR processes, the structure of the HR department, and finally, methods of measurement as the final (and possibly least important) conceptual element.

There may also be an element (preserving the idea of the "value chain") of understanding the way value is created, captured, and preserved.

However we suspect that many organizations do not reverse the direction of the "HR value chain." The HR strategy, and choices about how to organize and structure the function, is partially or wholly driven by theoretical models from the literature, or more likely from previous HR experience, with a substantial emphasis on the need to "prove" the value of these processes.

We should emphasize that this does not minimize the work of the HR professionals in these cases; it is simply a brutal fact that their senior line people do not consider HR to be integral to organization strategy. This question is now dealt with in Chapters 5 and 6, through the case example of a business model change and through an analysis of the power relationships necessary at the top of organizations for HR to exert such influence.

NOTES

1 Henderson, R.M. and Clark, K.B. (1990) Architectural innovation: The reconfiguration of existing product technologies and the failure of established firms. *Administrative Science Quarterly*, 35, 9–30.

2 Kang, S-C., Morris, S.S. and Snell, S.A. (2007) Relational archetypes, organizational learning, and value creation: Extending the human resource architecture. *Academy of Management Review*, 32 (1), 236–256.

3 See: Hooper, R.H., Hutton, D. and Smith, I.R. (2008) *The Challenges and Opportunities Facing UK Postal Services: An Initial Response to Evidence*; and Section 1: *Royal Mail's Proposed Solution to the Challenges Facing the UK Postal Services Sector.*

4 See: http://news.bbc.co.uk/1/hi/business/8017281.stm Accessed on 2 July 2009.

5 For discussion of this business model see: National Audit Office (2003) *Ministry of Defence Through Life Management*, Report by the Comptroller and Auditor General HC 698 Session 2002–2003; Ward, Y. and Graves, A. (2005) *Through-Life Management: The Provision of Integrated Customer Solutions by Aerospace Manufacturers*. University of Bath School of Management Working Paper 2005.14; Ministry of Defence (2006) *Through Life Capability Management (TLCM) Operating Framework*. Draft.04, 16th August; Nectise (2007) *Innovation Through Partnership, Network Enabled Capability Through Innovative Systems Engineering*. EPSRC and BAE Systems.

6 Becker, B.E., Huselid, M.A. and Ulrich, D. (2001) *The HR Scorecard: Linking People, Strategy, and Performance*. Boston, MA: Harvard Business School Press. p. 4.

7 Morris, M., Schindehutte, M., Richardson, J. and Allen, J. (2006) Is the business model a useful strategic concept? Conceptual, theorical, and empirical insights. *Journal of Small Business Strategy*, 17 (1), 27–50.

CHAPTER 5

NG Bailey: Constructing Business Model Change

CRAIG MARSH AND HELEN SWEENEY

5.1. Introduction

In the old days (not so long ago), an NG Bailey supervisor could sit in the portakabin, make a cup of tea, look out of the window, and see what his people were doing on site. If they stepped out of line, breaking one of the many procedures controlling the strictly regulated environment that characterized the construction trade, then he would quickly be able to point this out to the perpetrator. The future, however, looks somewhat different. Equipped with a PDA, the employee (who may or may not work directly for NG Bailey), skilled in customer relations, knowledgeable about the business of his client as well as his own trade, is sent off to the client in a company van. Unsupervised on site, he communicates with the company through his handheld computer; he is the "point man" for the company, the representative on site and the person the client will rely on to provide them with long-term value in their 25-year maintenance contract.

This vignette, contributed by Dave Evans, HR Business Partner, is of course stereotyping the complex changes taking place in NG Bailey; nonetheless, it is representative of the "front end" of the strategic shift in response to external and internal forces; it also is indicative of the HR challenges the company faces. We will start therefore by outlining the market conditions leading to the transformation of the company, before outlining NG Bailey's strategic response to those conditions including its value proposition, and the change to its business model. The third part of our case will then consider the Strategic HR element of this transformation.

After reinventing itself, the HR department plays a long game, led by an HR Director who finds herself in the position of balancing the need to respond to extremely urgent short-term pressures as well as offer steadfast support to the Executive and Board in its quest for business model change.

Engaging with business model change

Headline issue:

What impact does a transformational shift in the business model have on the role of HR?

Strategic imperative:

The transformation of the HR structure needs to be managed ahead of the business restructuring.

Must-win battle:

The ability to keep one's nerve by managing the short-term expectations of line managers while taking every opportunity to remind them of, and reinforce, the longer term objectives inherent in business model transformation.

In this chapter we will consider the latest issues and challenges of the transformation which have emerged to date from our research, especially given recent adverse market conditions. HR Directors can have a central role in shaping the business model at the early stage of transformation. We observe how the HR Director and the HR Department can help shape the implementation of a new business model, in the context of a legacy of a long history of family ownership, and strongly held values and external influences including deteriorating market conditions. All add weight to arguments for retaining the current business model, rather than moving to a new one.

The key messages that emerge from this chapter

We argue that

1) Providing an effective response to the political, economic, and social changes within the sector was the driving force behind the business and HR transformation.

2) HR Directors can have a central role in shaping the business model at the early stage of transformation.

3) Such transformations involve two major elements: moving up the value chain, and a consequent reprofiling of the organizational and individual capabilities needed.

4) The HR agenda then flows out from these issues into considerations of climate, talent, organization design, HR processes, performance management, and engagement.

5) The HR Delivery model, and associated centers of excellence and business partner structures, have to be aligned with this change process.

5.2. The construction industry: Changing traditions

The construction industry has been relatively slow to adopt the concept of supply chain management (SCM) by comparison with other large sectors of the UK economy, such as retail, manufacturing – especially vehicle manufacturing – and agriculture. It has been argued that this is a result of the unique context in which collaboration across the supply chain necessarily needs to be applied (termed the "temporary multiple organization").[1] The two most important aspects of the construction industry are customer specificity in the final product, and the involvement of a number of value-adding organizations. The SCM in the construction industry has been divided into "upstream" and "downstream" activities. "Upstream" covers activities and tasks leading to the preparation of the production on site involving construction clients and design team. "Downstream" consists of activities leading to the delivery of construction product, consisting of construction suppliers, subcontractors, and specialist contractors.[2]

The customer wields great influence on the physical aspects of the final product and on logistics (delivery dates, length of project, and so forth), often selecting the contractor, specialist suppliers, and materials suppliers, meaning long-term partnerships and coordinated action across the supply chain are vulnerable to disruption. Bottlenecks, including extensive preparation for approval procedures and conflicts of interests between suppliers, and the transient nature of production in a construction context all weigh against efficient SCM.

Quotations from published academic research into the construction industry reveal the traditional attitudes of senior players:

> the industry is, and always has been, dominated by competitive tendering and it is difficult to change people's attitudes.

> supply chain management is an academic theory that does not apply in practice in commercial contractor/supplier chains.[3]

NG Bailey was traditionally seen as a second-tier subcontractor in the construction industry, making its name and reputation by offering mechanical and electrical subcontracting to first-tier construction companies managing building projects. The company's experience reflects the observations from the literature. The construction market, they argue, has been dominated for many years by a particular business model. The client would put out for tender a building project, which would be responded to by a relatively small number of lead contractors. As the main criterion for selection of the contractor would be cost, this led to a set of consequences which were destructive of value for the client and the subcontractor, and potentially a huge risk for the main contractor in large construction projects where the future of the company was often on the table (Laing being a recent example of a project breaking the back of a long-established market player).

Main contractors, having cut initial proposals to the bone to compete for business, would look both to find as many gaps as possible in the contract to charge extra time for and also to squeeze the margins of smaller subcontractors, like NG Bailey, all in order to make a reasonable margin on a project. The objective of the clients, the contractors, and the subcontractors would therefore be completely divergent in a zero-sum search to extract the most value from the project.

5.3. NG Bailey's historical strategy and culture

NG Bailey developed a strong reputation in a particularly tough business environment characterized by fighting for one's corner. A family-owned business dating back 80 years, structurally the company had evolved a number of relatively independent business units identified by their technical speciality (mechanical and electrical controls, ceilings, and so forth). These units did develop their own business lines and clients independently and source the work from within their own department with little influence or support from the center. These units developed their own support structures, and conceived of their role as a supplier of products in a specialized part of the construction industry.

According to Karen Miles, the Director of Learning, NG Bailey's culture appeared to reflect the more supportive culture one might expect in a long-standing family business, and which seemed to be counter to the more prevalent adversarial nature of the industry. Certainly the nature of the engagement of employees with the company was generally one of long service, with generous benefits, life-long training and development, and a strong sense of loyalty to the company.

5.4. Transformation of the Industry, and NG Bailey's strategy: "For life in buildings"

In the first few years of the twenty-first century, several trends were observed by NG Bailey's senior management that have led to a fundamental re-evaluation of this old model; the convergence of these trends is referred to internally as "The Perfect Storm." The first is client-driven. Some companies, highly influential in that they had a high demand for construction projects, took the lead in driving a change to the business model. For example, in the oil industry in the early 1990s, BP Exploration restructured the "zero-sum" nature of oil platform construction by forming a consortium of contractors who worked in partnership over the duration of a project, including long-term operation and maintenance of a facility. Driven by a "gainshare" system of shared risk and shared reward, those players who took the chance of participating – and were successful in the selection process – found themselves working toward the same long-term objectives for the first time. This partnering process was then replicated in the onshore construction industry by some notable players, including BAA and Tesco.

Recent NG Bailey projects, such as their work on the Imperial War Museum North in Manchester, the redevelopment of Stirling Castle, and the Wales Millennium Centre in Cardiff, have shown how the company is moving toward the offering of an integrated services solution. For the last project, for example, the company delivered

> specialist theatre wiring, a fire alarm system, security systems, sprinklers, air conditioning, insulation refrigeration and ice storage. The key challenge of stringent acoustic requirements of major plant and equipment surrounding the

main auditorium and smaller rehearsal rooms was overcome through careful planning, commitment and quality engineering. Prefabrication was central to the project, with the plantroom, boiler room pipe work and all valve sets being delivered ready assembled, for ease of installation.[4]

A second driver of the transformation of the construction business model was the increasing public, and legislative, interest in the social and environmental impact of a building. It was no longer sufficient for construction companies to end their interest in a building the moment it is handed over to the client. Construction companies were being forced to take an interest in the long-term use of a building, including the impact and specific needs of its users and the way the building "relates" to its environment.

Providing an effective response to these political, economic, and social changes was the driving force behind the transformation of NG Bailey. To begin with there was a clear evolution, at least on paper, in the value proposition offered by the company; from a supplier of electrical and mechanical products and expertise to the construction industry on short-term contracts, to a company which, in their terms, "makes buildings come alive." Instead of the value offered to a project stopping at the opening ceremony, and maximized therefore only over the period of the construction, the value offering became a 25-year combined construction and maintenance offering. Knowledge of the particular requirements of a client moved to center stage, in order that the installation both reflected their needs, often sector-specific, and made long-term maintenance value adding both for the client and for the company.

5.5. NG Bailey's business model

This "perfect storm" required a rethinking of the business model of NG Bailey, recognizing that continued reliance on short-term mechanical and electrical engineering construction contracts ("one leg of the stool") with low margins was high risk in this environment. There were two major elements to the transformation:

1. The ultimate aim was to restructure the business to provide an integrated offering; integrated, that was both in its ability to offer a range of installation services to the same client in the area of its core expertise; and over time, was able to offer the necessary maintenance of those services.

2. The value offered by the company will also become sector-specific, that is, the company has and will develop construction and maintenance expertise in a particular field in order that the requirements of that sector can best be built into the offering. They referred to this transformation internally as "sectorization."

From the perspective of its competitive landscape, this transformation entails the move of NG Bailey to a different position on the value chain (see Figure 5.1). We define here the value chain as a key high-level component of the organization's

Figure 5.1: The shifts entailed in the current and future business models at NG Bailey

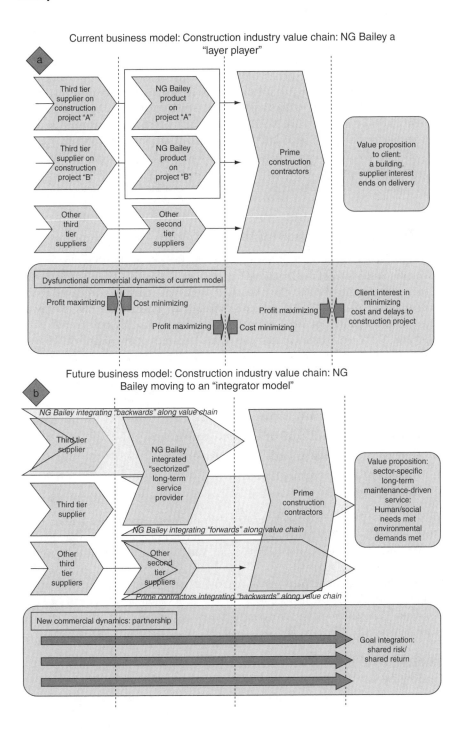

business model, frequently, as in this case, crossing specific company boundaries, from which organization architecture and capabilities can be derived. The two diagrams below represent the previous, and new, construction industry value chains, developed from the discussions with NG Bailey managers. Essentially the model shows both NG Bailey and the prime contractor market shifting their activities further along the chain in both directions, a classic shift from a "layer player" (specialist in one particular link in the chain) to an "integrator" model.[5] The threat (as well as the opportunity) that this represents to the company is well understood as the big contractors look to secure their "rear areas" by buying current second-tier players like NG Bailey. Members of the family are very clear that the business is not for sale; but this particular strategic intent contains the inherent risk that NG Bailey becomes isolated as all current competitors disappear. This created the need for the company to respond with its own move "up" the value chain and work (on some projects) directly with the end customer.

5.6. The change process in NG Bailey

The implementation of the transformation at NG Bailey began with prolonged discussion at the level of the Executive Management Team (EMT), but kicked off in earnest at the end of 2006. The EMT itself was a new creation, introduced by the chief executive officer (CEO), Mark Andrews, following his arrival at NG Bailey, and was itself symbolic of the move to internal integration and closer central influence. There were three key elements to the transformation plan. First, The EMT translated the "grand strategic vision" of NG Bailey into six "imperatives" or "strategic themes," as follows:

1. Diversification
2. Enhance specialist construction
3. Develop strong "Facilities Management" proposition
4. Develop and leverage strategic special relationships
5. Customer-focused organization
6. One NG Bailey[6]

Second, as one senior executive described, "various members of the EMT were given end accountability for delivering against the six imperatives, then we used the McKinsey 7S model, against which, again, various members of the team were given accountability."

The third element of the plan was referred to by NG Bailey as "the Six Ways," a set of value-oriented statements linked to the overall vision of "For Life in Buildings." These statements were clearly conceived therefore as a process central to implementation. The six ways are:

Leading the way by living our values and dedicated to working together
Leading the way by being focused on our customers

Leading the way by always improving
Leading the way by being committed to the long term
Leading the way by delivering sustainable solutions
Leading the way by maximizing the potential of our people[7]

5.7. HR added value to business model change: "Value from values"

The HR strategy element of the business model change process emerged as a dialogue between the HR function and senior Line people. Helen Sweeney, Group HR Director, described the HR piece of the transformation work as an "integrated framework model" – influencing:

1. Climate, which requires interventions in three main areas: on behavior; on culture; and on knowledge, skills, and competence;

2. Talent, through the assessment and development of the leadership population;

3. Organization Design – ensuring the structure is an enabler to achieve the strategy;

4. Processes – ensuring all HR processes are aligned to deliver the strategy; and

5. A major engagement initiative, "Leading the Way," taking the strategy and bringing it to life for individuals so they can understand and engage with it and start to see what it means for them.

As regards the value, added to NG Bailey of HR structures and processes in the context of their new business model, one senior executive was very clear about three potential contributions:

1. The first key area he identified was that of creating a performance management culture. At present, he observed, we "don't hold people accountable for poor performance, we don't do the GE thing of allocating people into four categories."

2. A second dimension where HR could add real value to support the strategy was in the area of resourcing. New skills were required, but the whole issue of growth in the industry and massive wage inflation requires a fundamental review of how we resource the business – the type and style of people and how they relate to the business.

3. A third, related area was to understand the nature of the capabilities that were needed to grow the business to achieve its ambitious turnover targets. Project management rather than engineering was to become the organization's key capability, and the transformation process would need to have a clearly identified strategy for acquiring and growing this capability. In a simple pyramid model of the organization, the bulk of the capability sat at the bottom; there was an area in the middle which was under-resourced and which did not have yet the capabilities needed to transform and grow the business.

An analysis by Helen Sweeney, the Group HR Director, of NG Bailey's strategic requirements in the area of HR led her to present the key HR strategic objectives to the Executive Team of NG Bailey. She listed the following as the top five:

1. Create an organizational structure which shows clarity in the relativity of roles across all business units within the group, providing an understanding of career progression and associated development;

2. Develop a robust strategy for recruitment and retention both during the current period of change and in line with future requirements of the group strategy;

3. Build on the current culture of busy, task focused, and friendly – toward encompassing strategic, long-term focus, and greater openness to change;

4. Develop a performance management system providing a clear line of sight from strategy to day-to-day activity; and

5. Develop an Engagement Program involving all people in the strategy, and in particular in "The 6 Ways."[8]

How these objectives were delivered in practice, and some of the difficulties encountered in implementation, will be discussed below.

5.8. HR department restructuring

At the most senior levels of the company, the HR function was recognized as a central part of both the transformation process and of day-to-day business. The Director of Learning and Development for NG Bailey, who worked closely with the CEO, Mark Andrews, in her current and previous positions, described how he regularly invited the HR Director into discussions on strategic decisions only tangentially related to the HR function. The internal appointment of a full-time HR Transformation Director (HRTD), Neil Lancaster, was testament to this degree of commitment.

The previous HR functional structure reflected the decentralized nature of the business, with each business unit having its own HR Manager and support team. HR needs were directed by these units and responded to locally, and the HR Director in the Center had an advisory role with little influence over individual business units. The company's HR administrative support was quite inefficient, with little opportunity taken to use technology to automate standard processes. The change of an employee's address, for instance, was still a form-filling exercise. This resulted in a relatively high HR headcount in relation to the size of the company. Relationships with line managers were generally very good but dependent on individual postholders to construct their influence with their internal clients, rather than as part of any overall approach to partnership.

To an extent, the transformation of the HR structure was ahead of the business restructuring. The main impetus was for centralization, the objective being to create control for consistency, and to develop a service delivery linked to overall business requirements, rather than to the needs of individual postholders in business units. A number of strategic priorities were identified for the function, oriented to adding value back into the business: "one HR team," and others around the theme of harmonization, engagement, and communication. To this end, the HR function constructed Centers of Excellence dealing with recruitment, reward, pensions, and so on, with IT systems introduced to manage the workflows; and business partners who dealt with HR strategy and worked alongside the Business Unit Managers. The structure was directly influenced by Ulrich's model of HR. business partners had just been identified and appointed during the period of the research.

5.9. Implementing change: The HR element

NG Bailey used the Balanced Scorecard approach to manage and measure the change process. Their approach supports our contention that HR evaluation and performance measurement should only be conceived and designed following the implementation of the other key strategic themes of HR – building in HR strategy to the business model design, developing an intimate working relationship between the CEO and the HR Director, and developing a strategy for the key supporting processes of talent management and engagement (see Chapter 9).

Each business unit developed its own scorecard; the HR scorecard is shown in Figure 5.2.

Figure 5.2: NG Bailey HR scorecard

Financial perspective	Customer perspective
• Progress against budget • Reduction in costs • Increased 'asset' usage	• Internal climate and external customer satisfaction scores/ service level performance • Retention and attendance scores • Invitations to engage with/be representative of industry and business events • Ease of recruitment
Internal perspective	Learning and growth perspective

• HR Productivity
   – proportion of activities completed by self-service
   – proportion of first line completion
   – reduction in rework
• Degree of understanding of services and procedures
• Attendance/sickness levels
• Retention across role types and time periods
• Diversity
• Exit interviews
• Employee conduct
	• Proportion of people completing agreed developmental programmes
	• Appraisals undertaken
	• Degree to which roles are filled internally
	• Acquisition of new skills required
	• Performance of our people
	• Increase in qualifications and registered institute status (under defined parameters)

Source: Helen Sweeney, "HR Strategy": presentation to NG Bailey Executive Team, 27 November 2007.

Each indicator on the scorecard is measured monthly across the business, and HR owned the collection, analysis, and accuracy of the figures derived in these areas. This way, NG Bailey could look out for movements in the numbers which may indicate early signs of a problem in a particular area that may need intervention. Helen Sweeney gave an example of the "culture/climate" indicator. The score was at the time 7.2 across the business (in answer to the question "I'm proud to be working for the organization"; the business had set a target for this to move to 8). The indicators can be broken down into functional areas, so if an area has a score of (say) 5.3, then there would an intervention to investigate why the figure was lower than the average. According to Sweeney, the trend in the figures was important, and she clearly saw this reporting as a trigger for a wider investigation of the data before any remedial action was decided upon, rather than "the answer" that a problem existed in the first instance.

Ownership of the data was also important. Although the responsibility for managing the data and conducting subsequent interventions was with HR, the area of "climate" was a line management responsibility to improve where it was deemed necessary.

The next stage was to position the detailed statistics themselves into a clear "red/amber/green" indicator of performance in each area of the scorecard.

5.10. Engagement and climate change

A significant part of the value HR was adding to the change process was to lead a company-wide development agenda for its managers. The process started at the highest level, with an in-depth survey and assessment of the top 60 managers. This comprised a 4-hour interview with a psychologist, and delivered a development agenda for the individual, including an evaluation of their competency profile, intellectual capacity and personality style, and a development discussion with their immediate line manager. Running over a year, the process resulted in several high-level departure, and a detailed understanding of the capabilities of the senior team. As Helen Sweeney commented, NG Bailey's long-term strategy demanded strengths in three key areas – strategic thinking, strategic influencing, and customer orientation. As in most organizations, these competencies were not in abundance. The Executive team was thus equipped with the information they needed to resource and develop their senior population in mission-critical directions.

An example of the development resulting from the survey was the need identified to develop the strategic influencing skills of this group, a key requisite as the organization moved to a matrix style structure. HR therefore sourced skills training for these managers designed precisely to close this competence gap.

By far the biggest intervention in scale, however, was the "Leading the Way" program which trained every manager in the organization (defined as those managing three people or more – around 300 managers in total) in a process of culture change. Assessed against the "six ways," each manager learned how to take his or her team through an assessment of their performance against the "ways" – what they needed to do more of, what they needed to stop doing, and what they needed to start doing.

5.11. Summary: HR contribution to business model change

According to Helen Sweeney, the three most significant learning points for her in her most recent experience of strategic change with NG Bailey are

1) senior team assessment and development – establishing a bench-strength view of strengths and weaknesses,

2) relationship with CEO and the Executive Team and supporting the strategic goals, and

3) knowing the industry, and keeping abreast of the changes happening in your sector.

Developing data on the performance profiles of the top 60 managers in the company, including the EMT, was key to making a number of hard decisions easier, argues Sweeney. This gave her a "bench-strength" view of the organization that allowed her then to develop a talent plan an understanding of where the organization was falling short of capabilities required to meet its ambitious targets. It also informed a discussion on succession planning, and made decisions about individuals easier, once it was realized (through the assessment process, rather than through "gut feel") that they weren't currently equipped for either current or future roles. Finally, it provided a new and more valuable developmental language to managers who began to discuss the organization's capacity for "strategic influencing" and "action orientation," thereby opening for debate for the first time certain capability areas that had previously been lacking, but not publicly recognized as such.

Second, a constant theme through this book has been the centrality of the relationship between the HR Director and the CEO, and the case of NG Bailey is no exception. Sweeney describes it not so much as a "yes-man" position but as a "trusted challenger," in her words, so that the HR Director can, where required, discuss a sensitive issue that is perhaps not working to plan, or highlight an issue to protect the organization – and the CEO.

The third area of contribution identified by the HR Director is that knowledge of the industry is critical to her success. Having moved through all the main sectors of the economy during her HR career, she is adamant that industry expertise prevents the HR Director from developing solutions which are simply transported from one context to another. NG Bailey has, as we have seen, characteristics which are individual to its market and to its ownership structure. Only a knowledge of the combination of these characteristics allows the HR Director to add strategic value.

However, as we have seen, even the deployment of these key capabilities and processes on the part of the HR Director has not been, and may not be, sufficient to guarantee the continuing success of NG Bailey. It has embarked on a challenging and brave course of change, and market conditions are extremely unsupportive of the chosen business model in the short term. It is quite striking that these circumstances dictate a particular response from HR – the need to continue to steer a steady course, toward a long-term vision, under severe short-term pressure.

On the one hand, the HR Director has to be seen to be responding to short-term demands. Take the issue of resourcing. Six months prior to the time of writing 250 vacancies were on the books in the organization. On the other hand, the long-term plan called for resourcing certain key capabilities – FM, project management – but the organization was risking grinding to a halt unless a short-term resourcing plan was put in place. So the HR Director has been attempting to do both. She built an effective resourcing unit and worked to fill the short-term need; but without necessarily making it obvious to some of the senior management in the company, she also began to identify and recruit people possessing the capabilities she knew NG Bailey needed for its long-term plan.

At the same time she has been ensuring that these key resources are directed – to the extent possible – toward the less profitable, but strategically important, parts of the business in the face of opposition from the more profitable areas.

So the path to long-term success in a business model change project such as this seems not only to be to possess the key capabilities of the HR Director as we have identified but also to develop, not without courage, the ability to keep one's nerve by managing the short-term expectations of client managers while taking every opportunity to remind them of, and reinforce, the longer term objectives so easily forgotten when the balance sheet is in the red. Not every HR Director will manage this and it is not even certain of course whether it will be a success at NG Bailey. But HR Directors can have no doubt that they will, in the course of strategic change, need to make similar choices.

NOTES

1 Cherns, A. and Bryant, D. (1983) Studying the clients role in construction management. *Construction Management and Economics*, 2, 177.

2 Akintoye, A., McIntosh, G. and Fitgerald, E. et al. (2000) A survey of supply chain collaboration and management in the UK construction industry, *European Journal of Purchasing and Supply Management*, 4, 159–168.

3 Ibid., p. 166.

4 See: www.baileybuildingservices.com/markets (accessed 27 January 2009).

5 Schweizer, L. (2005) Concept and evolution of business models, *Journal of General Management*, 31, 2, 37–56.

6 NG Bailey Supplier Project Briefing Document.

7 Ibid.

8 Helen Sweeney, "HR Strategy": presentation to NG Bailey Executive Team, 27 November 2007.

CHAPTER 6

Using Relationships Between Leaders to Leverage More Value from People: Building a Golden Triangle

ANTHONY HESKETH AND MARTIN HIRD

6.1. Introduction

I t has become a cliché of modern HR work that a "seat at the table" is a prerequisite for success, but with very little precise information about what this might mean exactly. The relationship between the chief executive officer (CEO) and the HR Director is the start point for the way HR work gets done in the organization, a situation which becomes particularly acute during a period of transformation. This chapter examines the importance and nature of these relationships.

A symbiotic CEO/HR Director working relationship

Headline issue:

Does the CEO "get" the people proposition? When they do, do they really think that the HR agenda is as important as any other part of their responsibility?

Strategic imperative:

HR's role in organization strategy, especially at a time of Business Model change, is largely dependent on the attitude of the CEO. If the answer to the headline issue is "yes," fine; HR strategy will eventually be indistinguishable from business strategy.

If the answer is "no," then do not even try and talk about HR's strategic role. Put in place good efficient processes, and look elsewhere if you really want to do strategy. Otherwise you can talk about it, but it won't happen.

Must-win battle:

Make sure that as HR Director you quickly develop an intuitive relationship with your CEO, as close as any other in the senior team.

Chapter 1 drew attention to the importance of "strategy talk" in organizations. However, there appear to be two facets of the relationship which explain the success, or otherwise, both of this critical relationship and of the characteristics of the HR strategy that follow:

1.   the attitude of the CEO to HR, and related

2.   how well the two people get on with each other.

One of the CEOs that we interviewed clearly believes in the centrality of HR:

> There's nobody that I'm more intimate with then my HR Director. Typically the person the GM is closest to is the FD. Part of my philosophy is that the two people I'm closest to are my finance man and my HR man.

There are of course likely to be many ways a CEO will approach the HR agenda. We have simplified these into two alternative stances:

1.   does the CEO believe that HR is part of and integral to the strategic agenda, or

2.   do they believe HR is separate from it?

The content of the HR strategy will be fundamentally affected by these two alternatives. A significant proportion of the HR Directors we have interviewed comment that they would never have joined the organization had they not heard the CEO's clear commitment to HR's integral strategic role in the business. We argue that

The key messages that emerge from this chapter

1)   There is a vacuum in our understanding of leadership capability, but this can in part be filled by identifying, exploring, and ultimately understanding and learning from the social processes engaged in by executives in the day-to-day relational activities of leadership.

2)   Leadership is not reducible simply to what leaders do, or in fact who they are or even the capabilities they possess. We should focus instead on whom leaders do leadership *with*, and how they achieve together what they cannot achieve alone.

3)   Our observations of these different strategic social relations have led to the detection of what we refer to as the "Golden Triangle" – an informal, tacit, or intangible network of executive relationships and conversations – typically, although not exclusively, operating between the chief executive, finance director, and their director or vice president of human resources (HR) as leaders recognize the increasing centrality of people to the execution of organizational strategy.

Returning to the CEO quoted above, their description of the levels of HR work is informative, given their stated attitude. For this CEO "HR Strategy" has no separate identity.

Q: What is on the HR agenda?

A: I usually describe HR at what I call three levels. There's the foundation level, what we used to call personnel, it's just pay and rations, recruitment, all that sort of stuff that makes the world go round, transactional work. Level 2 to me is tools, it could be engagement, reward, development, those sorts of things. Level 3 is the strategic engagement. When you say what's the HR agenda there'll be items on all three levels.

Q: What's going on at level 3 in terms of HR strategy?

A: Not HR strategy, business strategy. We have a small business in [country], we should either close it or expand it dramatically. It's a current business issue for us, and I want HR engaged in that debate.

Processes which for HR people are on the curriculum as "strategic" or as "transformational" are, for this CEO, tools (the CEO later clarifies explicitly that level 2 HR work is not "strategic"). "HR strategy" ceases to have any meaning for this CEO – there is business strategy, and a suite of HR tools at level 1 and level 2 which support it.

This is not, however, a situation that occurs regularly. This CEO believes it is rare to find such an attitude to HR at CEO level and finding an HR Director with the competence to engage at this level is even rarer, though one has been found in the current HR Director.

We draw attention throughout this chapter to the crucial part played by the relationship between the HR Director, the CEO, and the CFO. One CEO uses the word "intimate" to describe the relationship they have; another HR Director calls it "intuitive" and notes that they have to ensure that the function's business partners have a similar relationship with their senior line people:

> . . . It became very clear that [the CEO] and I connected, I used that as leverage, and then it became a matter of building relationships . . . if I take the top segment first of all, they get a lot of personal time with the HR Director – almost a coach to the senior person, they get a very personalised internal coaching service. The relationship can become intuitive. What you get with a high level HR business partner [is that] they get access to the discussion and debate on the market and the businesses right at the front end. So like the relationship I built with the CEO – high trust, pick up the phone – that's what I wanted the BPs to have with their managers.

An effective relationship with the CEO is a precondition of all the capabilities outlined throughout this book. The extent to which the HR Director has become socialized into operating through such a relationship helps them of course into a deeper understanding of the business model change, but can also enable HR Directors to lead the top team toward a progressive and people-based insight of the organizational issues involved.

However, if the credit crunch has taught us anything it is that the success of organizations and their leaders are inextricably linked with the performance of their counterparts. The construct of the heroic leader is now being subjected to new levels of scrutiny by markets, shareholders, analysts, customers, employees, and the academy. It appears many do not like what they find, as the chief executives of Citi, HBOS, Lehman Brothers, Merrill Lynch, UBS, and Northern Rock will testify.

Part of the problem lies in the conventional ways in which the personalities and roles of executives have been constructed. The executive literature is replete with the "secrets of leadership," be they observations of the innate skills and competences possessed by great men – and they usually are men – their charisma, or their transformation-inducing strategic visions. The faith once placed in these fixed, solid, and irreducible constructs is now unraveling leaving an operational vacuum where there was once merely a challenge, albeit a steep and competitive one, to identify and secure the requisite top talent to lead organizations.

6.2. Who leads people strategy?

There has in the last two decades been a growing recognition of the competitive advantage to organizations derived from their people. "Those with the best people win" is the new mantra replacing the old adage people are our most important asset. Nevertheless, there remains a vacuum in our understanding of the role played by those individuals primarily responsible for the construction and enablement of people-specific solutions inside executive management teams (EMT).

The reasons for this vacuum are complex. For example, if we are to believe emerging research findings, an increasing number of chief executives are cognizant of the primacy of having the requisite capability in place to achieve their strategic plans.[1] So much so that many what might be described as "people-oriented" chief executives assimilate human capital and its leadership under their wider remit of driving the future strategic direction and performance of their organizations, hence precluding the need at the boardroom table for a director or vice president of HR.

Despite these hard boardroom truths, as argued in Chapter 4, some HR Directors are exerting new levels of influence on the strategy formulation of their organizations. We explain how this largely informal and highly political influence comes to pass in leading blue-chip organizations we have studied at close quarters. Our work draws on interviews from our ongoing research with a range of organizational leaders – be they chief executives, HR directors, or other executive management board members – in an attempt to shed light on what has become a dark spot in our understanding of the activities and processes engaged in by executives when formulating and implementing business strategy.

In what follows, we report on our research exploring the decision-making processes of executives in general, and the role of people in this process, in particular. After exploring the current challenges now facing HR professionals, we suggest understanding the formulation of people strategy requires the establishing of the presence or otherwise of the Golden Triangle. We present the characteristics shaping the emergence of a Golden Triangle and introduce the case study of BAE SYSTEMS in the latter stages of this chapter.

6.3. Human remains

We want first to begin by contextualizing our work and challenging two long-standing assumptions that have dominated wider debates over leadership in general and the role of the HR function in particular. The two assumptions are inextricably linked.

First, HR has been dominated by debates concerning the credibility, some might even say, viability, of the Function. This has largely manifested itself in the furor over the contribution to organizational performance made by people,[2] but wider debates have also taken place regarding the design and service delivery of HR and their contribution to the top-line performance of organizations.[3] Clearly stated, the assumption is an improvement in the design and delivery of HR will lead to a *causal* improvement in the performance of the host organization.

Second, after work in the 1990s claiming to have established a formula for calculating the causal and *financial* rate of return to the investment in people, the elusive door to the boardroom was seemingly thought to be opened for a new generation of HR executives capable of establishing their contribution to the bottom line.[4] Thus a *measureable* link between an organization's people and its top-level financial returns was widely seen as the grounds on which HR executives could articulate a reason for their inclusion in developing the strategic direction of their organizations. Both of these assumptions have proved to be a miscalculation of spectacular proportions for two reasons.

On the one hand, despite the warnings from leading commentators that HR was being dragged into a political debate not of its own making, nor to be determined on its own terms, the Function ploughed head first into a concerted political campaign to establish its financial and strategic credentials in the boardroom. Whilst the debate over the strategic contribution made by people has developed into the tangential field of talent and its management – and, as we shall see below, has also become an area of responsibility largely acquired by chief executives – the future of the HR function and its services has been relegated to back-office status and seen as a major source of potential cost reduction via outsourcing.[5]

On the other hand, warnings over the magnitude of the task of attempting to take that which was largely seen as an intangible, albeit highly valuable, resource and make it tangible were ignored.[6] A "bet the ranch," all or nothing strategy, was invested in academic research which at best was problematic, and at worst, philosophically flawed.[7] The "science" underpinning the financial contribution of HR to the organization has not stood up to empirical scrutiny. Despite a number of research projects claiming to have established a demonstrative link between people management and organizational performance, John Boudreau and Phil Ramstead, in their discussion in *Beyond HR: The New Science of Human Capital* on the future of the HR Function, suggested that such measurement techniques:

> ... hit a wall ... despite ever more comprehensive databases, and ever more sophisticated data analysis and reporting, HR measures only rarely drive true strategic change[8]

The corollary has been the exclusion from the boardroom of senior HR executives.

6.4. Introducing executive strategic agency

The reality, of course, is much more complex than the mere symbolic status of the presence of HR in the boardroom. It is our contention that this "presence" is far more complex than mere access to the formal decision-making structures of an organization. Access to the boardroom is in fact a chimera to the role played by HR inside organizations. It distorts and relegates the debate over the importance of people in strategy development and deployment and organizational design to the mere symbolic status of a seat at the table.

To fully understand the role of people strategy within organizations in general and the role played by HR executives in particular, our focus needs to uncover the more relational and informal aspects of leadership between the individuals involved. In short we need to understand more about the complex interplay between HR executives and their fellow executive peers across different functions. This involves examining the "zones of maneuver"[9] that are located outside formal structures of the boardroom, yet available only to a few organizational elites and the relative capabilities they utilize when seeking to achieve their own personal strategies as well as realizing the institutional, material, and political goals of the functions they are responsible for. These personal strategies involve executives in power struggles over limited resources and involve the deployment of material, symbolic, and ideological power to secure distributional advantages for both themselves and the functions they represent.

This area of work has been overlooked in previous research for one understandable reason, and two rather surprising ones. First, we can understand why researchers have found access to the political processes through which executives mobilize and enhance their collective power within their own networks and across the organizations in which they work. Such "ruling minorities" not only benefit from operating in what is to all intents and purposes a tacit and subliminal world, but they also benefit from the control of such organizational hierarchies, which in turn governs access to the dynamics which control power struggles within organizations. Competition for resources, the mobilization of power and socio-political struggles and affiliations of the executive world take place behind closed doors. One cannot subject the discursive regimes, elite agency, and practices that shape subjects' subjectivities to empirical scrutiny without access to those same individuals who participate in such power struggles.

What is less clear to us, however, is the oversight first of the importance of these networks in constructing, shaping, and ultimately determining the outcome of material resources, or, secondly, why their ultimate value to the organizations which posses such power networks has been under estimated.

6.5. Introducing the Golden Triangle

The position that HR occupies in terms of its power and influence within organizations is highly contested both within and without organizations. What we do know is that across corporations and industries the position and status of HR is highly differentiated.

Furthermore it is evident that this differentiation is not always due to purposeful decision-making, by, for instance, the chief executive officer (CEO) or the board, based upon established policies or strategies. It is often more random than this – almost an accident of history! For example, some CEOs may be operating with a board-level HR VP/Director who will determinedly lead HR and People strategies on behalf of the board while in other companies of similar size, product-market, and so forth, HR is not on the board, is far from powerful and remains little more than a "gopher" function operating as an implementer of predetermined people strategies and policies.

It may be a symptom of this erratic power and influence position of HR that has led significant business commentators to predict the demise of the HR function. For Rosabeth Moss Kanter, "the end of the aging and ailing HR empire" is imminent.[10] In recent years we have seen a number of significantly sized organizations appoint non-HR professionals to the top HR position validating Moss Kanter's prognosis. This has been further exacerbated by the power and influence of HR being negatively impacted by a widely held view of the function's organizational isolation, a point not lost on Dave Ulrich and Wayne Brockbank in their influential *HR: The Value Proposition,* where it was identified that all too frequently HR professionals and their stakeholders have operated in separate worlds.

What is an absolute truism is that an effective HR VP/Director must achieve power and influence within their organizations if they are to play a meaningful role. With that power and influence their HR function can lead rather than simply follow. Without power and influence HR executives are merely implementing policies and strategies for the organization that have been determined by others.

We believe that this facility on behalf of HR to lead rather than follow is given major impetus if an organization operates at a senior level, with what we term a "Golden Triangle." The Golden Triangle can operate at corporate board level or within a business unit management team. In essence it is an informal component of the formal organizational structure. The key characteristics will vary from company to company depending upon local cultural and environmental circumstances but will certainly include the following:

> ### Key characteristics of a Golden Triangle
>
> 1. a close working relationship both formally and informally between the CEO, CFO, and senior HR executive;
> 2. a pattern where members meet frequently, often in an informal and relaxed manner;
> 3. a culture of mutual trust and respect;
> 4. the triangle focusing upon reflection, "temperature" assessment, counsel, discussing linkages to the corporate center, business performance "hot spots," and being a mini think tank for the organization;
> 5. the HR Director acting as a coach, counselor, and, in some special cases, as "consiglieri" to the CEO in particular;
> 6. micro and strategic people issues will be part of the ongoing agenda; and,
> 7. where the HR executive is clearly perceived as a key member of the senior team.

6.6. Operationalizing the Golden Triangle

The role of the HR executive in shaping the development of a Golden Triangle turns on the capability of an individual to have key influencing and leadership skills across four key organizational contexts, each of which transverse conventional functional demarcation lines. These are in executive level recognition, strategy, operations, and performance (see Table 6.1).

6.6.1. Executive cadre recognition

It is worth recording here our view that the triangle will operate with optimum efficiency and effectiveness if other senior team members accept the legitimacy of

Table 6.1: Operationalizing the Golden Triangle the role of the CHRO

Context	Operating	Not Operating
Executive Cadre	Participating in strategic discussions	"Talked about" but not "talked to"
Strategy	Strategic Progenitor	Strategic Implementer
Operations	Operational Leadership	Operational Expert
Performance	Performance Orchestrator	Performance Enabler

the existence of the Golden Triangle. It requires political acumen on the part of the HR executive to ensure that this acceptance is achieved and maintained. This political legitimacy lies at the heart of the distinction between whether or not HR executives or their equivalents inside organizations are included in the zones of maneuver over strategic resources. The obvious indicator of the recognition by executive cadre-level colleagues of HR being an equal player is a position on the Board with equal voting rights such as, for example, when Allan Leighton appointed Tony McCarthy as HR Director of the Royal Mail Group in the United Kingdom.

An HR executive on the Board is not an automatic indicator of a Golden Triangle in operation, however. On the contrary, as we shall see below, some HR executives find widening their strategic agencies to matters outside the Function to one encompassing the Corporation as a whole as a step too far for their business acumen. Similarly, not being on the Board does not automatically preclude the existence of a Golden Triangle. A number of organizations, to quote Lee Patterson of Shell, "may not be at the table, but are certainly in the room." Indeed, this lack of a formal position on the Board heightens the importance of the Golden Triangle in accessing top table executives if HR is to find a strategic voice in the Boardroom. As one CEO put it to us:

> There's nobody that I'm more intimate with than my HR Director. Typically the person the General Manager is closest to is the Finance Director. Part of my philosophy is that the two people I'm closest to are my finance man and my HR man.

6.6.2. Strategy

Even if we accept it is reasonable to head HR structures with non-HR professionals and although it is absolutely clear that HR isolation is damaging to all parties, those charged with leading the Function need to have access to the discussions and subsequent decisions that determine not only how HR is managed but also to play a major role in their organization's strategy formulation and implementation, governance, and management decision-making. Or, as a minimum, CEOs need to consciously determine the nature of the role HR is to play.

The defining hallmark of a Golden Triangle in play here is the capacity of the HR to lead strategic thinking with the full support and recognition of their CEO and finance director. As opposed to those who follow or implement others' ideas, *strategic progenitors* see corporate-level strategic possibilities before other executives. They understand the financial implications of their ideas and choices not just for their own Function, but also for others. Strategic progenitors contribute not just to innovation at corporate level for their own Function, but they contribute to the articulation and shaping of underpinning strategies and business models across other parts of the business with co-progenitors from other functions. Indeed, our research has revealed a new generation of commercially savvy HR executives is emerging with clear aspirations to move outside HR across the Boardroom table into other executive functional roles. This is a major development and one made possible by the Golden Triangle as relational capabilities involved in articulating strategic agency are developed and enhanced across those with access to its informal executive networks.

Those on the outside of the triangle are simply implementers – they execute the ideas, choices, and decisions of others – without first having helped to shape them. This is not to say that high quality execution is not celebrated – indeed it is what the majority of CEOs wish from their HR functions. But to be an operational Golden Triangle HR executives need to be at the vanguard of strategy formulation, not simply informing others on the people connotations – but thinking first about the business and then the concomitant people issues.

6.6.3. Operations

Those in Golden Triangles seek more than operational expertise; they seek operational leadership. Leadership here involves new and innovative thinking around how to deliver operational imperatives of the business. HR executives have increasingly become progenitors of new operational delivery business models, which themselves require new and innovative accounting methods as well as world-class execution.

Golden Triangles generate new models such as service delivery, enterprise partnerships, and technical solutions, as key players unite in their understanding of both the underlying strategic, operational, financial, *and* people issues. Indeed, one possible observation here might be that people and talent have become the new operations of the business as IT and other e-enabled systems and processes are increasingly outsourced.

An effectively operating Golden Triangle recognizes the centrality of people issues and the need for the HR executive to play an increasing role in articulating and shaping the underpinning strategies and business models of new and evolving operational models. This extends well beyond the comfort zone of traditional HR administration – although a classic indicator of a successfully operating Golden Triangle is a high degree of satisfaction with HR held by line managers – and out into complex service delivery and financial models which comprise recent large-scale outsourcing agreements such as that undertaken by Dupont with Convergys and Unilever with Accenture.

Fresh from the successes of negotiating these large-scale deals with senior executive colleagues, there is a new generation of HR executives who do not simply have aspirations to rise to the top of HR, but view the other seats around the boardroom table as possible trajectories for themselves. These individuals are highly politicized, understand and possess the leadership traits of empathy and wider forms of social capital, and convert/commodify their economies of experiences into executive leadership signaling devices. The emergence of Golden Triangles is as much a testimony to their increasing political skills as it is to the rising status of people issues inside organizations.

6.6.4. Performance

The role of HR in driving the performance of organizations has reached almost fever pitch in the decade since Ulrich published *Human Resource Champions*. But HR leadership is more about simply articulating, or even accounting for, HR's value proposition. It is even more than enabling the business to perform and enable different business scorecard-holding stakeholders to deliver service-critical operations. It is, rather, about the orchestrating of performance-enhancing transformations of people and operations and their underpinning architectural forms. It is leading performance transformation with, if not even ahead of the CEO. *Performance orchestrators* see strategic possibilities before other executive colleagues; they understand how changes in operations, IT, strategy, and a whole host of other things can be shaped before others, and they know what the costs and potential return on investment will be. This is not just in terms of HR streamlining, but in terms of the currencies of the CEO and finance director – they understand how their interventions will orchestrate profitability within the business, drive share price, and enable the other Golden Triangle players' agenda of driving p/e ratios. In the words of one finance director:

> . . . HR can talk to me in Excel, not PowerPoint

One additional observation we need to acknowledge before examining the evidence for the existence of Golden Triangles is required, notably, the willingness of HR executives to find themselves in the middle of the political power games executive networks inevitably entail. Participation in a Golden Triangle is not always of an individual HR executive's choosing.

On the contrary, whether HR likes being propelled to the front of service businesses or not, the role of people strategy has become paramount in the face of growing emphases on human capital management, intellectual capital, and the knowledge-based economy. Propulsion works both ways. Those HR executives who actively court engagement in Golden Triangles and fail, or those who are invited only to fail to live up to expectations, can equally find themselves forced outside the Golden Triangle.

Those HR executives who make the step up to CEO only to step back again will testify to the height of the stakes and the intensity of the performance expectations. Consequently, Golden Triangles are temporal – they may or may not last. They remain highly contingent on context and a whole raft of other externalities to the relationship between the three individuals in question each of which are subject to a number of changes including a change in market performance, mergers and acquisitions, career progression, and so forth.

6.7. Evidence for the existence of golden triangles

By their very nature Golden Triangles are highly contingent, tacit, intangible, and consequently highly problematic to identify and examine. Three questions immediately spring to mind when reflecting upon the existence of the Golden Triangle:

1.   Can we discern companies that have operated with a Golden Triangle and those that have not?
2.   Where Golden Triangles do exist, is their life finite?
3.   Do Golden Triangles bring effective people strategies to the fore?

The answers to these questions are, respectively, yes, yes, and definitely maybe! We will return to the first two questions below but it is worth exploring first the legitimacy of the Golden Triangle in the eyes of executives in terms of its capacity to facilitate effective people strategies.

Do these relationships make a strategic contribution? Our hesitancy over the contingency of the positive impact of the Golden Triangle lies in the competence of the HR executive in question. Generally the existence of the Golden Triangle with a credible and competent HR executive as part of the trio will enhance the emphasis upon people strategies. However, in a company where the Golden Triangle is absent, there may be in position a very people-oriented and people-knowledgeable CEO or, possibly, a chief operations officer who will compensate for the absence from the inner sanctum of the HR VP/Director.

Do these relationships have a finite life? We believe so. There are influencers for the existence of the Golden Triangle that can change rapidly and that preclude, in our minds, the notion that the triangle is a permanent fixture in any organization's formal or informal structure. We will turn our attention to these influencers in the next section.

6.8. Golden Triangle influencers

In our view there are certain influencers that will impact upon the likelihood of an organization operating with a Golden Triangle. The influencers will be as follows:

1.   *Structural* (organizational aspects that include characteristics such as size, culture, environment, and industry and are likely to only change over a period of some time).
2.   *Relational* (individual and group characteristics present within the organization at any given time – the current "politics" and personalities – and therefore could change in an instant).

It is the Relationals that give the Golden Triangle its sense of impermanency and its essential fragility. Some key influencers are outlined below (see Figure 6.1).

Many structural influencers, while predictable after a period of time, are slower to change. Structural factors often but not always represent a key target for transformation for those in Golden Triangles. Alternatively, relational factors are those C-suite players seek to embed in their organizations – for example, customer focus, engagement – and, typically, are those factors which are typically

Figure 6.1: Golden Triangle influencers

Influencers	Structural	Relational
POSITIVE	Large (10,000+ employees)	"People-oriented" CEO
	High labor costs	Credible, respected, politically skilled HR executive
	Powerful trade unions	"Team-oriented CFO"
	"HR at the table" culture	"Accepting" C-suite
	People-confident CEO	Less emphasis on measurement, more on quality
	Distant, non-confident people line managers	Adequate HR executive/HRD
	Centralized shared services/third-party provider	Customer-focused and entrepreneurial mindset
NEGATIVE	People-confident and competent line managers	"Bottom line" Only CEO
	Function "X" dominated company	Inadequate HR service delivery
	Global Listing	Inadequate, devolved, and expensive HR delivery
	No history of HR influence	Low personal credibility of those in HR

unpredictable and subject to constant, even rapid change! We now examine those structural and relational factors that have a positive and negative influence.

6.8.1. Structural pluses

Large-size organizations tend to have evolved as complex organizational structures and, as part of that process, will have recognized HR as a significant role to play in terms of optimally managing what is likely to be a large and stratified group of employees. However this factor of size could be linked to a long history of downplaying HR so although a plus, large size is not a major plus factor for engendering Golden Triangles.

High labor costs are often associated with the negative aspects of HR. Enlightened CFOs recognize the distinction between the costs of their human capital and its return on investment. Conversations in Golden Triangles focus less on the typical costs of HR per FTE (estimated to be roughly $1,000 in a typical US organization), or the value added by each employee (£56,700 in the top EU 750 in 2007). Instead, those in Golden Triangles understand the key metric to be the extent to which the investment in people and equipment is leveraged; quite literally, the return per £1 spent on people (currently on average in the EU 750 in 2007 at £1.63). Even smarter HR executives learn from their corridor meetings with the CFO how this *People Leverage* figure is changing over time (which is nearly as important as the actual amount leveraged), informing them about the direction in which the performance of the company's, and not just the HR Function's, talent is progressing. They will also understand that there is a very high correlation between the changes in their company's market capitalization and people leverage and will keep this relationship under constant review.

Powerful labor unions frequently make CEOs nervous, particularly if they are short on experience of dealing with industrial relations. There is an international mystique regarding the conduct of industrial relations that can create a powerful position for HR professionals who are seen to have the competence to conduct effective relationships with unions. Thus strong unions can lead to prominent HR activity, which can cement the creation of a Golden Triangle when CEOs rely heavily on their HR executives to drive through negotiations on change, "rightsizing," and remuneration.

A "HR at the table" culture is, in a sense, a self-evident influencer. If the company has a history of HR as a major player then this will support the existence of the triangle.

We have been involved in a number of companies where distant/non-confident line managers are largely recruited from a cadre of highly qualified scientists/technologists, who often lack in-depth preparation for people management roles. They can often lack both the confidence and the motivation to deal with people management issues and therefore become highly reliant upon HR to support them in these issues including labor relations, development, remuneration, career advice, and general engagement. This reliance can permeate the whole company structure and can only lead to increased HR power and influence. This all may seem somewhat *Machiavellian* on the part of HR – to seize influence based on managerial incompetence. However if a void exists that requires HR filling it then it is a pragmatic reality that this will extend HR influence within the company.

6.8.2. Structural minuses

People-confident and competent line managers – and yes they do exist in companies that have a strong people managerial tradition – supported by rigorous managerial preparation and training represent a potential threat to the development of Golden Triangles. In this environment HR may be seen to play a support role only with the line handling all people management activities and where people strategies are initiated and developed by the whole senior team. An absence of hostile labor relations or indeed non-recognition of unions is likely to characterize this sort of company.

Global-listing as a minus is clearly open to debate. However we base the categorization upon the notion that many global corporations delegate HR to an in-country activity, which in many ways weakens the corporate influence of HR.

A low history of HR influence can characterize some companies who have developed quite successfully with a low level of HR influence and strategic involvement. This low involvement becomes a cultural facet that is hard to change – as long as "satisfactory" performance is maintained!

6.8.3. Relational pluses

A people-oriented CEO is almost always predisposed to place a high value upon HR's contribution and will tend to be the major driver in creating a Golden Triangle. It is also probable that the very confidence that is part of the CEO's personality will enable them to make a "strong" appointment as HR executive. Needless to say this influencer is a crucial one.

A credible HR executive is the critical influencer! Even if the company has a culture that supports the existence of a Golden Triangle an inadequate incumbent can demolish the triangle's very existence. Newly appointed HR senior team members need to make an immediate impact in terms of delivery, respect, teamworking, coaching, and strategic contribution in the eyes of both the CEO and the CFO: no small feat.

A "team-oriented" CFO heads off the Achilles' Heel of Golden Triangles: that they can be subject to acts of sabotage! If the working relationship between the HR executive and the CFO suffers from negative "chemistry" then the triangle will have a diminished effectiveness. The HR executive may have to take a decision as to whether the triad will ever operate effectively as long as the personalities remain the same and they may need to work on forging a strong dyadic relationship with the CEO.

An "accepting" C-suite is paramount in the formation/existence of the Golden Triangle and may cause some discomfort within the remainder of the senior team with VPs/Directors responsible for Operations, Commercial/Marketing, Procurement, IT, and so forth, puzzled and resentful. This is a delicate issue and needs to be managed carefully by particularly the CEO and HR executive. An "adult" senior team may be calmly accepting but if there is an issue then the CEO may need to discuss their motives and purpose openly with his/her senior colleagues.

6.8.4. Relational minuses

A "bottom line only" CEO driven only by financial returns for shareholders, particularly on an annual or even quarterly basis, and who see the future prosperity of the company as being derived by external market and financial factors, may be inclined to undervalue the contribution of both effective people strategies and HR leadership. In situations such as this the HR executive, if indeed the organization has one, must focus upon a longer term policy of strong HR advocacy and delivery tightly focused on business success/performance criteria.

An inadequate HR executive is very much the opposite to the positive influencer of a credible HR leader. In a performance-oriented organization an HR leader who fails to contribute, convince, and coach the team will at some point fail the standards expected by his or her executive colleagues and depart the Golden Triangle – and it will be very difficult for their successor to win that position back.

At the next level down, an inadequate HR Team/HR Delivery will eventually undermine the credibility of a HR executive, however good an advocate regarding the crucial contribution of HR. If their team consistently fails to deliver in the medium and long term then life in the triangle will become very stressful indeed! Their choice is very simple: either revamp and improve the team or face exit from the triangle.

The emergence of a Golden Triangle at BAE SYSTEMS

An excellent example of a company where HR has been of major influence and, where a Golden Triangle culture exists is British Aerospace/BAE Systems (BAE Systems was formed in 1999/2000 with the merger of British Aerospace and Marconi Defence).

From the early 1990s through to the present day one can discern the existence of Golden Triangle characteristics in terms of the key strategic and tactical role that HR plays. The organization possesses many of the structural and relational pluses outlined in this chapter. In terms of structural pluses BAE is characterized by the following:

1. Large size/employee numbers as one would expect from the second largest global defense company.

2. With high labor costs based on a well-educated labor force.

3. In UK terms still powerful trade unions who were relatively untouched by "Thatcherism."

4. From 2002 a centralized shared services provider in the form of Xchanging.

BAE from the early 1990s also possessed many of the relational pluses including:

1. A series of people-oriented CEOs including Sir Richard Evans, John Weston, and latterly Mike Turner who really believed in BAE people as a key competitive asset. From the 1990s there also existed within key strategic business units people-committed Managing Directors such as Kevin Smith at Military Aircraft Division and Chris Geoghan at Airbus division.

2. Throughout this period the HR Director role was occupied by highly credible individuals such as Rob Meakin, Terry Morgan, Tony McCarthy, and the present incumbent Alistair Imrie. All had clear views on a range of issues and were well able to contribute to all elements of the key strategic debates.

3. Because of the clearly visible orientation of the CEOs and the MDs, linked to the credibility of senior HR leadership, it is fair to say that overall functional leaders at BAE were accepting of the core strategic role of the HR function.

As a result of possessing these significant pluses HR visibly participated in all major decisions and led in a number of key activities both at corporate and at business unit levels. HR was a prime architect in the major corporate change initiative at the then British Aerospace recorded in the book *Vertical Take Off* authored by Sir Richard Evans and Colin Price, published in 1999.

The Benchmark Change Program led to a major leadership cadre-sponsored role for HR as Terry Morgan highlights: "I've experienced several change programs in other companies. The difference about Benchmark that sets it aside from the others is the amount of time and effort that has been spent by the leaders – making their mark and giving it their stamp. There has not been what I have seen elsewhere, delegating change management to a set of willing champions. Very soon those champions hit a wall because they don't get the support they are entitled to."

An interesting example of the strong relationships that existed between HR and top management at BAE was when Rob Meakin in 1996 passed the baton of day-to-day leadership of the benchmark program to Kevin Smith, previously the very high-profile managing director of the Military Aircraft Division. According to Damien Turner, himself a managing director at BAE SYSTEMS, "Perhaps it was the single biggest thing in the Program – to take the man who was running the largest part of the business and say that this culture change program is so important that it merits this guy's undivided focus. This carried an awful lot of weight."

A progressive and confident HR at BAE SYSTEMS was also exemplified by an early commitment to the 3-Box model (see Chapters 2 and 3) which was initiated in 1999 and was reinforced by a pioneering move to an HR outsourcing agreement with Xchanging with discussions/negotiations commencing in 1999 and culminating in the launch of a formal joint venture in 2001.

Before drawing some general conclusions in terms of the Golden Triangle and its implications for CEOs and HR executives it is worth reflecting upon the interactions deriving from the influencers as outlined. We have demonstrated in an earlier section of the article that within individual companies the existence or not of the Golden Triangle can alter over relatively short periods of time. We believe the life cycle is governed by the interaction of the influencers and that fragility is more often derived from interpersonal influencers. Clearly if the long-term culture of the organization is favorable to the triangle's existence, then this is a major boost to HR power and influence. But if the interpersonal relationships are counterproductive and the CEO loses confidence in the HR leader, then the triangle is likely to collapse, at least, until the actors change.

6.9. Conclusion

In terms of our thinking regarding the Golden Triangle we would draw a number of insights. Firstly, whatever the future governance and leadership of HR by HR professionals or not, the Golden Triangle will still continue to exist as an organizational facet in a high proportion of large organizations. Secondly, the Golden Triangle ensures that the "separate world" issue of David Ulrich and Wayne Brockbank is negated.

Thirdly, the existence of the Golden Triangle within companies, leading to a powerful and influential HR function, is unpredictable, random to a great extent, and varies over time. We can predict, with a high level of confidence, that the Marketing VP/Director in global fast-moving consumer goods companies will be part of the senior team "inner sanctum." One could not make the same confident prediction regarding the HR executive in those same companies. The concept of the Golden Triangle merely highlights the importance of HR achieving authentic credibility. Finally, and very importantly, the Golden Triangle highlights qualities of wisdom, business awareness, coaching, and respect that any leader, HR or otherwise, must possess. That HR is the Function charged with the responsibility of developing these qualities provides HR executives with their mandate to create lasting value through the strategic enablement of theirs and their colleagues' commercial aspirations.

NOTES

1 IBM (2006) *The IBM Global CEO Study.* London: IBM.

2 For example, see Huselid, M. (1995). The impact of human resource management practices on turnover, productivity and corporate financial performance, *Academy of Management Journal*, 38: 635–72; Ulrich, D. (1997). *Human Resource Champions – The Next Agenda for Adding Value and Delivering Results*, Harvard Business School Press, Boston, MA; Becker, B., Huselid, M. and Ulrich, D. (2001) *HR Scorecard.* Boston, MA: Harvard Business School Press. The latest manifestation of this approach can be found in Purcell, Kinnie, Swart, Rayton and Hutchinson (2009) *People Management and Performance.* London: Routledge.

3 This debate was initiated by Ulrich (1997), complimented by Becker, Huselid and Ulrich (2001), and several other publications culminating in Ulrich, Brockbank, Johnson, Sandholtz and Younger's (2008) *HR Competencies: Mastery at the Intersection of People and Business.* Alexandria, VA: RBL/SHRM.

4 An extensive discussion of the development of these events can be found in Fleetwood and Hesketh (2009).

5 Lawler, Ulrich, Fitz-Enz and Madden (2004) *Human Resources Business Process Outsourcing: Transforming How HR Gets Its Work Done.* San Francisco, CA: Jossey Bass.

6 The best example of this can be found in Pfeffer (1997), a theme he picked up again with even more venom in Pfeffer (2000). The pursuit and later abandonment by the UK government's Treasury to impose a strict system of *Accounting for People* also reveals the philosophical aporia that the debate over measuring the financial impact of HR has become.

7 See: Fleetwood and Hesketh (2009).

8 Bourdreau, J. and Ramstad, P. (2007) *Beyond HR: The New Science of Human Capital.* Boston, MA; Harvard Business School Press, p. 189.

9 Clark, P. (2000). *Organisations in Action: Competition between Contexts*, Routledge, London.

10 Moss Kanter R. (2003). Leadership and the psychology of turnarounds. *Harvard Business. Review*, 81(6): 57–66.

CHAPTER 7

BAE: Using Senior Management Assessment as Part of a Talent Strategy

MARTIN HIRD, JOHN WHELAN, AND SHERIEF HAMMADY

7.1. Introduction

I n one of the organizations studied by CPHR, a Managing Director made a very telling remark about the centrality of talent to the issue of business model change:

> ... Where the business model is about differentiation, it is very people dependent ... With certain roles you can choose from a wide spectrum of people but when you move to senior management, then the quality of people is crucial, particularly when the industry is made up of companies where a lot of people are pretty average.

Picking up on this, one of the HR Directors expressed the issue succinctly as "the task is to future-proof talent," and we believe this is apposite to a central concern of many organizations: the building of capability in the organization to support business model change. This was seen as a central issue in the survey data in Chapter 4 and also in Chapter 5, which examined NG Bailey. Before we explore this issue at BAE SYSTEMS, what then is the headline issue, the strategic imperative, and the must-win battled for HR in general that results from this need to future-proof talent.

Future-proofing talent

Headline issue:

To what extent does HR concentrate on building strategic capability – as opposed to building its internal talent management practices, functional capability, and knowledge?

Strategic imperative:

Dealing merely with the HR agenda of competence or talent management fails to engage properly with the immediate issue of strategic capability, which is an organizational characteristic of which the people agenda is only part.

How one measures the competitiveness of the top cadre and the degree of formal assessment that is applied to these "stewards" of effective business strategy is a key question for those *Leading HR*.

Must-win battle:

There is a strong level of awareness on the part of senior operational executives that, based upon the now-accepted notion of the possession of talent being a key component of competitive advantage, HR makes a vital contribution to business model health by establishing and managing a talent pipeline that provides for both present and future business model requirements.

However, future-proofing talent requires that HR Directors understand how new business-critical skills get formed, and then take out all options necessary to manage this process.

In many ways Talent Management has been the "fashionable" HR activity for the last 10 years or so. The scene was set by the seminal *War for Talent* publication by McKinsey[1] and then reinforced not only by academic and other publications but also by the appointment in many HR departments of high profile Talent Directors, Heads of Talent, or Heads of Resourcing. We have also witnessed the rapid emergence of Talent architecture within organizations, architecture that has included processes for high potential identification, succession planning, creating talent pools, onboarding, and key role analysis. Inevitably to service these architectural requirements a range of Talent consulting services have arisen, some of which have been based upon occupational psychology expertise, some emerging from the major search companies. We argue that

The key messages that emerge from this chapter

1) Debate about past Performance versus future Potential still provokes lively discussions amongst both HR Professionals and occupational psychologists, and in recent years organizations have made a number of process changes to integrate talent systems more closely with the corporation's executive performance management architecture.

2) The provision of talent systems is now split across three categories of potential supplier – Psychologists, Search Companies, and Management Consultancies – each with their own views on what talent management should really be about.

3) For *Leading HR*, the design of more individualized development interactions has become an important element of helping Future-proof Talent around future organizational requirements.

4) It is crucial to link envisaged future business strategy with top management selection criteria and competences. This requires thinking about both organization design (OD) and associated key roles in a future time frame, which can then be converted and more finely honed strategic drivers and future role requirements.

The key messages that emerge from this chapter: (Continued)

5)   *Leading HR* requires the development of HR tracking systems that can demonstrate how, via development processes, people have moved closer to these requirements in terms of behavioral competence.

6)   It becomes ever more possible even for high-level HR processes such as this to be (jointly) provided by external providers, optimizing systems, and blending internal work on the strategic leadership with external talent data.

7)   Credible diagnosis, based on observed information, is possible to judge Strategic insight – how senior business leaders conceptualize a business problem and then move to a practical solution to that problem.

One focus for Talent Management will always be the senior cadre of specific organizations – the top 100/200 who should contain within their membership board successors and who should benchmark adequately against product/market competitors. An interesting debate surrounds how one measures this competitiveness of the top cadre and the degree of formal assessment that is applied to these "stewards" of effective business strategy.

This chapter is, in essence, a case history of formal talent processes, including assessment, that were applied to two senior groupings within BAE SYSTEMS, namely, the corporate "Top 100" and secondly the senior leaders within the Military Air Solutions (MAS) business of the company. In both instances the chosen external provider was Hay Group who worked closely with the internal BAE SYSTEMS HR team and the line/operational managers of BAE.

Two in-depth interviews were conducted with John Whelan who was in a corporate HR role when the process commenced and then moved in 2007 to take up the post of HR Director for MAS and Sherief Hammady who was the Coordinating Consultant for Hay Group throughout the process. In this chapter, we consider the history and background of the project, the selection of the external provider, the resulting Talent architecture, the integration of the process with the existing BAE SYSTEMS Talent system (which is called "Spectrum"), the degree to which the process was based upon psychological testing, and views about the process' business value. The chapter is structured as follows:

1.   We provide a brief background to the Talent Management System that has operated at BAE SYSTEMS since the mid-1990s.

2.   We outline the client perspective, based on John Whelan's evaluation of the process.

3.   Finally we outline the consultant perspective, based on the reflections of Sherief Hammady of the Hay Group.

7.2. Background to the BAE SYSTEMS talent process

BAE SYSTEMS utilizes a well-established Talent System entitled Spectrum. The model has been in operation for 15 years or so and was developed in the early to mid-1990s. In its time it was a much-admired system and to ensure its continuing relevance the system has been reviewed and overhauled on a number of occasions by the BAE SYSTEMS HR team.

The people performance potential model has been used, in various forms, inside organizations for many years. Its precise origins are unknown. The model appears in different formats, with different terminology for staff categories, and different titles (such as the performance potential model, the human resources portfolio, etc.). The purpose of the model is to enable an assessment and representation of the mixture of types (according to potential and performance) within any work group or team. It co-opts the language used to evaluate products in terms of their market share and their potential for market growth, and applies this to the categorization of human talent. It is variously attributed to, claimed or adapted by Boston Consulting Group (BCG), George Odiorne (famous for the management by objectives concept), Jack Welch, Doug Stewart, and Nicholas Barnes. The core concepts that underpinned the Spectrum system at BAE SYSTEMS were derived from an article by George Odiorne[2] in which he recommended utilizing the BCG matrix as the basis for constructing what he terms a "Human Resources Portfolio" (See Figure 7.1). Understandably British Aerospace, as it then was, did not adopt all of the category labeling utilized by Odiorne!

In recent times many HR functions have based their high potential identification around quadrants such as Odiorne's but, in the context of the early 1990s, this portfolio approach was quite an innovatory framework for Talent System architecture.

It is interesting to note the emphasis that Odiorne places upon differentiating Performance from Potential in terms of succession planning. The debate about past Performance versus future Potential still provokes a lively debate amongst both HR professionals and occupational psychologists. When researching and writing in the 1980s Odiorne defined potential as

> the likelihood of the job holder making a future contribution to the organisation.

Odiorne's six factor approach to identifying potential

1. Past Performance;
2. Intelligence and aptitude;
3. Future "availability" to the organization;
4. Interests and desires;
5. Supply and demand factors; and
6. Biographical information.

Figure 7.1:

a) The BCG Matrix

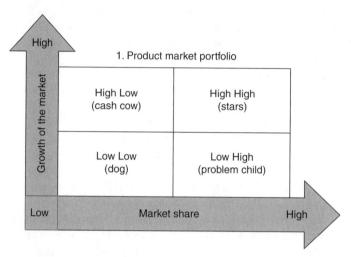

b) Odiorne's Proposed Adaption

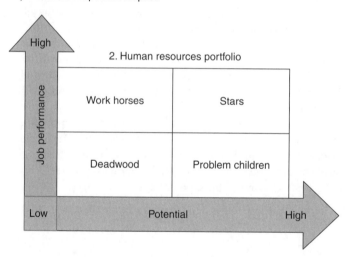

In terms of Talent Management, at what was then British Aerospace, the embryonic Spectrum System was initially developed within the Military Aircraft Division in 1994 and then integrated into the remaining divisions of the company during 1995 and 1996. The system revolved around a performance/potential matrix as advocated by Odiorne and a set of supporting processes were developed to underpin the system including various proforma and guidelines.

The key characteristics of the system included the following:

1. Color coding of the key categories:

   – Deep Gold/Light Gold for high potential/high performance
   – Green for high performance/lower potential

- Red for high potential/low performance
- Blue for low potential/low performance

2. Criteria were developed for allocating individuals to each category.

3. The Target Group was the British Aerospace senior management population.

4. A common proforma for all individuals to be assessed in the process was developed which covered name, age, executive grade, desired move pattern, assessment (color) code, aspirations, personal development plan, and tangible successes (the tangible successes ascribed to a particular individual were regarded as a crucial section of the process).

5. Core to the system was group calibration where for every individual his/her "parent" manager would submit their rating to a cognate group of parent peers, for example, heads of manufacturing, whose views in turn, were chaired by the "grand parent" manager, in this example, the manufacturing director. In essence the Spectrum "groups" revolved around advocacy, debate, and decisions that were regulated by a senior chair with an HR expert in attendance.

6. Development strategies for each category were developed and published.

7. Forced distribution was a key part of the system to ensure British Aerospace wide comparisons would be optimized.

8. A corporate training program was developed for HR Professionals across the company to ensure they were able to contribute effectively to the functional Spectrum groups that were in operation.

9. Spectrum brochures with management guidelines for the whole process were distributed across the corporation.

By 1996 the Spectrum System operated across the company and by 1999 had also migrated into GEC/Marconi which eased the introduction of common people strategies when British Aerospace and Marconi Defence merged in 2000 to form BAE SYSTEMS. Annual Management Resource Reviews were based upon Spectrum outputs and in a positive sense the system became institutionalized and continues to the present day.

In 2001 the system was subject to a comprehensive review that resulted in a number of process changes and additionally Spectrum was integrated more closely with the corporation's executive performance management architecture.

The merger between British Aerospace and Marconi Defence had involved a rigorous executive appointments process based upon a 15 per cent reduction in that executive population and that process had, in many ways, established the more systematic perspective with regard to executive appointments and formed the starting point for executive/top management assessments that form the core focus of this case history.

At this juncture it is appropriate to turn to Section 7.3 in which we explore post-2000 executive talent initiatives from the client/internal BAE SYSTEMS perspective.

7.3. The client perspective

John Whelan is currently HR Director for the Military Air Solutions business at BAE SYSTEMS. The business employs 16,700 people and operates three key businesses – Air Mission Support and Services, Autonomous Systems and Future Capability, and Typhoon Mission Support and International Programmes. The business operates on 8 UK sites: Warton/Samlesbury, Brough, Woodford, Farnborough, Chadderton, Malvern, and Yeovil and also has teams operating in North America, Europe, Asia, and the Middle East.

John became MAS HR Director in 2007. He was previously located at BAE SYSTEMS Corporate Center as HR Director Organization Development and Learning with responsibility for Leadership Development and Talent Management. He occupied his corporate role from 2001 and thus has had oversight, at different times, over senior talent assessment processes from both a corporate and a MAS perspective.

For John the story of Senior Talent Management began with the executive appointment process that was introduced at the time of the British Aerospace/Marconi Defence merger. That rigorous selection process was complex to manage but did introduce in John's view a highly systematic approach from late 1999 to 2000. John describes his view that the process was "more scientific, more thoughtful."

This systematic thread continued into 2001 when a formal assessment process with external providers was introduced for key senior BAE SYSTEMS selection decisions. However these centers were very "test" oriented – both ability and personality instruments were used in what could only be described as an intensive manner. John believes that the process was unpopular with those senior candidates and for some, the outcomes were damaging.

In July 2004 a new Chairman of BAE SYSTEMS was appointed, Dick Olver, who had previously been Deputy Chief Executive of BP. Olver was understandably very interested in the quality of BAE SYSTEMS top management talent pool particularly in terms of board and top management role succession potential. He was briefed on the Spectrum System and its inputs and outputs, but wanted to install a process of external validation to accurately measure the quality of the BAE senior cadre and ensure that succession plans were robust. John Whelan was tasked to manage the selection of an external provider for this validation exercise. He was aware that an increasingly wide range of consultancies were operating in the talent arena, ranging from specialist occupational psychology companies through to some of the major global search companies. To provide a range of choice John deliberately sought bids from three categories of potential supplier: Psychologists, Search Companies, and Management Consultancies with an established talent management track record. Eventually the contract went to a provider from the latter category, Hay Group.

We will outline in greater detail the components of the approach that Hay utilized in our next section, but it is important to highlight some of the broader principles of the process.

The initial target group for assessment was BAE SYSTEMS "Top 100" Group, who clearly occupied the most senior roles within the corporation. The actual assessment was based on a premise that John described as "not now a classical assessment center." The one-day interactive part of the process tended to take place in the individual manager's office rather than at an off-site location.

John Whelan outlines the rationale for this:

> ... We went for a more individually based process because we felt it was more palatable for the senior team. Putting our senior people through classic assessment centre scenarios and role plays did not seem right or appropriate. Any psychometrics are completed online prior to a session with a Hay consultant. Overall it feels less like an assessment centre and more like an individual development interaction.

John believes the key issue is ensuring that the process integrates with BAE SYSTEMS Spectrum System. His view is that the role of the "parent" manager is crucial in terms of this integration being successful. The "parent" owns the outcome of the process which promotes consistency with the Spectrum evaluation for his/her specific report. Thus the manager is responsible for that very integration process and this avoids the possible conflict between the well-respected Spectrum System and what could be perceived as an imposed external assessment process. John observes that in nine cases out of ten, the parent manager and the external assessor come to very similar conclusions about the potential of particular candidates. However there have been occasions when there are differing perspectives between parent and assessor. On these rare occasions the differences are discussed and usually resolved, but in the end it is expected that the external assessors will "stick to their guns."

An interesting element of the process is the degree to which aspects of clinical psychology are utilized. The clinical component is relatively minor. Apart from the tests the main thrust is a behavioral event interview evaluating elements of both business and personal life where things have gone well, and not so well, but the main emphasis of the behavioral event analysis is focused upon business life. Therefore in the corporate (Top 100) programs, the only clinical element is the use of a picture story exercise.

Great store was placed on the assessment criteria being formulated around future organizational requirements that will be demanded of BAE SYSTEMS Managers. Therefore a strong link was forged between the ongoing strategic planning process at both corporate and business level and the development planning process.

John Whelan explains:

> ... We need to be sure that we are preparing people for 3–5 years hence. It's no good basing everything on how things look today because the business will change.

Senior Directors were pushed to think about both organization design and associated key roles in a future time frame and then they were interviewed by senior Hay associates who were able to convert those strategic drivers into future role requirements. One cannot over-emphasize the importance that BAE SYSTEMS and HAY place upon this link between future strategy requirements and key development competences.

An important issue – one that in many ways is the core issue – is that of effectiveness of the process. John believes it has been effective from two perspectives:

Judging the success of talent assessment

1. HR tracking systems have demonstrated that, via the emerging development process, people have moved closer in behavioral competence to the requirements of succession roles than they were prior to the development process being introduced.

2. On the whole, individuals who were rated highly in terms of their position on Spectrum succession plans have attained high ratings/scores in the development planning process. This correlation validates the robust characteristics of the Spectrum System and also offers a reassurance that the overall talent architecture is identifying, broadly the key future players.

A final discussion point with John was the role of external providers in terms of constructing Talent architecture. As we have seen BAE SYSTEMS is a very large international company with, what would be termed, a sophisticated HR resource, and the legacy of an internally designed Talent Structure. So how does John see the balance of internal/external Talent provision?

> ... It's certainly possible to design Talent Systems internally when you have a substantial HR resource – well educated and professionally qualified in areas such as behavioural sciences and psychology. I also think one can over complicate the design of Talent Systems. They can, and should be, simple and straightforward in construction.

There are some exceptions to this though:

> ... However there may be specifics within the whole architecture – tools or sub processes that would benefit from the support of specialists who may be best available from outside the company. You want to be sure that what you are measuring is the characteristic you thought you were measuring and you want to be able to prove that for two reasons: you want it to be right; you need to prove to internal clients that your system has validity and reliability.

An overview of the assessment process is outlined below in Figure 7.2:

Figure 7.2: An overview of the assessment process

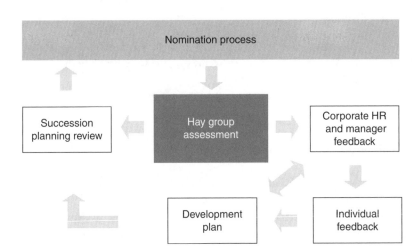

7.4. The consultant perspective

Sherief Hammady is an Associate Director and a member of the United Kingdom's Private Sector Consulting Leadership Team with Hay Group and leads their work with BAE SYSTEMS. Sherief has been employed with Hay Group for 8 years.

The Hay Group is a specialist people consultancy organization with a major focus upon three service lines:

1. Building effective organizations, with a key focus upon OD/development.

2. Leadership and Talent Practice, focusing upon talent development/executive development.

3. Reward/Compensation.

As with all global consultancy operations Hay Group has extensive databases to support its service lines and also has strong links with key academics and business schools.

It is important to explore the pattern of Hay's relationship with BAE SYSTEMS. The relationship between the two organizations has a long history, not least because British Aerospace utilized the Hay Job Evaluation System for its executive grading processes for many years and also regarded the Hay approach as a potential organization design aid.

In 2005 Hay won the contract for the corporate performance development activity and then since 2007 has been involved in developing Performance Development Centers within MAS transferring the learning that had developed from the corporate activity. Sherief was centrally involved with the tender process for the MAS work and has been the main contact point for John Whelan since the tender was won.

Sherief believes that a key part of the process is to identify the candidates with the greatest potential to lead MAS from 2011 onward. His familiarity and experience with the senior team at MAS lend support to optimizing the effectiveness of the development process.

He perceives two elements to this optimization process.

Optimizing the talent assessment process

1. A Talent Identification Agenda, which is central to MAS's future in terms of identifying future leadership potential;

2. Providing the most appropriate development plans for those future leaders. Hay are involved in this process working closely with BAE SYSTEMS senior line managers as well as HR/Learning and Development personnel.

In the MAS Personal Development process Hay work with BAE SYSTEMS to blend the internal work on the strategic leadership requirements for the future with Hay research data on the personal competencies that are indicators of success in senior management roles, for instance leadership impact. This should then optimize the declared aim of wedding MAS's future strategic requirement to the most appropriate senior management selection choices.

Emphasis is also placed upon the individual's ability to translate their cognitive competencies into action and also the individual's strategic insight – how they conceptualize a business problem and then move to a practical solution to that problem.

Discussions are held with the individuals in the process about their suitability for what is termed "business leadership" which involves possessing distinct strategic insights and capabilities as against more "functional leadership" which could have an operational focus or value that is achieved through "influencing" decision-making rather than leading it. The discussion with the individual regarding their future career orientation must be based, Sherief believes, upon credible diagnostic and observed information so that the ensuing discussion is both honest and well informed.

The physical output of the process is a written report to be sent to the "assessed" individual by Hay but also the "parent" manager, who is involved throughout the process. In addition it is important to highlight that BAE SYSTEMS line managers are trained as assessors (by Hay) and thus the whole process is, in a sense, triangular with the candidate, the external consultant and the internal line assessor. As John Whelan stressed the overall evaluation of the candidate is an output of a discussion between the external consultant and the internal assessor.

What does the assessment process consist of? The prime event for the candidate is likely to be perceived as the assessment "day" but prior to that a number of activities occur.

Diagnostic information is gathered internally from managers, peers, and team members. Psychometric tests are administered online, and a discussion is held with the individual to gather data about their background and their future aspirations. On the actual day the candidates complete a series of exercises, tackle a key business problem, and are subject to an observed simulation which involves business actors. An interesting facet is that the candidates get immediate feedback from the actors. This is perceived as quite an important part of the overall feedback process.

An area of mutual interest has been the issue of key criteria that can be used to identify high potentials generally, and therefore one wondered what position BAE SYSTEMS and Hay took on high-potential criteria. Companies and consultancies use a range of labels for high-potential criteria that range from innate qualities, such as internal drive and EI through to "abilities" including strategic and learning ability. Sherief has clear views about one of the classic high-potential criteria debates. When asked what is more important – intellectual ability or emotional intelligence? – in his view:

> . . . Well it's interesting this issue. Hay has conducted a substantial amount of research in this area and Daniel Goleman[3] who is an associate of our company, has used the research to spread awareness of the concept of emotional intelligence. We hold a database for Goleman's research and that data provides an accurate insight into the effectiveness of what intellectual ability and emotional intelligence bring to managerial performance. We believe that intellectual ability must be at a high level but, in essence, it's a base line. High potentials must have a high quality intellect but when you are looking at leadership it's about the ability to connect with others, interface, understand what is happening around you, empathise. Those qualities are linked to high emotional intelligence, so as a leader the individual must possess high EI.

Sherief's view on the importance of EI as a key criteria for successful leadership is broadly supported by recent work by Claudio Fernandez Araoz[4] who undertook a research project involving a sample of 250 managers. Following the project Araoz concludes:

> . . . EI was present in successful managers with a higher frequency than IQ as one of the most salient characteristics (almost two-thirds versus 50%). It seemed that for successful managers EI mattered more than IQ.

Sherief also outlined the importance of working on a joint basis with the BAE SYSTEMS team on the overall design of the process. One key benefit of this methodology is ownership by both BAE SYSTEMS Line Management and the HR Team. An interesting facet of the project was that Sherief believes the process "provided a language for the executives succession and development processes" and now that "language" also needed to integrate with the Spectrum Process. Overall Sherief emphasizes the importance of "providing rigorous information that feeds into decision-making regarding succession and development." He explains:

> ... It's not just about the assessment context; there is something that we call "holistic assessment"; so you look at the person, the background, all of the data that's coming out, and the likely transition that they experience. It really must be a holistic process that is linked to long-term planning.

Finally, Sherief outlines how he saw the future relationship with BAE SYSTEMS unfolding:

> ... It's to keep asking what the company need from its talent for the future. BAE SYSTEMS have managed to implement the right process for the organisation, which is very important. It is a process that effectively fits the culture. It isn't a check in the box exercise; we both need to question what we are doing and to keep questioning the validity of the process and its fit to the needs of the future.

7.5. Conclusions

This case history has focused upon the issue of assessing very senior managers within a large international company in terms of their fitness and suitability for future strategic leadership roles. Some may argue that formal assessment of long-serving top-level managers is inappropriate – that, at the most senior levels it is "track record" allied to appraisal and performance management to date that will suffice to make effective senior role decisions. BAE SYSTEMS thought otherwise and believe in the value of being "more scientific, more thoughtful." The case outlines the process that emerged from that philosophy. Drawing upon our collective experience, we draw four important conclusions in terms of talent management:

1. There is a "delicacy" involved in assessing senior managers that must be taken into account in terms of overall design, labeling, terminology, venue, and content if one is to attain internal credibility. BAE SYSTEMS seemed to get the right balance.

2. It is important to give a great deal of thought to integrating new talent processes with existing talent architecture and therefore avoiding issues of "babies and bath water."

3. It is crucial to link envisaged future business strategy with top management selection criteria and competences. BAE SYSTEMS and Hay have been very aware of this and there has been a strong internal link at BAE SYSTEMS between strategic planning and HR.

4. Line Management ownership and involvement is crucial in building a successful structure. HR cannot "carry" such an intervention unsupported.

NOTES

1 Michaels, E. Hanheld-Jones, H. and Axelrod, E. (2001) *The War for Talent*. Boston: Harvard Business School Press.

2 Odiorne, G.S. (1984) *Human Resources Strategy: A Portfolio Approach*. San Francisco: Jossey-Bass Inc.

3 Goleman, D. (1996) *Emotional Intelligence: Why It Can Matter More Than IQ*. London: Bloomsbury Publishing PLC.

4 Araoz, C.F. (2007) *Great People Decisions: Why They Matter So Much, Why They Are So Hard, and How You Can Master Them*. John Wiley and Sons Inc., New Jersey, U.S.A.

CHAPTER 8

Integrated Organization Design: The New Strategic Priority for HR Directors

CRAIG MARSH, PAUL SPARROW, AND MARTIN HIRD

8.1. Introduction

This chapter focuses on what we see as a primary capability that human resource (HR) Directors need to develop in their function – that of organization design.

Organization design as a prime capability

Headline issue:

What are the key steps to take, and in what order, to support business model change?
To what extent does the HR function march in lockstep with the change?
What does the organization design capability need to look like?

Strategic imperative:

Some of the key capabilities and competences outlined in this book are essential whatever the business model situation that the organization finds itself to be in, whereas others are more appropriate to specific business model situations.

However, organization design (we shorten this to ODS in this chapter in order to differentiate it from organization development, which is shortened to ODV) capability is most required in the Fluid and the Changing Rules of the Game political spaces outlined in Chapter 4, but particularly in the Fluid space, where both structures and teams change constantly in orientation and membership.

The ODS team must possess high levels of credibility.

Must-win battle:

The HR Director must recognize the primacy of ODS expertise in business model change

They must agree what is implied by this capability. We use the term *Architectural Design* to signal that the understanding of this capability is still vague, but its contours are being shaped by the need to develop the architectural knowledge that is required to deliver changing business models.

This capability might not be seen as being anything to do with HR. HR Directors need to lay claim by having a good ODS resource or recruit one fast. The ODS discussion is at the heart of the strategic discussion.

The key messages that emerge from this chapter

1) The half-life of organization designs seems to be eroding at an ever-faster rate. The time has come for a fresh look at two key HR capabilities. We analyze what is important in organization design (abbreviated to ODS) and organization development (abbreviated to ODV).

2) They present a major opportunity for HR Directors to make a contribution to strategic debates about business model change.

3) However, there has been much questioning of the relevance of ODV. We argue that as a field it is still healthy and vibrant and has a continuing role to play. However, it now needs to be subordinated to an ODS capability, especially in the context of business model change.

4) In a post credit-crunch world there will be inevitable industry restructuring and attention to organizational issues, but there are also deeper and more longstanding pressures. ODS has increasing financial utility, and is a central component of the ability to effect successful business model change.

5) However, ODS too is actually a fragmented field. The idea of ODS as an integrating idea that pulls together every area of business strategy and operations has been lost as the field has become fragmented. Functional areas and academic disciplines have been pushing their own agendas. As a consequence the capability has become devalued, with not altogether positive experiences in recent decades with consultants' offerings and business fads such as Business Process Re-engineering.

6) This raises three challenges for HR Directors: the capability of their HR teams, the relevance of their knowledge base, and the position of the HR Director in entering these debates at Boardroom level. We ask how HR Directors can get into the appropriate "space" inside their organizations.

7) The well-established Star Model helps establish what a base ODV capability involves, but we need to, then use this to, generate a series of questions that signal the sorts of knowledge that HR Directors need in their function to consider design issues.

8) It draws on different assumptions and technical know-how that comes from those with a decision-making or technology and information-processing background. HR needs to engage with these different types of expertise. This is all the more important because

The key messages that emerge from this chapter: (Continued)

we are seeing experimentation in what are called organizational forms – often extending well beyond any one single organization – and this has raised the importance of a number of new ways of understanding the knowledge and information markets that talent now operates within.

9) In the context of business model change, both ODS and ODV capabilities, historically distinct and fragmented across departments and intellectual traditions, now need to be assembled into one "seamless" capability in support of rapid organization restructuring. We call this combined capability "Architectural Design."

10) It does not have to "sit" in the HR department of course, but we think there is an opportunity for HR to co-opt this agenda for itself, especially if the alternative is allowing it to be externalized to strategic consultancies. Given that this integrated capability carries high strategic importance and is something that HR Directors should ensure exists in-house.

11) HR Directors should now bring together the various technical disciplines – HR thinking included – that have taken responsibility for questions about design. The HR department generally, and the HR Director in particular, is in an ideal position to exploit the imperative to think holistically and in an integrated way, about the organization's strategy and business model, its design and structure, and the people agenda. The contribution to be made by HR Directors is partly based on their observations on the business case, but is also based on the necessary personality, attitudes, and thinking style that underpin sound ODS insight.

We are told incessantly that the key asset the organization possesses is knowledge, not plant or products. However, in the knowledge environment, quite simply, your people are your structure. Any effort to construct or reconstruct a business model without some careful analysis upfront about the most effective way of designing a people-orientated model will be only partially effective. Just as an architect would not dream of producing a building design without integrating form and function, so any restructuring efforts ought to build in both outcomes – the value proposition and the best organization of its people to deliver them.

8.2. Getting into the right frame of mind

HR Directors are increasingly involved in some fairly tough discussions with their Executive teams, as previous business models and plans are re-evaluated, "red-inked," or simply thrown aside. Chapter 4 showed that the rules of the game are changing all around us; the temptation (and the practice) may be toward short-term measures to reduce costs quickly. Items that were previously top of HR Director "to-do" lists – talent, engagement, and performance for growth – may take second priority for a while as the realities of uncertain credit facilities, rapidly declining asset values, and shrinking markets begin to take hold.

Restructuring will also be part of these new discussions. ODS has always been a central topic in organization theory and the study of performance capabilities. Now is a good time to take a fresh look at an old concept – Organization Design – in a way that, we believe, has substantial implications for HR Directors in managing their strategic agenda. Building this capability will take a few years – so understanding what it looks like now is crucial.

The words "Organization Design" may appear to be a return – even a retrograde step, perhaps – to the classic texts of the mid- to late twentieth century by Jay Galbraith, Kurt Lewin, Warren Bennis, Richard Daft, and others – which became such a familiar and central plank in the foundation of work on, and theorizing about, organizations.[1] Many of the models developed at the time are still very much part of practitioner thinking today – witness the hundreds of management texts, websites, and consultants' pitches available on the Galbraith Star model, for example, recent work by the likes of McKinsey[2] featuring the words organization design. McKinsey conclude:

> ... The centerpiece of corporate strategy for most large companies should become the redesign of their organisations.[3]

The McKinsey dialogue about wealth from talent and ODS

Chief executive officers (CEOs) are being advised today to analyze their relative profitability and their ability to create high profits per employee. McKinsey argue that coping with the challenge of complexity has little to do with industry or sector, but is driven by internal capabilities – the organization structures, talent, business models, and other intangibles. To incentivize attention to ODS consulting, they argue that for a company with 100,000 employees, the ability to add $30,000 more profit per employee (the difference between being in the top 30 as opposed to top 60 firms on this measure) adds $3 billion to profits. ODS is being pushed as the new Holy Grail – a way of leveraging step-changes in additional earnings through marginal investments in capital and labor (the marginal cost argument will sound attractive to CEOs in these days of financial stricture).

Their recipe for step-change draws upon a number of generic principles that have been around in the organizational theory academic literature for a while – but are now being operationalized in strategic consulting. The challenge is to

1. improve on the use of hierarchy,
2. devolve and customize control to frontline "field-commanders,"
3. improve cross business-unit governance,
4. use management processes that manage portfolios of ideas through staged investment mechanisms,
5. make better use of networks,
6. operate talent markets and knowledge markets, and
7. redesign performance management and financial control measures.

Three things (consulting models apart) have combined to elevate ODS to the top of the "wanted" list of key organization capabilities:

1. The recent turmoil in world markets is forcing a fresh look at extracting the most value out of the organization.

2. There is increasing emphasis on business model change as a strategic agenda item, compelling executive team members to think broadly and systemically about the external and internal structuring, relationships, and linkages that hold their business together and sensitize it to the necessary stakeholders involved in the business model.

3. The strategic positioning of the HR Director offers these professionals a unique opportunity to influence design conversations at the highest level.

This confluence of factors however presents a threefold challenge to the HR Director.

Three challenges for HR Directors: How do you ensure that . . .

1. Capabilities – or at least that of their HR teams: Does it include both sufficient knowledge of all areas of the business and its external market, and also the ability to translate that knowledge into value-adding ODS concepts?

2. Knowledge and expertise in the field of ODS as a whole: How is this more than just the traditional HR agenda? How is this knowledge retained and deployed in their departments?

3. Influence: How do they develop and maintain a position to allow facilitation of debates about the direction, structuring, and restructuring of the organization's business model? How do they utilize close partnerships with the CEO and probably the Chief Information Officer (CIO) or Chief Knowledge Officer (CKO)?

Whether the HR Director is a convert or not to this way of thinking, the dialogue is taking place in Boardrooms. So how should those *Leading HR* lay their stall out to match these strategic dialogues? We need to go back to the future – which is why in this chapter we revisit history to trace what a modern ODS capability should, and should not, look like. For HR people, especially, we need to be clear what we mean when we talk about "Organization Design" as opposed to "Organization Development" – using the familiar abbreviation of "OD" may not always help to distinguish which term is really being referred to. At the end of the chapter we lay out what a combined design and development capability looks like, and shall call it "Architectural Design." For now, however, we must still talk of ODS and ODV as separate capabilities.

Much writing on HR in recent years has emphasized the need for HR people to think as business people first and foremost, with as much an eye on the bottom line as the CFO. This emphasis fails to recognize one fundamental, admittedly relatively unscientific, notion – that HR people look at the world slightly differently from many or most other people on the Executive team.

Why are HR Directors potentially well-equipped to deal with Architectural Design?

1. Due to their functional background, HR Directors are more likely to be what psychologists call "dual geared."[4] This refers to being particularly adept at moving easily between two opposite but complementary thinking styles – the analytical, data-driven approach, and the more intuitive, creative, "synthesizing" style that is useful for integrating new business models into structural designs.

2. They tend to be more aware of factors that motivate, engage, and incentivize people, essential in making sure that the design intentions associated with restructuring the knowledge of the organization stand a chance of actually being converted into behavior.

This difference should be recognized and exploited by executive teams, not minimized or sidelined, and is a key reason why HR Directors have the potential to work effectively with business model restructuring, where this style of thinking is a uniquely valuable addition to the discussion. As one VP of HR told us:

> The OD people . . . must be in the space, not only advising on different organisational models, but in the strategic direction of the business, and advising that that thinking should be going on around organizational change . . . if you're at the heart of the OD thinking the rest follows – the resourcing, the engagement piece. It's all about the relationship with the key guys: the rest follows.

8.3. Where have we come from? The ODS tradition

We lay out the essentials of an Organization Design (ODS) capability later in the chapter, but first clarify what is meant by that other "OD," Organization Development. (ODV) Historically, the field of ODV came first – design has been a more recent concern. The very familiarity of ODV to HR Directors begs the question of how we define it, especially in relation to ODS, and what the implications of the relationship between the two topics are for HR capabilities.

During the 1960s and early 1970s the ODV field was prescribed by the group of academics who contributed to the Addison-Wesley Series on ODV, edited by Edgar Schein and Richard Beckhard. The group was also active in the consulting field as well as publishing academic material. By the 1970s, publications were emerging in the series with a focus on design and structure including an early publication by Jay Galbraith "Designing Complex Organizations" and "Matrix" by

Stanley Davis and Paul Lawrence. These publications could be viewed as a bridge or linkage to an ODS perspective, exemplified by the 7-S Framework by Pascale and Athos, the Burke–Litwin model and Galbraith's later work on "The Star Model."

This led to a simple distinction, in which ODS generally referred to static "mapping" processes of the organization; whilst ODV was traditionally linked with dynamic concepts of change management. Precise definitions have shown a degree of affinity with the particular perspective of the expert doing the defining.

Traditionally, ODV has had "some of the features of a religious movement"[5] as it is a discipline founded on a set of strongly held values. As a consequence of its value-driven foundation, most definitions share similar characteristics. One of the original 1960s definitions from Richard Beckhard is:

> Organisation Development is an effort 1) planned, 2) organisation wide and 3) managed from the top, to 4) increase organisation development and health through 5) planned interventions in the organisation's "process" using behavioural science knowledge[6]

At the same time, Warren Bennis defined it as:

> a response to change, a complex educational strategy intended to change the beliefs, attitudes, values and structure of organisations so that they can better adapt to new technologies, markets and challenges, and the dizzying rate of change itself.[7]

ODV is about promoting commitment to top-down and planned change, so it is embedded within a simple input–output systems model of organizations.[8]

The collection of approaches on which it is based relies heavily upon the assumption that conflicts between the individual and the organization, and conflicts between groups in the organization, can and should be reconciled. In certain cases it appears that these values become, in the eyes of its proponents, ends in themselves, disconnected from the actual "bottom-line" value to the organization.

Even by the 1990s, there was much continuity in the values-driven orientation of ODV. Although definitions had been updated to include more recent discussions of culture, teams, and facilitation, the definition by Wendell French and Cecil Bell[9] still noticeably fails to mention organization performance:

> Organisation Development is a long-term effort, led and supported by top management, to improve an organisation's visioning, learning, and problem-solving processes, through an ongoing, collaborative management of organisation culture – with special emphasis on the culture of intact work teams and other team configurations – utilising the consultant-facilitator role and the theory and technology of applied behavioural science, including action research.

However, by the 1990s, the challenge for the ODV agenda represented by new forms of organization design was being signaled.[10] A shift away from traditional hierarchical structures and control cultures to more flexible, commitment-orientated organizations saw attention being given to topics not traditionally within the ODV remit – total quality management, employee empowerment and involvement, "whole task" job divisions, network structures, the need to acquire and retain talent, and attempts to create a "learning organization."

Despite this marginal development, ODV has been subject to much criticism. Orientated to process and tools, rather than results, and qualitative rather than quantitative approaches, ODV has risked becoming marginalized in the march toward profit, and becoming over-reliant on single-intervention consultants' reports rather than more rigorous research. Some commentators begun to argue that the field is in crisis. The critical view notes that:

> OD practitioners identified with employees at the margins; OD was something that practitioners felt and lived as much as they believed.[11]

The charges leveled against ODV:

1. It is founded in a unitarist and managerialist view of the organization "which has no place in modern paradigms."[12]

2. The field has no integrative models or theories, and it is confused about its values.[13]

3. The agenda frequently demonstrates slightly introspective, evangelistic characteristics of an exclusive club or sect, where techniques are considered to be ends in themselves rather than a means to deliver organization performance.

4. Those who call themselves ODV consultants are not really doing OD.

We do not believe that the field of ODV has passed its sell-by date. Far from it. It just needs to be re-positioned as an HR capability. Keyword searches of the literature[14] still find that the field of writing on ODV, though clearly fragmented, is extremely healthy and demonstrates some longstanding favorite topics of ODV practitioners at the top of the list of subjects covered – team building, process interventions, and international and cultural issues. There will still be a central role for the traditional strengths of ODV practitioners in leadership development, team dynamics, and, perhaps most of all, techniques and processes to facilitate the design work itself.

The real question is how should ODV expertise be fitted in with other key HR capabilities? Richard Beckard famously constantly asked "where is the O in OD?" We think the real question is what does the D mean and which D takes precedence?

Early definitions all tended to subordinate the ODS agenda to the ODV one. For some commentators, this still holds true.[15] Writing for an HR audience, Ruona and Gibson[16] note evidence of the convergence of the domains of ODV and ODS in recent years. Whilst not implying that HR should be the integrating function that owns both capabilities, they note that HR is becoming:

> a meta-profession, if you will, that can accommodate multiple fields under its umbrella.[17]

8.4. Understanding ODS capability

In order to understand why we believe HR Directors must move into the territory of ODS, we must provide some history, definition, and explanation of the term. The terrain laid out by literature on ODS has prominent contours which in turn have significantly impacted the practice of Strategic HR Management. Impact, in two senses:

1. creating the boundaries which have defined ODS work and
2. creating spaces into which HR professionals have rarely ventured.

Academic disciplines associated with the field can trace their origins to separate domains of expertise, a separation that has persisted in organization functions to this day. This separation is now inappropriate.

"ODS" as a phrase can contain the ambiguity of both description and implementation – as does the word "strategy." Are we referring to the static "phenomenon" pointed to by the word "design" or do we mean the process by which organizations come to be formed and reformed? Professionals tend to come from one of these backgrounds. The challenge for HR is to now bring the insights from each of these perspectives together into an integrated capability.

Three perspectives on ODS:

1. Decision-making,
2. Information-processing, and
3. Strategists and the "organization form" view.

Richard Butler – coming from a decision management perspective – defines ODS as "the setting of appropriate structures within which decisions are made and executed."[18] From this perspective, HR Directors need to see their organization's "structure" as a

> ... set of decision rules, or "rules of the game", that guide the behaviour of an organisation's participants during decision making and provide both opportunities and constraints for action; structures become observable as patterns in participants' behaviours.

Framed within a relatively static meaning of ODS, this literature limits the terrain by concentrating on *the nature of organization structure and form* rather than on defining the value web (see Chapter 1) on which this structure hangs.

IT-centered approaches also attempt to isolate, and then take ownership of, the topic ODS. Here, we see a different perspective.

IT-centered approaches to ODS focus on

1. the redesign of strategic organizational processes or
2. the competing value of information inside the organization and
3. how structures can help make sure managers attend to the most important information.

Many of the more strident statements about the revolution brought about by IT have been rejected.[19] The impact of technology has been exaggerated beyond the limits of human capacity and behavior. People can only take in, process, and communicate roughly the same amount of information as at any time in modern history. The main effects of the "information revolution" are therefore limited to the storage of databases and the ability for almost unlimited search and retrieval of information. Networking and communication improvements will always be limited by our natural (human) capacity for information exchange. This, in turn, places a natural limitation on the success of "fads" such as networked teams and virtual organizations.

The third piece of the jigsaw comes from strategists, who have given attention to new organizational forms – such as the network form (N form).

Organization form

This refers to the combination of strategy, structure, and internal control and coordination systems that provide an organization with its operating logic, its rules of resource allocation and its mechanism of corporate governance. Managers are the primary designers of this "form," through the choices they make about the structure, processes, and job design. These forms traditionally emerge to protect the organization from, and create a buffer against, external uncertainty.

Strategists also highlight the importance of the integration mechanisms that bring together the varied knowledge of small numbers of individuals to produce organizational solutions. They argue that organizations need to be designed around strategically important "information markets."[20] Organizations should be designed around markets because

1. there are distinct sets of suppliers of information (practice groups, networks, functions, etc.),
2. these suppliers have to compete for attention in a crowded space, and
3. both information suppliers and users have to receive rewards to participate in this market.

But the scarcest resource in organizations is attention to information. The ability to control and manage the quantity and quality of information that flows through these markets is central to organizational survival.[21] Moreover, ODS continually erode in their efficiency, so a redesign capability is also an ongoing and crucial need:

> Organisation re-design is the set of managerial actions intentionally used to alter organisational technologies, processes and structures[22]

These last two observations show it is time for HR professionals to "move into" (or perhaps "return to") the territory of ODS.

Why must HR move into the organization design debate?

HR departments understandably focus attention on the retention and management of talent and the development of leadership capability. But in the knowledge organization, it is the creating, capturing, and sharing of knowledge that has become vital for performance. The distinction between the inhabitants of the building (to extend our architectural analogy somewhat), and the building itself, has therefore become much more fuzzy. Architects and building experts would not think of placing people inside a badly designed and maintained structure, and they pay close attention to the relationship between the structure and its people to avoid this problem. Recruiting and developing the most talented people loses much of its impact if the organization they find themselves in is not suited to their needs. Often the supposed experts in motivation, behavior, and the limitations in human interaction (i.e., HR people) have not been involved in the organization's construction. Structures, processes, and hierarchies interfere with, rather than facilitate, work getting done effectively.

8.5. Bringing the different ODS perspectives together

An analysis of tools still prevalent in the field[23] cited a 1999 survey that suggested that 25 per cent of firms use the Weisbord Six-Box Model, 19 per cent the McKinsey 7-S model, 10 per cent the Galbraith Star Model, and 10 per cent the Nadlet and Tushman Congruence model. The Star Model is still very much in use. Although in the 35 years or so since it first appeared the model has undergone several adaptations, its fundamental principle remains unchanged.

The star model of ODS

Jay Galbraith[24] devised the most widely exploited model of ODS, the "star" model. This lays out a series of design policies that influence employee behavior but can be controlled by managers. Managers have to use each policy like a tool to shape the decisions and behavior intended by ODS:

1. Strategy: to determine direction.
2. Structure: to determine the location of decision-making power.
3. Processes: to manage the necessary flow of information and quality of decision-making.
4. Reward: to provide motivation and incentives for performance and goal-directed behavior.
5. People (i.e., HR policies): to influence mindset and skillset.

The model has been criticized for promoting an overly deterministic and machine-like view of design. The nature of the "fit" between each of these elements has also evolved – organizations in a globalized environment need to be more fluid and flexible than ever. Nevertheless, the model is instructive when we compare it with domain-specific literature on ODS. It shows that ODS must be more than structure, strategy, process, or other element separately considered. Its success derives from the combination of these elements working in conjunction with each other. This model signals the questions that a good HR Director can feed into the organization and its strategy debate.

In order to understand better the HR capability implied by this model, we have analyzed key work and applications of design thinking over the last 15 years to identify, for each element, the essential knowledge that constitutes an ODS capability. HR functions need to have a range of analytical tools, experience, and insight into a number of important consequences of design.

The Strategy-Design link needs HR Directors to demonstrate an understanding of how the goals and processes that are used to design the organization can influence effectiveness.

Strategy-design questions:

1. How do specific design options influence the "mental processes" of the organization (e.g., the ways that efficiency and productivity, creativity and innovation, or learning are dealt with)? This mindset might be embedded in the behavior of managers, or may become more deeply institutionalized

2. What are the necessary changes in priority-setting and focus of attention that must accompany any new mindset?

3. What are the most appropriate types of performance measurement?

4. What is the basis of power that each part of the structure has, power either by design or by default?

5. What is their influence on the culture, and what impact does this have on important outcomes such as scale and scope, productivity, creativity, and innovation?

The Structure-Design link needs HR Directors to understand the performance outcomes created by each component of the change.

Structure-design questions:

1. What are the basic pros and cons of all *structural alternatives* (such as function, product division, matrix, task force, and networks)?

2. How do different types of *organization control system*,[25] get formed and applied to work groupings (such as teams, clusters, or segments)? How does the formation of these control systems affect the timing and sequence of strategic delivery?

3. What impact will changes in the most visible new structures that flow from mergers, joint ventures, strategic alliances, outsourcing, virtual organization, and cross-sector cooperative arrangements have (this is called *inter-firm form*)?

4. What impact will changes in the most visible new structures that flow from downsizing, delayering, and the new arrangements that specify the design and coordination of jobs have (this is called *intra-firm* form)?

5. What are the consequences of the structural alternatives, organization control systems, inter-firm form and intra-firm form for the requisite levels of *trust*, *task competence*, and *values-congruence*?

The Process-Design link needs HR Directors to demonstrate an understanding of how the flow of activity reconciles important functional or business unit priorities.

Process-design questions:

1. Which interactions and dialogues between key people and perspectives are needed in order to add value, leverage the value, or protect the value inherent in the business strategy?

2. How is the necessary social network of exchanges enabled?

3. How are conflict, power, and political issues across this network to be resolved and mitigated?

4. What are the costs associated with failure of newly designed work systems and processes? What processes exist to mitigate new risks such as the increased costs of individual error, downtime, damage to technology, or reputation that might exist in the new design?

The Rewards-Design link needs HR Directors to understand how to avoid discrepancies between formal and informal incentives and the behaviors required by design.

Rewards-design questions:

1. How can people be incentivized to share knowledge in the ways deemed important by the new design?

2. How does the new design change career aspirations and create opportunity for other non-financial rewards?

3. Given the natural inclination of people not to break the habits of their past and present roles, how can your reward systems shape the new behaviors?

4. How will any significant shifts in power, influence, and credibility need to be rewarded and recognized?

The People-Design link needs HR Directors to understand the ways in which HRM systems integrate the new bundles of jobs into the strategic process,[26] how the rebundling of roles and jobs reshapes employee competencies and commitment, and what capacities have become necessary to handle the decision-making and power afforded by the design.

People-design questions:

1. Why do employees need to be exposed to new sources of information and new networks of relationships?

2. Why and how does such exposure shape and change the roles that employees are expected to play?

3. How must managers think differently about the tasks that need to be done?

4. What are the required decision-making processes that must be altered?

5. What are the time spans of discretion before the consequence of an inappropriate decision become known, and how are these time spans being altered? With what associated modifications to the people management process?

6. What are the new critical criteria for effectiveness, such as the judgment and leadership capabilities needed by employees, and how are these being altered?

7. What are the shifts in actual work content and business process flow?

8. How should the choice of performance management criteria and measurement metrics be changed?

8.6. Key messages from the ODS literature

In all too many organizations, ODS stops with the drawing of new boxes in a structure chart. We argue that this is just the beginning. The design needs to start with a reasoned answer to the above questions. When this is so, and when this reasoning has been shared with, and is built on the intelligence of, the line, then the ODV task becomes so much the easier.

Unfortunately, however, both the theory and practice of ODS has been characterized by an overreliance on division of interest and responsibility into its constituent elements represented by the different functional specialists: Strategy (often Marketing-led), IT, Operations Management, and (often lastly) HR. The HR element has been characteristically "relegated" to people process work after all the other major structural elements have been dealt with by their respective "experts." One of the consequences of this has been a systemic failure of HR people to grasp the opportunity to become involved in wider ODS work.

There is an opportunity for a more fruitful relationship, for example, between the Head of Technology and the Head of HR in ODS work, in which the people, behavioral, and organizational knowledge of the HR expert can be combined with the systems and process engineering capabilities found in technology managers.

Commentators such as McKinsey argue that managers need to place ODS at the center of strategy, with a clear HR element to the definition of the necessary design work:

> Managers must think holistically about designs incorporating market mechanisms that nurture talent and knowledge, governance structures that undo unproductive complexity, and new performance metrics – notably profit per employee – that are suited to a business environment where talent, not capital, is the scarce resource.[27]

Drawing upon the developments in theory we noted above, they have sketched out the key elements of any design work to overcome what they refer to as the "unproductive complexity" of organizations – arguing it is important to make organizations into a single profit center, streamline hierarchy, expand its capabilities horizontally, delegate authority to the front line, have a one-company structure and culture, and introduce internal market mechanisms including a "knowledge and talent marketplace."

How might this be done? It is time to bring ODS capability in-house. The opportunity is now re-presenting itself with the growth in organizational ideas such as the resource-based view of strategy, the recognition of the strategic importance of capabilities, and, more especially, the attention paid to the construction of the organization's business model.

HR people are potentially, at least, uniquely placed to look across all aspects of the organization's functioning, a key prerequisite to be able to participate in the full range of organization design tasks. An essential requirement is the ability to look upward – to look above the concerns of an historical, divisional, or functional agenda.

This perspective is routinely offered by external consultants and it is questionable whether this expertise should be left in the hands of outsiders. As one commentator notes:

Too often, HR simply use the designs that others create – often on the fly or by implementing recipes from outside consultants – and deal with the resulting people, rewards, and management issues that come about from a poor fit of problem and solution.[28]

As organizations become more dynamic, we need to

1. merge the two areas of ODS and ODV explained in this chapter into one strategic capability, which HR should group into one structure or center of excellence;

2. the ODS capability must take precedence, not ODV; and

3. the capabilities required to lead ODS work require now need some integration across the traditional functional disciplines that have been used to study it.

Any strategic restructuring – especially that which involves changes to the organization's value proposition – will now inevitably result, to some degree, in the need for this combined Design and Development capability. Bringing the ODV agenda into the fold of ODS work, not the other way round, may be seen as heresy to experts in the field, but it serves to give ODS its rightful place in business model change.

There is a problem, however. A survey of senior executives inviting them to comment on their key ODS priorities and who they turn to for help for each suggests that HR and separately defined ODS specialists come a long way down the list for strategic restructuring:

> When looking for assistance in positioning industry consolidation, mergers and acquisitions and strategic alignment for success from a cultural perspective, business leaders turn to line management first, to consulting firms second, to HR third, and OD fourth.[29]

HR has been obsessed – understandably – by the talent agenda in recent years. However the areas of organization design work in Galbraith's Star Model and the capabilities presented above are the context in which talent is managed.

Another reason to bring ODS in-house is the work that is now necessary to manage business models (see Chapter 4).

There are three strategically different situations faced when building on current success:[30]

1. retaining the current business model;

2. refining the current business model;

3. or seeking to develop New Program Platforms.

Each situation determines the broad approach to ODS. In the first and second case, ODS is focused on both process and product innovation. HR's role is in the assistance they provide to the leaders of change. These are typically the Chief Operating Officer (COO) for process innovation (through the provision of total quality management training) and the Chief Technology Officer (CTO) for product innovation (through ensuring talent is supplied in the right field). In the third case, where New Program Platforms are pursued as part of a growth strategy, the organization needs to innovate in its value proposition to the market, that is, it changes its business model. In this last case – that of business model change – they argue strongly for HR's contribution to ODS:

> Strategic HR leaders will need to push the boundaries of their influence . . . a key challenge for HR will be to recognise and reconcile the differences in mindset in the core business and the less well-defined and less-confined domains and work in the new programme platform world. To do this they will have to start by looking in the mirror. Who in their HR organisation has experience in building new businesses and ventures, operating external networks, and supporting centers of excellence for growth?[31]

8.7. Three levels of design capability

We call the evolving capability that results from combining ODS and ODV capabilities *Architectural Design*. This capability does not have to "sit" in the HR department of course, but we do think there is an opportunity for HR to co-opt this agenda for itself, especially if the alternative is allowing it to be externalized to strategic consultancies.

The precise nature of this capability is still evolving, driven by the drumbeat of building the knowledge required to manage business model change. Chapter 1 introduced the concept of business model, and Chapter 4 highlighted a range political spaces that they create for HR. The attention of HR Directors should be directed to understanding and working with the idea of business models. What must this capability entail? We believe the frameworks, tools, and techniques to look at business models as they operate at three different levels of analysis:[32]

1. Industry or market value chain (Level 1).

2. The organization's own value proposition (Level 2).

3. The organization's internal structure (Level 3).

HR needs to develop tools and techniques that enable it to diagnose what is happening at each level of analysis, and to be able to highlight the necessary HR implications. It needs to then be able to use this analysis to contribute to, and be actively involved in, the strategic debates. By expanding these three elements, we now signal the layers of expertise and capability that HR needs in order to truly have an ODS capability.

The work of Schweizer[33] shows there are four different ways in which an organization might position itself within an industry value-chain: integrated, orchestrator, layer player, or market maker. These value chains – or what more recently have become called webs of value – are expanding across organization boundaries. The first level of analysis therefore necessitates a broad understanding of where the value flows are in the industry, and where the company wishes to position itself within those value flows in the long term. Two of the contributing organizations to this book – NG Bailey in construction and BAE SYSTEMS in manufacturing – are moving from a "layer player" position to more of an "integrator" position by extending their offering to a complete service delivery to the end customer.

For example, NG Bailey has placed the "whole life of buildings" at the center of their company strategy for the next few years, a "cradle to grave" value proposition to their customers, that also enables change in the traditional contractor industry model. For BAE SYSTEMS the Through-Life Capability Model represents a new integrated proposition.

At the second level HR needs to diagnose the specific value proposition and implication of its necessary strategic processes for people management. George Yip[34] argues that once changes to the industry structure and the company's positioning are understood, then more detailed mapping or modeling of strategic flows and processes can take place (see Chapter 1). For another organization featured in the book, Vodafone, the ODS work of the HR Director started at this level, with a discussion, spanning several executive meetings, about the nature of these elements in their business in a rapidly changing environment. These high-level concepts were then translated into operationally viable structures to deliver the company's value proposition. In another organization, United Utilities, the CIO – in partnership with the HR Director – led a project to identify, map, and implement six strategic processes that target value delivery and result in improving the power of frontline employees to make on the spot decisions affecting customers.

Finally, at the third level of analysis attention is turned to the specific components or structure of the business model and its operations. This last level of analysis enters territory traditionally more familiar to HR experts. For example, IBM's component business model[35] divides the organization horizontally into key components (business administration, new business development, relationship management, servicing and sales, product fulfillment, and financial control and accounting) and vertically into strategic direction, strategic control, and strategic execution. The strategic direction components set the direction in the business model, and the strategic control components translate these into actions and the day-to-day activities. The strategic execution contains all the business components that execute the plans and activities in the business model. All component units (often processes or functions) in this two-dimensional matrix have to be made consistent with, and support, the strategic processes developed at level 2. This work can only start, however, once the analyses at level 1 and 2 are completed.

For HR to be truly strategic, the function needs to develop the capability of influencing business model design at each of these levels, understanding how they represent new challenges to HR thinking, organization, and capabilities.

8.8. HR's role in linking ODS to business model change

How can HR Directors evolve the new Architectural Design skills? ODS and ODV, despite their historically distinct intellectual traditions and skills that are fragmented across departments, now need to be assembled into one "seamless" capability in support of rapid organization restructuring.

We look at a profession for whom such combined capability is a base requirement. The ideas and practices of evolutionary Architectural Design have been around for several years.[36] Buildings are constructed using biological principles to create a "symbiotic" and interactive relationship between space, the people inside, and the structure itself. They challenge the traditional architectural approach of fixed, immovable, and predetermined objects, designed and built by experts who have no further part to play once the construction has been handed over to the client. The distinction between a static ODS and dynamic ODV capability similarly needs to evolve.

This Architectural Design capability can be defined as the possession of insight into firm-wide routines that coordinate and combine the various functional components of a business model, and awareness of their consequences for organizational behavior, through the possession of knowledge of the bigger picture. By its nature, business model change entails building new capability of this type and then "routinizing" the knowledge so that the capability is greater than any one person, or set of people, in the organization.

An HR Director offers a good example of the "integrating" nature of this type of capability:

> ... We realised that supply chain management was a key capability. A lot of people misunderstand what this capability needs. Beyond just having better procurement, you also have to integrate all of your functions together. You have to be able to optimise your assets. It is inventory management that drives the costs and these costs can be predicted when you look forward.

For this organization the business model had thrown up a new capability that was based on an amalgam of high-level functional insights.

HR added value therefore must comprise a clearly thought out, broadly business based explanation of how strategy translates into a new business model using business architecture design, and thence into HR structures and processes. HR strategy, in this model, is coexistent with and subsumed by organizational strategy and business model design.

The pattern of HR's contribution to business model change

1. Ensure the function possesses a combined ODS and ODV capability. There will be an HR orientation to this expertise; however, business model change also incorporates changes to commercial and customer-oriented structures as well as organizational ones. The broader the business knowledge, the better.

2. An intuitive relationship with the CEO or senior line directors is a necessary condition for the next step – to develop a high level set of organizational principles with the Board. The HR Director acts as a facilitator to this discussion and uses it as a way of

further developing relationships with senior players. The process will be iterative, consultative, and will involve expert members of the HR team in a consultative role.

3. A new business model is drafted out which is consistent with the principles agreed at step two. In one organization, the HR Director "bunkered down," to use their term, with their HR team for a month as they developed several design options to be represented to the Board.

4. Analyze whether the business possesses the required capabilities and knowledge to deliver the new business model. Frequently, the capability gap represented by business model change entails not only talent gaps, but a shift in the nature of knowledge from localized, specialist "component" capability to more "architectural" capability (see Chapter 1).

5. Having handled the Organization D for *Design* questions, manage the change as a "classic" Organization D for *Development* intervention.

It is also clear that the nature of Architectural Design input will vary according to the stage of business model change in the organization, something underlying, but not made explicit, in the description above.

Facilitating input on Architectural Design seems to be crucial for HR Directors. However, being realistic, in several cases the HR Directors in our research encountered ambivalent, lukewarm, or inconsistent responses at this stage of the process. Board members do not necessarily buy in either to the role of HR or the nature of business model change, particularly if the CEO is not attentive to driving the change through consistently. So at one organization an HR Director laments:

> . . . If only . . . the Board knew what role HR plays. This is what we're wrestling with now, the work we're doing is owned by, let's be honest, the CEO, the HR Director, the CIO and [the management consultants]. End. That's what we're dealing with. I don't think the organisation has talked about what the business model is.

The CIO in the very same organization however acknowledges the realization of the need for HR input:

> . . . We've set ourselves some ambitious goals. When I first mentioned those to the Executive Management Team I was met with a few gasps and shakes of the head. Take customer satisfaction for example. 70% of our customers say they're satisfied with their experience of [the organisation]. Which means 30% are not. So we've set ourselves a target of 90% which is the highest in the industry. And our customer services people are saying "how the hell are we going to do that?" And it suddenly dawned on them that . . . they have to start thinking in ways they haven't thought before. So they're no longer thinking of the management of the customer relationship, they're thinking about the whole redesign of the customer relationship, because we've set them this target.

At another organization experiencing business model change, the Transformation Director felt that this was a key failing in the change process – once step one (ensuring organization design capability) had been completed:

> ... If you look at the reports coming through [from the Executive], they don't talk about [the organisation design], they don't try and measure [it] ... a number of attempts to start to tweak it are not being driven through with nearly enough fire and passion. Certain individuals are doing their own thing and driving things through; others aren't. As a result the people below that level aren't seeing the changes. They've seen a couple of people they liked leave the business and wonder what it was all for, and they haven't really seen any pressure or benefit to changing.

Consequently, a key issue for the HR Director becomes the management of performance of the Board, perhaps through helping them to develop new knowledge of Architectural Design.

HR is being repositioned in this way, not just because of internal organization design pressures, but also as a consequence of changes in the importance of external interdependence and partnership. The analysis of business model change in Chapter 1 noted that organizational "value web" is, in almost every case, extended across traditional organizational boundaries. This interdependence is a defining characteristic of business model change. Relationships with external bodies which were previously characterized as adversarial at best are suddenly having to be redesigned under a partnership model, as long-term contracts are developed with other organizations in the same value web. For example, at BAE SYSTEMS (see Chapter 7) the concept of through-life contract management is driving a "partnering" culture; for many employees this partnering culture may well involve a physical change in location from a factory site to a partner site. NG Bailey (see Chapter 5) is experiencing precisely the same shift from "adversarial" to "partnering" relationships with outside bodies. At the same time, new relationships are being forged with organizations which would previously have been kept at a distance.

HR Directors therefore have a strategic imperative to grasp the nature of such new capabilities and how they may be developed. HR refers regularly to the management of "talent," itself a crucial part of the HR agenda, but this risks confusing organizational capability with something existing at a lower level of analysis: competence, or component capability.

Understanding the necessary capabilities

HR needs insight into the ways these capabilities are being developed. Typically this is through the following:

1. A deep understanding of two or three crucial ingredients – perhaps specific advanced technological skills resident within a handful of high-talent on which the organization must place a bet or take an option to ensure the success of its business model[37] (an insurance premium, if you like, an option that the organization wishes to take in the talent market, the purchase of which might need to break the HR systems).

2. A hybrid skill or insight, created by the bringing together of different component skills. The task for HR is to capture the nature of new insight by being involved in the business dialogues that have helped to articulate it, and to assess the best route to sourcing it.

3. The transformation or evolution of an existing skill or knowledge base into a new mindset, and it is that new mindset that forms the "glue" that ties together the business model. Often the talent question cannot be separated from the issue of engagement – and the need to manage the way in which the broader workforce identifies with the new capabilities necessary for the business model.

8.9. Conclusions

Most managers are from financial, engineering, or scientific backgrounds, and their original discipline trains them to be analyzers – knowing how to take something apart and see how it works, or how to build a tangible, working construct – rather than synthesizers, that is, the skill of understanding how to assemble intangible component parts into an integrated, future-orientated picture.

Architects are trained to undertake synthesis by profession.[38] They talk of the idea of "imperfect design" – a structure which does not have every single element in place, which accommodates space for the developments of patterns of work or routines. We are reminded of the analogy of the business park developer who did not put in place paths between buildings. After 3 months the architect observed where the grass had been worn by the occupiers, and he placed the paths along the worn spaces.

Managers need also to resist the temptation to fix processes that are overly deterministic and rigid in order that people find their own ways through the structure. Most importantly, the skill of ODS – as a synthesis of complex patterns – is acquired over a long period, not, as most managers assume, as an adjunct to their day-to-day work and which can be completed in 30 minutes with the sketch of a new organization chart or matrix.

This is where HR Directors can come into their own. It is likely that they are naturally inclined to think in patterns – the "people" function seems to attract this type of capacity more than the other specialist functions – and they are likely also to have a finely honed perception that it is individuals, not boxes or lines on an organization chart, who comprise the organization's architecture. There are, however, a number of questions that HR Directors may choose to ask themselves about their HR strategy vis-à-vis this Architectural Design:

The key questions about Architectural Design capability

1) Is their organization, or a strategic element of it, likely to be undertaking business model redesign in the near future?

2) If yes – will the HR unit be able to contribute an Architectural Design capability to the discussion?

3) If no – who is going to provide it?

4) If yes – how will HR integrate or balance the separate traditions of ODS and ODV into one value-adding contribution to the discussion? Where are the skills in each area right now?

5) How should the necessary skills be structured in the unit – together, in a Center of Excellence, or part of the business partners' area of expertise, or a combination of the two?

6) Should any element of this capability be outsourced? If so, which ones?

7) In any case, how will *Leading HR* make sure these skills are brought into the "HR space"?

The challenge to HR Directors therefore is threefold:

1. **Think bigger**: Traditionally, the HR Director's contribution to ODS work has been restricted to functionally driven expertise in the area of ODV. This has involved developing models of organization structure that have been influenced by a single-minded values-driven orientation of empowerment and teamwork, without due regard for the bottom line. HR Directors need to think bigger and make sure that the function is capable of applying business model design skills, first at level 2, and ideally also at level 1.

2. **Think broader**: In order to achieve this the HR Director will need to acquire or develop a broad type of knowledge – architectural knowledge – of the way the organization fits together. The process of ODS is often outsourced to consultants, and yet this capability, though hard to develop, will add considerable advantage if it can be retained in-house. It is most unlikely to be obtained quickly and effectively by an external party. The HR Director needs to determine whether they need to possess this capability personally, or to have it available through some other mechanism within the HR function.

3. **Think more integrated**: Most importantly, HR is a boundary-spanning function. Possibly in close partnership with the CIO or CKO, the HR Director is well positioned to see how the various elements of the business fit together. It will demand a high degree of board-level facilitation skills, and the ability to merge diverse political and economic interests. It is also likely to involve a degree of courage, as vested interests in the executive team vie with each other

to defend entrenched positions. The essential element or condition is likely to be the commitment of the CEO to the HR Director in allowing him or her to perform this integrating role. The HR Director needs to manage their reputation to take on such responsibility successfully in periods of business model change.

In the final analysis, we must always remember that the primary purpose of an *Architectural Design* capability – that is, combined ODS/ODV skills – is to make the organization optimally effective. HR must never lose sight of this.

NOTES

1 See for example: Bennis, W. (op.cit.) *Organisation Development: Its Nature, Origins and Prospects.* Reading, MA: Addison-Wesley; Lewin, K. (op.cit.) *Field Theory in Social Science.* New York: Harper and Row; Galbraith, J.R. (1973) *Designing Complex Organisations.* Addison Wesley; Daft, R. (2006) *Organisation Theory and Design: Understanding the Theory and Design of Organisations.* Michigan: West Publishing Company.

2 Bryan, L.L. and Joyce, C.I. (2007) *Mobilising Minds: Creating Wealth from Talent in the 21st Century Organisation.* New York: McGraw-Hill.

3 Ibid., p. 1.

4 Sadler-Smith, E. and Sparrow, P.R. (2008) Intuition in organisational decision making, in Hodgkinson, G. and Starbuck, W.H. (eds) *The Oxford Handbook of Organisational Decision Making.* Oxford: Oxford University Press. pp. 304–323.

5 Buchanan, D. and Huczynski, A. (1997) *Organisational Behaviour: An Introductory Text. 3rd Edition.* Harlow: Prentice Hall. p. 487.

6 Beckhard, R. (1969) *Organisation Development: Strategies and Models.* Reading, MA: Addison-Wesley. p. 9.

7 Bennis, W. (op.cit.)

8 Lewin, K. (op.cit.)

9 French, W.L. and Bell, C.H (1995) *Organisation Development: Behavioural Science Interventions for Organisational Improvement.* Englewood Cliffs: Prentice Hall. p. 28.

10 Morley, M.J. and Garavan, T.N. (1995) Current Themes in Organisational Design: Implications for Human Resource Development. *Journal of European Industrial Training*, 19 (11): 3–13.

11 Weidner II, C.K. (2004) A Brand in Dire Straits: Organisation Development at Sixty. *Journal of Organisation Development*, 22 (2): 37–47.

12 Iles, P. and Yolles, M. (2003) Complexity, HRD and Organisation Development: Towards a Viable Systems Approach to Learning, Development, and Change, in M. Lee (ed.) *HRD in a Complex World.* London: Routledge. pp. 25–41.

13 See: Rothwell, W.J. and Sullivan, B.L. (2005) (eds) *Practicing Organisation Development: A Guide for Consultants. 2nd Edition.* Chichester: Pfeiffer/Wiley imprint; Bunker, B.B., Alban, B.T. and Lewicki, R.J. (2004) Ideas in Currency and OD Practice: Has the Well Gone Dry? *Journal of Applied Behavioral Sciences*, 40 (4): 7.

14 Piotrowski, C. and Armstrong, T.R. (2004) The Research Literature in Organisation Development: Recent Trends and Current Directions. *Journal of Organisation Development*, 22 (2): 48–54.

15 Yaeger, T. and Sorensen, P. (2006) Strategic Organisation Development: Past to Present. *Organisation Development Journal*, 24 (4): 15.

16 Ruona, W.E.A. and Gibson, S.K. (2004) The Making of Twenty-First Century HR: The Convergence of HRM, HRD, and OD. *Human Resource Management*, 43 (1): 49–66.

17 Ibid., p. 60.

18 Butler, R. (1991) *Designing Organisations: A Decision-Making Perspective*. London: Routledge, p. 2.

19 Groth, L. (1999) *Future Organization Design*. Chichester: John Wiley and Sons.

20 Hansen, M.T. and Haas, M.R. (2001) Competing for Attention in Knowledge Markets: Electronic Document Dissemination in a Management Consulting Company. *Administrative Science Quarterly*, 46 (1): 1–28.

21 Ibid.

22 Huber, G.P. and Glick, W.H. (1996) (eds) *Organisational Change and Redesign: Ideas and Insights for Improving Performance*. New York: Oxford University Press. p. 11.

23 Noolan, J.A.C. (2006) Organisation Diagnosis and Its Place in the Organisation Development Process, in B.B. Jones and M. Brazzel (eds) *The NTL Handbook of Organisation Development and Change*. London: Pfeffer/Wiley.

24 For example Galbraith, J.R. (1973) *Designing Complex Organisations*. Addison Wesley: Reading, MA; Galbraith, J.R. and Kazanjian, R.K. (1986) Organising to Implement Strategies of Diversity and Globalisation: The Role of Matrix Designs. *Human Resource Management*, 25 (1): 37–55.

25 Daft, R. (2006) *Organisation Theory and Design: Understanding the Theory and Design of Organisations*. Michigan: West Publishing Company.

26 Sparrow, P.R. (1998) The Pursuit of Multiple and Parallel Organisational Flexibilities: Reconstituting Jobs. *European Journal of Work and Organisational Psychology*, 7 (1): 79–95.

27 Bryan, L.L. and Joyce, C. (2007) Better Strategy Through Organisational Design. *McKinsey Quarterly*, 2007 (2): 52–63.

28 Mohrman, S.A. (2007) Designing Organisations for Growth: The Human Resource Contribution. *Human Resource Planning*, 30 (4): 43.

29 Wirtenberg, J., Lipsky D., Abrams L., Conway M. and Slepian J. (2007) The Future of Organisation Development: Enabling Sustainable Business Performance Through People. *Organisation Development Journal*, 25 (2): 11–27.

30 Laurie, D.L. and Lynch, R. (2007) Aligning HR to the CEO Growth Agenda. *Human Resource Planning*, 30 (4): 25–33.

31 Ibid., p. 33.

32 Schweizer, L. (2005) Concept and Evolution of Business Models. *Journal of General Management*, 31 (2): 37–56.

33 Ibid.

34 Yip, G. (2004) Using Strategy to Change Your Business Model. *Business Strategy Review*, 15 (2): 17–24.

35 IBM website: http://www-935.ibm.com/services/us/igs/cbm/html/bizmodel.html, accessed 1 October 2007.

36 For example Frazer, J. (1995) An Evolutionary Architecture, Architectural Association, London (available on the web at http://www.aaschool.ac.uk/publications) accessed 24th March 2008.

37 See: Kogut, B. and Kulatilaka, N. (2001) Capabilities as Real Options. *Organisation Science*, 12: 744–758; and Bhattacharya, M. and Wright, P.M. (2005) Managing Human Assets in an Uncertain World: Applying Real Options Theory to HRM. *International Journal of HRM*, 16 (6): 929–948.

38 See: Yokoyama, Y. (1992) An Architect Looks at Organisation Design. *McKinsey Quarterly*. 1992 (4): 116–127.

CHAPTER 9

Understanding the Value of Engagement: Building Belief in Performance

SHASHI BALAIN AND PAUL SPARROW

9.1. Introduction: Why is employee engagement seen as important by organizations?

Chapter 1 argued that the complexities of business model change often involve a change in "mindset" or an employee's "mental model" of exactly what the organization's business model is. There is an essential process of communication and involvement of the workforce in which the human resource (HR) Director plays a leading role, attempting to create this mental mobility in the attitudes held by the workforce. This becomes especially true when, as argued in Chapter 4, there are likely to be relatively few people – especially at the outset of a change – who have really grasped the nature of the change and have made the "mental" shift to a new model.

The challenge for chief executive officers (CEOs) and HR Directors in periods of rapid change is to ask whether they can take their people with them. The aim of this chapter is to help us understand – and test – the assumptions that HR engagement strategies are based on.

Understanding the value of engagement

Headline issue:

Is engagement a future-proof HR strategy?

Strategic imperative:

Construct and develop much better insight into how it influences organizational performance – reverse engineer the performance recipes that managers have in mind.

Investigate the "performance recipes" in the organization with transformation, capability, and operational directorates. Help line managers understand the complex business performance benchmarks that they report to, and how these performance

---

outcomes are best engineered through people management. Help employees understand the benefits of engaging with that particular view of performance.

Design engagement surveys using the analogy of a medical diagnosis, including the complaint, history, examination of the condition, ancillary tests if needed, diagnosis, treatment, and prognosis with and without treatment in a single examination.

Deal with the issue of employee identification with the organization – why should employees live the organization's values if it does not live theirs?

Research how customer satisfaction affects the relationship between employee experiences and financial performance, and how employee satisfaction is associated with specific components of the service model.

Step into the void that currently exists in the prediction of organizational performance on the back of strategic change management projects. Work side-by-side with corporate communications, internal and external marketing, and operations experts and share respective models and insights into how employees truly impact operational and strategic performance

Must-win battle:

The HR Director "reverse engineer" the type of performance that the organization is trying to create, and to understand the depth to which – and the ways in which – the organization needs to foster links and bonds with its employees.

In examining the issues raised by this challenge, we argue that

The key messages that emerge from this chapter

1) Engagement is used in practice inside organizations in three different ways: as internal marketing, as process improvement, and as being predictive of corporate performance. Each makes very different assumptions about what needs to be measured under the label "engagement," what the consequence of positive or negative scores on such measurement will be, and what remedial action by the organization needs to be made dependent on that measurement.

2) Work from Harvard introduced the concept of the Service-profit chain and Balanced Scorecard and proved influential for HR Directors in assuming that business performance has direct and less direct causes and these can be put in a cause-effect order. Employee factors act as important antecedents.

3) Psychologists begged to differ in some of the conclusions that might get drawn. They had been working on the topic of engagement for many years, under the guise of specific employee constructs, such as employee job satisfaction, commitment, or burnout and only saw intermediate performance effects, not a link to organizational performance.

4) Practitioner approaches, rather than being driven by theory, have been more empirical. Items in the questionnaire are a measure of attitudinal outcomes

The key messages that emerge from this chapter: (Continued)

(principally satisfaction, loyalty, pride, customer service intent, and intent to stay with the company). It lumps items that are significantly related to performance together to form the core of what is then called engagement.

5) Engagement is brought down to: belief in the organization, a desire to work to make things better, understanding of business context and the "bigger picture," being respectful of, and helpful to, colleagues, a willingness to "go the extra mile," and keeping up-to-date with developments in the field. HR practitioners make different assumptions as to how this type of engagement is best created.

6) There is a risk that organizations are "asking" too much when they expect significant proportions of their people to be so "engaged." What is being measured at the moment may lead to misdirected effort.

7) Psychological approaches either view engagement as an attitude (having the three components of cognition, affect, and behavior) and is therefore similar to the concept of job satisfaction, or is more akin to motivation (i.e., is a heightened state of goal-directed behavior as in vigor).

8) The idea that employees are either engaged or not, and that once engaged, the impact on performance is linear (a bit more engagement equals just that bit more performance) is of course absurd (yet much of the practitioner literature presents this picture).

9) Many definitions confuse the condition of engagement with the outcome that it is supposed to create. Some of these desired outcomes can be seen to exist at the individual or employee level, whilst others really exist (and are best managed) at a group or collective level.

10) Empirical evidence suggests that the service-profit chain is generally supported at the business unit level. But there have been few tests of the whole chain, and those carried out provide a more sober conclusion on the size of effect between individual-level engagement and organizational performance outcomes.

Credit crunches and recessions have a habit of breaking acts of faith. Is engagement a future-proof HR strategy? We argue that it is, but we must be far more critical about the construct and develop much better insight into how it influences organizational performance. We have taken far too much on trust. There are three streams of management thinking that have all led to the importance of employee engagement as both an idea, and as a basis for HR strategy:

1. Engagement as internal marketing;
2. Engagement as process improvement; and
3. Engagement as predictive of service and corporate performance.

In practice, organizations, or the people made responsible for managing engagement strategies, often see a little of each of these three purposes within their HR strategy. This is understandable, yet we argue also dangerous. The danger is that each of the three purposes makes very different assumptions about what needs to be measured under the label "engagement," what the consequence of positive or negative scores on such measurement will be, and what remedial action by the organization needs to be made dependent on that measurement.

Given the general lack of development in employee communication mechanisms, the first type of engagement strategy used by many organizations, sees it as a process to help articulate and sell complex change and strategy to the workforce, with the intention of creating a sense of emotional attachment and identification to the goals of the change.

Engagement as internal marketing

1. Goal is to develop a shared mental model of the change or strategy;

2. Employees asked to "engage with" something – a brand, a particular strategy, a value proposition;

3. Employee engagement process must be preceded by an important prior period of business engagement (education of the line and of employees about the strategy);

4. Organization uses customer relationship management (CRM) principles, to see how employees (as internal customers) feel about the proposition;

5. Organization assesses whether both sides deliver the "deal" that is seen as necessary, that is, behaviors and emotions desired by the organization and the employee need for internal support;

6. Internal marketing is used to target and shape communications in ways that resonate with key employee communities;

7. The engagement survey represents an employee feedback mechanism, and a management control device;

8. Periodic assessment is used as a barometer to show how well the organization seems to be doing against the strategy.

The second strategy carries a performance expectation, but engagement is still seen as having an indirect contribution to performance. The assumption made by the organization is that motivated employees, when also encouraged to act as good citizens, will self-manage, thereby taking initiative to improve on processes.

Engagement as process improvement

1. Engagement is seen as part of a quid pro exchange relationship. The organization has to create a "blanket of trust" before motivated employees will pay back the investments made by the organization to motivate them by taking care of the organization and its customers.

Engagement as process improvement: (Continued)

2. Seen as a necessary ingredient for – or precursor of – subsequent performance but *no* claims are made by managers that engagement necessarily improves bottom-line organizational performance.

3. Rather, senior managers believe that indirectly it makes the execution of a strategic change smoother and easier, and that they are capable of putting in place more complex and testing changes once engagement scores are high.

A third view comes from the customer services literature and draws upon models of what is called "emotional contagion" and "service climate." This suggests that there is a direct and causal "service-profit chain." HR practitioners have picked up on this and assumed that the message must be that more employee engagement means more business unit performance.

Engagement predictive of service and corporate performance

1. Asserts that there is an association between employee perceptions of the organization climate (especially its focus on service) and subsequent levels of employee satisfaction, and then between employee satisfaction and customer satisfaction levels.

2. Asserts that there is then an association between customer satisfaction and customer behaviors, such as intention to purchase, which in turn has an impact on financial performance.

3. HR practitioners assume the whole chain is triggered, such that more employee engagement means more business unit performance.

4. Certain HRM practices that create engagement must also have the power to influence employee behavior in a desired manner, so that good HR equals good engagement.

This view developed out of the simple proposition by James Heskett and colleagues[1] from Harvard University that organizational profitability can be influenced by chain of events starting with internal service quality proved to be a landmark paper for HRM. They argued that this chain involved strong and direct relationships between:

> ... profit; growth; customer loyalty; customer satisfaction; the value of goods and services delivered to customers; and employee capability, satisfaction, loyalty and productivity.

Within this hypothesized causal sequence lie important employee variables such as employee satisfaction. These are considered vital to achieve important customer outcomes, which in turn directly influence profitability and revenue growth of a company. The original work by Heskett and colleagues provided persuasive case-study-based evidence to support their proposed model and created a new research agenda, which is now popularly referred to as "the service-profit chain." It proved very influential for HR Directors and many refer to it when describing their engagement strategy.

Soon after, following similar research methodology, Robert Kaplan and David Norton,[2] also from Harvard, introduced the concept of Balanced Scorecard. The basic idea was the same: business performance has direct and less direct causes and these can be put in a cause-effect order. In their model too, employees figured prominently under the learning and growth perspective. Their ideas proved very influential on HR thinking and were developed by Brian Becker, Mark Huselid, and David Ulrich[3] with the publication of their book the HR Scorecard, which again inferred a chain of cause-effect constructs that finally lead to organizational performance. All of these authors argue that certain HRM practices have the power to influence employee behavior in a desired manner, such that it finally leads to improved organizational performance.

At the same time as this work on service-profit chain and HR strategy, psychologists began to raise their sights beyond the individual. They begged to differ in some of the conclusions that might get drawn. They had been working on the topic of engagement for many years, under the guise of specific employee constructs, such as employee job satisfaction, commitment, or burnout. However, this was a critical difference. Psychologists had been reporting some tenuous links between employee attitudes toward their work with a range of what were called *employee-level (intermediate) performance outcomes* – such as organizational commitment, job satisfaction, and low intention to leave. However, the idea that employee attitudes could also influence *organizational-level performance* was still seen as an untested proposition.

As new work was carried out, ambitious claims were made about the "effect sizes" that attitudes such as satisfaction and commitment had on organizational-level outcomes (effect size is a measure of the strength of the relationship between two variables showing not only whether this relationship has a statistically significant effect, but also the size of any observed effect when replicated across samples).

This generated a huge research and consultancy interest. Research was then initiated to find the mechanisms through which individual-level attitudes could possibly translate into organizational-level performance outcomes. A plethora of new constructs came into existence to fill this void. *Employee engagement* was one of them.

9.2. Engagement in the practitioner perspective

In this chapter we analyze how the concept of engagement has been understood, defined and used from the perspective of, practitioners, researchers, and organizations. This is not to say that one perspective is better than the other, but it is important to highlight that the approaches *might not reflect the same thing and may be based on different assumptions about how engagement works as a process.* Even within the practitioner or academic field, different approaches are often taken. Organizations should benchmark their scores on engagement with caution.

The term "employee engagement" initially caught the eye of practitioners. A stream of consultancy reports seemed to find out how important it was for organizational performance and how a lack of it could lead to disastrous consequences. For example, a study conducted by Sirota Consultancy reported that organizations that have highly engaged employees exhibited a 16 per cent rise in their share prices as compared to an industry average of 6 per cent. Similar outstanding results were claimed by other consultancy and research organizations. It seemed that HR functions had found a tool that could guarantee them a voice at the highest echelons of management. Now they had in their power something that could influence shareholder value! Every progressive organization with a responsible HR function started significant exercises to measure, and yearly benchmark, the level of engagement of their employees.

The strategic use of engagement benchmarking

As employee engagement was being shown to influence shareholder value, many organizations chose to make it an important benchmark in their annual Human Capital Reports (HCR). Engagement became a "must improve" agenda on every HR function's performance dashboard. It has been used by organizations as their employer brand endorsement – being seen as one of the best companies to work for. It became an essential indicator for any organization aspiring to achieve various employer brand recognitions. Consultancies offered internal HCRs using engagement as predictive and diagnostic data, as a risk mitigation strategy, intended to identify parts of the organization, or key pools of talent, who might be suspected of under-performing in future, or of leaving, given engagement survey data trends.

One might assume they were all measuring the same thing. We take it for granted that there is a universally accepted operational and empirical definition. Leaving aside the question of whether it is empirically useful or not, there is not. So what is engagement?

We begin with the practitioner view. An organization that many practitioners' draw upon is that of Gallup Inc. The questionnaire to measure employee engagement developed by Gallup – known as Gallup Workplace Audit (GWA, also popularly known as the Q12) – comprises of 12 questions plus an overall satisfaction question. The items were found to have a highly significant relation to unit level measures of a company's performance.[4] Rather than being driven by theory, Gallup's approach has been more empirical. The items measure attitudinal outcomes (principally satisfaction, loyalty, pride, customer service intent, and intent to stay with the company), chosen in part because they measure issues that are within the remit of a supervisor in charge of a given business unit. Gallup had a rich database of employee surveys built up over 30 years. Based on their understanding of those employee behaviors that had maximal impact on a firm's performance, they defined engagement as

the individual's involvement and satisfaction with as well as enthusiasm for work.[5]

Three different types of employee

Based on their national survey of US workers using their engagement questionnaire, Gallup argues there are three types of employees:

1. *Engaged*: employees work with passion and feel profound connection to their company. They drive innovation and move the company forward.

2. *Not-engaged*: employees are essentially "checked out." They are sleepwalking through their workday, putting time – but not energy or passion – into their work.

3. *Actively disengaged*: employees aren't just unhappy at work; they are busy acting out their unhappiness. Every day, these workers undermine what their engaged coworkers accomplish.

Towers Perrin[6] adopted a similar approach and define employee engagement in terms of the *preferred characteristics* that engaged employees exhibit, as different from the non-engaged employees. They note three key features of such engagement.

Three key features of an engaged workforce: Towers Perrin

1. Rational/cognitive understanding of the organization's strategic goals, values, and their "fit" within it (also known as the "Think" sector);

2. Emotional/affective attachment to the organization's strategic goals, values, and their "fit" within it (also known as the "Feel" sector); and

3. The motivation/willingness to do more than the minimum effort in their role (i.e., to be willing to invest discretionary effort, to "go the extra mile") for the organization (also known as the "Act" sector).

The Institute of Employment Studies[7] argues that three important requirements must be met before engagement can exist:

1. A healthy "psychological contract," that is, an unwritten, fragile relationship between the employee and employer that is underpinned by a two-way and trustful relationship;

2.   A need for employees to identify with their organization and its values, believe in its products and services, that is, to embrace what the organization stands for;

3.   A need for employees to understand the context in which the organization operates: that is, not just show a commitment to the organization, but a desire for business appreciation.

The IES view of engagement

1.   Belief in the organization
2.   Desire to work to make things better
3.   Understanding of business context and the "bigger picture"
4.   Respectful of, and helpful to, colleagues
5.   Willingness to "go the extra mile"
6.   Keeping up-to-date with developments in the field

IES pointed out, however, that HR practitioners make different assumptions as to how this type of engagement is best created, subscribing to one of two contrasting views:

1.   A "Bottom-up" philosophy, which contends that levels of engagement are primarily a function of employees' experiences in their jobs. In which case engagement is therefore largely a result of factors controlled by first-level supervisors.

2.   A "Top-down" philosophy, which contends that engagement is created by behavior of an organization and its top-level leaders. In which case engagement primarily flows out of the organization's values and the quality of its strategic leadership.

Making your mind up as to which view you subscribe to is important. If it is the first one, then the reaction to a set of low engagement scores tends to focus on the (re-)education of first line management, and the skilling of the line to enable them to both sell the strategy down and manage the employee needs upward. If it is the second one, then the reaction is to create an attractive and compelling vision that employees will find desirable and meaningful.

The practitioner view has progressively expanded the range of constructs measured under the umbrella term of engagement – in many instances stressing not just a sense of "cognitive attachment" and "identification" to the organization and its mission – but also a strong emotional element as well. The Conference Board offers a synthesized definition – derived from those scale items, amongst all those used by its various clients to measure the engagement level of their employees that could be seen as common – that sees employee engagement as a heightened emotional connection that an employee feels for his or her organization, that influences him or her to exert greater discretionary effort to his or her work.

To summarize, practitioner and consultancy views on engagement are largely driven from their respective survey databases, designed for problem description, tracking, and benchmarking, and are based on non-theoretical but empirical models.

Problems with the practitioner approach to engagement

Practitioner work looks for key differences in employee surveys between high- and low-performing business units, then lumps the items that are significantly related to performance together to form the core of what is then called engagement. There are three major problems with this:

1. Most survey-based research tends to infer causality in a way that suggests that it is the answers to the engagement items that can be presumed to "cause" performance, not merely correlated with it. *However, there is very little support from their research designs that in reality enables them to make such a strong assertion.*

2. There is little "construct validity" behind the items being clubbed under a single name of engagement. The scale items are not embedded in any validated theory, so it is unclear exactly *how* they enable and deliver performance. Performance cannot always be predicted. *If you don't know how a measure delivers its assumed outcome, you can't manage the use of it.*

3. Perhaps reflecting this, although all the major consultancies *use different items in their measures, they all label it as engagement.*

This creates a problem for *Leading HR*. Much good work has been done by the consultancies on behalf of HR in bringing the issue of engagement to the attention of line managers. But here is the problem. In difficult economic times, imagine that you were asked to bet your organization's money that an increase in a collection of attitude survey items answered by individuals, and then averaged together, automatically, and in all future circumstances, leads to higher business performance. Would you do it? Then imagine you had to bet your own dwindling personal financial resources, your future pension, on the same proposition. Would you still do it, or would you want to know a bit more about how this engagement game really works? We believe the wise person would want to do the latter.

More proactive strategies that ultimately revolve around engagement are covered in Chapters 10, 11, and 12. However, for many organizations, measuring top-sliced scales of engagement, based on a small subset of empirically useful data, their HR functions may get dragged into managing the symptoms and side effects as expressed by each and every patient, rather than the disease and its curative treatments! There is no point in measuring engagement if its management can not be modeled – what is needed is measurement of a generic model of human functioning, with engagement being one of the functions that is modeled, but the impact of each factor upon the other understood beforehand. Surveys that measure long lists of factors – or short composite scales – that may have something to do with employee engagement can serve to merely confuse.

9.3. What is engagement? The academic perspective

The definitions of engagement used by academic researchers are sadly not necessarily any better than practitioner ones in producing an operational definition that clearly differentiates engagement from other (similar) practices. In this section we

1. analyze the main research that has investigated the condition, causes, and consequences of engagement at the individual level and
2. present a model that helps to capture and model the various individual-level factors that are being measured by organizations.

A more theoretical approach helps to understand the phenomenon of engagement. Only then can we better understand what needs to be managed as part of an engagement strategy. However, psychologists have examined engagement at the *individual level of analysis*. We shall argue that the more fruitful way of thinking about engagement is to see it as a team or business-unit level construct – rather than something to be managed at the individual level.

But most organizations have not yet made this jump. They still think about engagement at the individual level – they see it as gaining the "hearts and minds" of their employees.

> **How does your engagement survey measure up?**
>
> Engagement surveys need to be designed using the analogy of a medical diagnosis. What is the point in running a survey that tells you about the state a patient is in, if the diagnosis does not also consider all the other symptoms that exist, and if the measurement is not guided by a model of how these all fit together and so can best be treated? The medical analogy suggests a single examination of the complaint, history, examination of the condition, ancillary tests if needed, diagnosis, treatment, and prognosis with and without treatment. It aims to find the treatments for diagnosed symptoms and syndromes and treats the human as a very complex mechanism. Engagement thinking needs to follow the same logic.

Whilst we persist in focusing on the individual, we should at least use a medical model to think about engagement. If you want to measure all the things that will give you the "hearts and minds" of your employees, what are the key things that have to happen for people to be "engaged"?

Reviewing the evidence in the next section, we might ask:

1. Are organizations "asking" much when they expect significant proportions of their people to be so "engaged"?

2. Is what is being measured at the moment by many organizations going to lead to misdirected effort? Items included in surveys may produce results that look good on the surface – but hide the more difficult and enduring employee pathology that lies beneath.

Surveys may therefore not prove to be a sustainable diagnosis, especially as organizations experience the more testing "hard times" associated with a recession and recovery.

To be confident that the survey findings are authentic, organizations need to be clear about some basic principles:

1. Is engagement primarily a psychological reaction to job design and role, readily switched on or off?

2. Is engagement the opposite of burnout, and so a more diffuse and difficult to address outcome?

3. Is engagement more like an attitude (e.g., job satisfaction), or is it a state of motivation?

4. How is engagement any different to related ideas, such as job involvement, job commitment, and organizational citizenship behavior (OCB)?

That we still have to ask such fundamental questions shows that we are pursuing an HR strategy about which we know less than we think.

What are the psychological reactions that create the condition of engagement? Two sets of assumptions:

The first psychological approach considers the condition of engagement as a psychological reaction to the job role people are required to play in their work. It is akin to the concept of "psychological presence" – a dedicated focus on the job which enables people to move away from any mental distractions that may lower job performance. Such a condition comprises three aspects common to all attitudes (each of which must be measured to understand if the condition of engagement exists):

1. cognitive (i.e., relating to mental processes of perception, memory, judgment, and reasoning);

2. affective (i.e., relating to mood, emotion, feeling, and sensibilities); and

3. behavioral.

(Continued)

This is a very different condition to the second way in which the idea of engagement is discussed, which has its basis within the realm of job stress research. This group of researchers define the condition of engagement[8] as: . . . *a positive, fulfilling, work-related state of mind that is characterized by vigour, dedication, and absorption* (p. 74). There are significant differences between these two definitions of engagement.

In the first definition, job engagement is very role specific – it is in fact the role that determines what type of self will be elicited (engaged versus disengaged). The condition of engagement is therefore more easily switched on and off. In the second, the condition of engagement (as the opposite to burnout) is a diffuse and long-lasting state, and it has more pervasive impacts.

To compound the problem, many definitions of engagement do not take enough care to distinguish it as a condition in relation to a number of other similar ideas – such as job involvement, job commitment, and OCB. In terms of our medical analogy, these related conditions form some of the ancillary tests that are necessary in order to produce an accurate diagnosis.

9.4. Can we model engagement?

To understand what causes engagement, and therefore what it causes in turn, we need to embed the idea in a well-founded theory. The "condition" of engagement forms part of the social exchange that takes place within the organization. Fortunately, the nature of this exchange is much better understood. Feelings of loyalty, commitment, and discretionary effort are all in some form a social reciprocation by employees to a good employer. Being an engaged employee is one of the ways employees repay their organization, and according to Saks[9] there are two ways in which this engagement is paid back:

1. job engagement, which is specific to the role task an employee is principally hired to perform;
2. organizational engagement, which is a more diffuse concept referring to other roles that an employee plays being a part of the larger organization.

Employee engagement is not the same thing as job satisfaction or organizational commitment; rather it is best thought of as an antecedent cause for these intermediate performance outcomes.

So if engagement helps cause satisfaction and commitment, what first causes engagement? Psychologists tend to focus on five factors. If these antecedents are not in place, HR Directors should not even think about building future engagement.

Aspects of the social climate that act as antecedents to employee engagement

1. The perception that the organization's systems, procedures, and ways of allocating resources (financial and non-financial) are fair i.e., that there is no perceived breach in key forms of justice.[10] When employees look at the budget mechanisms, the rewards systems, the promotions and performance systems, do they think they are fair, reliable and equitable?

2. The perceived support received from the organization (this is called Perceived Organizational Support (POS)[11]). This describes the quality of the employee–organization relationship and is defined as a general perception by the employee about the extent to which the organization values their general contribution and cares about their well-being. Employees might understand that times are hard and there is little their organization can do for them at the moment, but they may still sincerely believe that if the organization could do something, it would.

3. The support received from the supervisory relationship. This describes the perceived supervisor support, but also importantly also describes the quality of – and the existence of a positive two-way relationship – between a supervisor and an employee. It is often measured using the construct of what psychologists call Leader–Member Exchange (LMX).[12]

4. The level of trust that exists in the employment relationship,[13] notwithstanding the fact that the nature and focus of trust these days is changing (employees might be more likely to trust their profession, their team, their project or mission, rather than necessarily trust their organization).

5. The existence of sound job characteristics and designs that provide employees with the necessary job variety and challenge, autonomy, control, and power to deliver the strategy the organization wants them to engage with.

Returning to our medical analogy, in terms of conducting ancillary tests, organizations need to measure (all) the primary antecedents to engagement – perceptions of job characteristics, organizational support, quality of leadership, fairness, rewards, and trust. They also need to understand the bonds that these are intended to create – the sorts of linkages between the individual and the organization that good performance dictates. Not all performance requires the same level of engagement.

Psychologists still question whether the condition of engagement

1. is an attitude (having the three components of cognition, affect, and behavior as noted earlier) and therefore is similar to the concept of job satisfaction), or

2. is more akin to motivation (i.e., is a heightened state of goal directed behavior as in vigor).

However, they agree on a number of different types of relationship, bond, or attachment to the organization that capture the human experience and social exchange. This is a "Hearts and Minds" way of thinking about engagement. For an employee to be "engaged" with their organization – for the organization to have their hearts and minds – four bonds, or states of mind (psychologists see these as different types and levels of employee–organization linkage) arguably have to be in place. Again, any measurement of engagement needs to assure the organization that the necessary linkages that enable performance are actually operating, or to help diagnose which linkages are not working! There is no point in measuring engagement if the diagnosis does not suggest the cure.

The necessary bonds of engagement: Progressive levels of linkage

1. *Motivation and incentive to bond:* first, people have to have a reason and a desire for social membership (with the organization), which includes feelings and/or beliefs regarding the reasons why they want to maintain a relationship with, or their membership of the organization.[14]

2. *Organizational identification:* then, people have to think about the use of characteristics of the organization to define themselves and where people socially classify themselves in terms of what they believe to be distinctive and admirable attributes of the organization.[15] Are employees engaging with your mission, your values, your goals, your brand? Just because senior managers engage with a new business model, why should they expect that most employees will or should identify with the sorts of performance that now needs to be engineered?

3. *Internalization:* the personal learning, internal recognition, and personal adoption of the values and goals of the organization.[16] Do employees "live" the organization's values – are they enacted in key situations?

4. *Psychological ownership:* an attitudinal state of mind involving feelings of being psychologically tied to an object.[17] Do employees treat the organisation's resources as if they were their own? Is there a sense of responsibility and obligation that comes from the feeling of ownership?

For each of these linkages, imagine the call for more sophisticated measurement and assessment approaches. The good news is that they are all considered to be learned responses, more than they are inherited predispositions.[18]

Of these bonds, psychologists currently stress the importance of the second – the issue of employee identification with the organization – noting that it is often under-stated in the work that has been carried out on engagement. The idea that employees are either engaged or not, and that once engaged, the impact on per-formance is linear (a bit more engagement equals just that bit more performance) is absurd (yet much of the practitioner literature presents this picture).

Leading HR involves the ability to "reverse engineer" the type of performance that the organization is trying to create, and to understand the depth to which – and the ways in which – the organization needs to foster links and bonds with its employees.

9.5. The consequences of engagement: Intermediate performance effects

Many definitions therefore confuse the condition of engagement with the outcome that it is supposed to create. Some of these desired outcomes can be seen to exist at the individual or employee level, whilst others really exist (and are best managed) at a group or collective level. These individual and group-level conditions are created through very different types of HRM intervention.

Is engagement best seen as an employee or group-level intermediate performance outcome?

Which of these outcomes do HR Directors try and create through an engagement strategy? How does each intermediate outcome impact actual organizational performance metrics?

Employee-level variables with intermediate performance effects
Whereby HR practices improve factors such as

1. job satisfaction (how content an individual is with his/her job),

2. motivation (a state of arousal and reason to act toward a desired goal),

3. discretionary effort, and

4. job and organizational commitment (being bound intellectually or emotionally to a course of action and displaying sincere and steadfast purpose).

Collective or group-level variables with intermediate effects
which are in turn strongly influenced by the culture and climate of an organization. The factors involved here have variously been called

1. morale (group climate exhibited by confidence, cheerfulness, discipline, and willingness to perform assigned tasks);

2. OCBs (being a "good soldier" through positive social behaviors such as helping others, innovating, and volunteering); and

3. closely related to the above, contextual performance (defined as discretionary behaviors that go above and beyond the requirements of the job description, such as following organizational rules and procedures even when personally inconvenient and assisting and cooperating with coworkers).

An important challenge facing employers is to better understand the individual factors that are associated with, shape and explain the employee's relationship with the organization, and produce outcomes that appear to fit the practitioners' view

Figure 9.1: The antecedents, bonds, condition and consequences of individual-level engagement at intermediate level

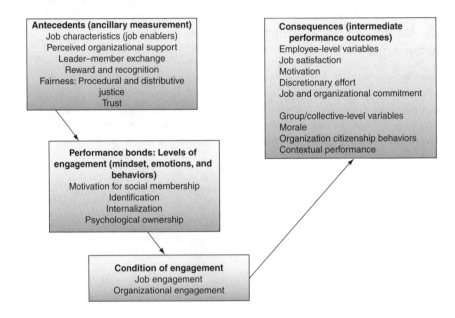

of engagement. We believe that organizations interested in managing engagement as part of a HR strategy should consider it to operate according to the model shown in Figure 9.1.

Important questions remain to be addressed:

1. How does this model fit in with the existing understanding of the link between HRM practices and organizational performance?
2. How must this link be moderated and mediated by employee reactions to these HR practices?
3. How is employee engagement assumed to predict organization-level performance outcomes?
4. And does good HRM impact this particular view of engaged performance and organizational performance?
5. If so, do the HR practices themselves impact engagement, or do they have an impact through the conditions they create (such as a good employer brand)?

The role of HR practices and policies in influencing organizational performance has been of interest to both researchers and practitioners alike for many years. There has been an increase in research publications that have claimed significant causal links between HR practices/policies and a firm's performance. However, an exhaustive systematic review of research on this topic from the early 1940s to the year 2006 found that there are very few longitudinal studies in this field to affirmatively claim a causal link between any definite set of HR practices to a company's financial performance.[19]

What this research does show is a robust statistical and theoretical link between various HR practices and *intermediate*-level performance outcomes, such as job satisfaction, organizational commitment, motivation, absenteeism, and employee turnover. Most of these intermediate outcomes are at the level of the employee and not the organization. Good HR practices may lead to high employee commitment and low employee turnover, but the question as to whether it will it lead to better organizational performance is a totally different one.

If engagement is created by influences beyond the traditional range of HR practices and policies (rewards, talent management, performance management, etc.) that the HR function designs and implements – for example, if engagement is primarily created by factors such as corporate reputation, the quality of strategic leadership, or simply be existing good performance of the organization – then HR functions should only claim an indirect role in managing engagement.

9.6. Understanding organizational performance recipes

It should be clear that we believe that when measured at the individual level, engagement is too complex, too big a concept, to be able to consistently and reliably explain much corporate performance. Consider all the components that have to be measured (as suggested in Figure 9.1), compound this with the problem that different employee segments exist alongside multiple internal models of engagement even within a single organization. It should be clear that we measure the symptoms of performance, not the causes.

Is there robust evidence of a link between engagement and organizational performance? We began this chapter by noting that many HR functions – and supportive line managers – fall back upon the service-profit chain to argue a link between engagement and performance.

The basic tenets and assumptions of service-profit chain theory:

It assumes there is a clear link between employee's work experiences and financial performance in the service sector, with customer satisfaction acting as a critical intervening variable. This is based on a series of presumed causal links:

1. An association between employee satisfaction and customer satisfaction.[20, 21, 22]

2. An association between employee perceptions of the organization climate (especially its focus on service) and customer satisfaction levels,[23] followed by an association between favorable climates and levels of employee satisfaction and commitment.[24, 25]

3. An association between customer satisfaction and financial performance.[26, 27, 28]

Figure 9.2: The service-profit chain

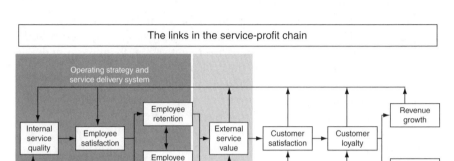

Empirical evidence generally supports the existence of some key components of the service-profit chain (see Figure 9.2) at the business unit level. However, there have been very few tests of the whole chain, and those tests that have been carried out provide a much more sober conclusion on the size of effect between individual-level engagement and organizational performance outcomes. Despite strident claims in the practitioner literature that engagement (as measured by respective scales) is a key contributor to the financial bottom lines of the organizations from where the data have been collected, such claims fail to stand up in the face of rigorous checks on the methodology adopted and the scales used to carry out the research work.

What is not known with any certainty is how customer satisfaction affects the relationship between employee experiences and financial performance, and how employee satisfaction is associated with specific components of the service model.[29]

Why should engagement have the same performance impact across different service models? We need to be more circumspect in overstating the impact that individual-level engagement can have on corporate performance measures. There is a general relationship assumed between employee satisfaction and customer satisfaction, but

1. is there any difference in the sensitivity or influence that employee engagement has over organization performance – especially when organizations operate to different service (industry) models?

2. why should we expect the same impact across all service (and indeed less service-orientated) settings?

Table 9.1: Contextual differences in service model that impact the engagement–performance relationship?

Personal versus nonpersonal/possessions[30]

1. Personal services (e.g., healthcare and fitness): Require "up-close" interactions between employee and customer throughout the encounter and high visibility of service processes to the customer. Versus . . .
2. Nonpersonal/possession services (e.g., equipment repair and call center) where service production can take place away from the customer, interactions can be limited to the transactional, and service processes can remain hidden in a service factory.

Encounter versus relationship[31]

1. Encounter (e.g., airlines and fast food). Convenience is a main driver for choice of service provider. Systems designed to satisfy customer's needs, employees can be scripted. Transactions mainly brief and transactional. Versus . . .
2. Relationship Business (e.g., hairstylist, doctor, and dentist). Customers incentivized to seek same service provider for each encounter; employees more able to internalize customer's personal needs and expectations; personal and commercial bonds can be formed; and display of emotions have more lasting impact on customer perceptions.

Collaborative versus single service interface relationship[32]

1. Employees working in a collaborative, team-based and mutually supportive work process can create "inter-dependence" effects, realizing synergies by feeding off mood state of one or two lynchpin employees. Versus . . .
2. Single employee interface more dependent on personality and mood state of one employee.

Relative strength of B2B or B2C interactions at different points of the value chain[33]

1. Business to Consumer (B2C). Dependent on above distinctions at the point of customer interface. Versus . . .
2. Business to Business (B2B). Organizational buying potentially more impersonal and objective. Subject to B2C dynamics but buying behavior also determined by personal networks and corporate reputation attributes.

There are a number of different service business models in which the potential contribution that employee engagement should make to organizational performance must differ (see Table 9.1).

In some sectors the intensity or richness of customer contact creates unique conditions. The airlines industry (an "encounter" services model) was famous for the original customer service work by SAS on "moments of truth"[34] and the importance of "thin slices of employee behavior." Jan Carlson famously pointed out that each of his 10 million customers on average only ever interacted with 5 customer service facing employees. In the US Airline industry – an industry famed for poor service – a recent study using the SERVQUAL measures of expected versus experienced service quality, found that employee personal touch (individual attention, helpfulness, courtesy, and promptness) explains 54 per cent of reported airline passenger satisfaction.[35] But:

1. Should service quality and customer satisfaction be expected to be less closely associated with employee satisfaction in an encounter service business compared to a relationship service business model? The evidence surprisingly says that this difference in service model does not make a difference, nor does it differ across B2B versus B2C service models.

2. Why should customer-perceived service quality always result from employee satisfaction? Walmart finds that it has been able to computerize schedules to vary staff numbers according to the number of shoppers in the store, because the increases in customer satisfaction caused by having an optimal number of staff on hand outweigh minor losses in employee satisfaction caused by having less predictable work schedules and pay.

Research evidence then shows that employee satisfaction determines the perception of service quality – this *perception* comes first (like service value, service quality is a mental judgment and assessment of the service delivered). Once made this judgment then explains three quarters of measured customer satisfaction (a more emotional response to overall service). Service quality and customer satisfaction are different ways in which employee performance may be evaluated by customers, and employee satisfaction is assumed to be linked to both these outcomes through three main processes: helping behaviours, the display of certain emotions as part of your job (called emotional labour), and commitment to a service ethic.

Engagement can have positive impacts on organizational performance outcomes – but these effects are not as large as often claimed, and they work through complex dynamics and sets of causal processes. Relying on simple models that are assumed to apply across all business and service models and across all groups of employees whatever their talent or strategic centrality, is naïve.

So HR Directors have a fantastic opportunity to step into the void that currently exists. On the back of strategic change management projects, new alliances are being forged between HR professionals and other professional groups. They now work side-by-side with corporate communications, internal and external marketing, and operations experts, all sharing their models and insights into how employees truly impact operational and strategic performance. *Leading HR* can shape this thinking, but from a more realistic perspective than current human capital and employee engagement work suggests.

Performance recipes: Managerial "theories of action"

Managers believe that specific business performance outcomes only result from engaged employees – what we call a "performance recipe." Some of these presumed links between employees and organizational-level performance outcomes may be misguided, and not supported by data, but other knowledge is extremely insightful. HR professionals need to help line managers understand the complex business performance benchmarks that they report to, and how these performance outcomes are best engineered through people management. And employees need to understand the benefits of engaging with that particular view of performance.

If engagement is to continue to be a strategic priority for HR Directors, it has to be designed to work at the level of strategic business units (SBU) or the team. HR Directors need to "reverse engineer" the sorts of performance that is required by the particular service model that their organization pursues. They need to understand the logic that suggests why a range of employee attributes (whether you call them engagement or not) must serve a central purpose in delivering that type of performance.

9.7. Conclusion

Engagement is a widely accepted concept by practitioners in industry. Having reviewed the approaches taken by the likes of Gallup, Towers Perrin, and Conference Board we believe that the construct of engagement needs to have clearer boundaries as to what it is and what it is not. In this there is much to learn from other disciplines that have been working on similar concepts but in a different context.

We believe that such work provides a convincing case for us in the HR profession to delayer the idea of engagement. It is time to move away from using a hotchpotch of multiple definitions comprising of cognitions, affect, and behavior. In times of significant business change, the most fruitful way of thinking about engagement is to look at it just as a cognitive construct. The appropriate feelings, emotion, and behavior should be seen as an outcome of – and an accompaniment of – the employee's perceptions. Engagement should have the following core components:

Five core components of engagement

1. **Engagement should be seen as a "belief" and not an attitude.** Therefore it is largely a cognitive construct (it needs to be information-based) rather than an affective or behavioral one. Obviously, it will have affective and behavioral outcomes, but for the sake of clarity of construct, we need to separate out the cause from the effect.

2. **Very importantly, it is best seen as a "shared belief of a team" and therefore should be managed as a team-level idea.** To distinguish engagement from other similar ideas we need to agree on a space where it exists. We have drawn attention to a number of individual-level items (such as job satisfaction, job involvement, and job commitment)

Five core components of engagement: (Continued)

and also organizational-level (such as organizational commitment, culture, and climate). In order to explain individual-level performance (task performance), the individual employee items modeled in Figure 9.1 may be the right measures. However, in order to predict group-level performance outcomes, such as the performance of SBU as a whole, we need to have a collective team-level idea of engagement.

3. **This collective perception of employees of their workplace and organization can have silent but far-reaching consequences for any organization.** In large multinational corporations it might not be very productive or even possible to understand each employee's judgment process. But if a significant number of employees have a common judgment about their work place, then understanding what these perceptions are and why employees think what they think can be extremely valuable information for refining the HR practices at the given organization.

4. **We need to have a more fine-grain analysis of the various levels of performance outcomes in a work setting.** Engagement is being used by organizations as a proxy for their performance. Yet there is little theoretical rationale for why any employee-level item should directly influence organizational-level performance outcomes, such as annual profits. Some of these outcomes will not be directly influenced by employee efforts alone; some will be outcomes which can be directly influenced by employees' abilities and effort.

5. **It makes more sense to treat engagement as an aggregated perception that certain core team abilities, resource availability, goal clarity, and leadership attributes, when directed toward achieving some common goal, are within the instrumental capacity of the employees.** Therefore, engagement needs to be directly linked to measurable performance outcomes, customized to measure team-level performance (as distinct from individual and organizational-level performance outcomes).

Given these core components, we redefine engagement as follows:

Engagement is a shared belief of a team that it has the required ability, resources, goal clarity and leadership to achieve the desired performance outcomes.

The rationale behind providing this definition of engagement is to help us disentangle it from the current state of affairs – where it is seen as an all-encompassing cognitive, behavioral, affective, motivational, values, and identity phenomenon. Instead we should identify employees' beliefs and attitudes about their work, their colleagues, and their own abilities as instrumental in "engaging" them on the task at hand, and thereby delivering the desired level of performance. Our definition above – intended to provide us with an operational definition and a reliable and valid measure – draws much upon research that has been carried out in the field of work design, attributions, and teams

In our view engagement is a shared belief amongst team members that they have the right resources to achieve the targets expected of them. Such resources may be adequate staff and/or staffing mix in a busy hospital, retail superstore, or a restaurant; it may be tools for mechanics on a shop floor or technicians in a lab; or a good library and access to the required journals for a researcher!

All jobs have their own unique set of resource requirements, and every job needs to be analyzed to know what they are. Statements asking employees about the availability of these resources need to be more specific to the job in question; this again reinforces our view that rather than having a very generic questionnaire that asks broad questions about resource requirements, employee engagement surveys need to be more customized to the job that a given team of employees is required to do.

To achieve a given goal requires more than resources. Goal theory advocates that clear and precise goals are a prerequisite for good performance. These shared beliefs, in our definition of engagement, therefore extend to other requirements for better performance. An engaged team should also have clearly defined goals.

Employees should also believe that they have the required control over their work environment and backing of the team leadership to achieve the desired results. This part of the definition draws from both the goal theory and the demand and control research, which advocate that employees should have the relevant resources and control on their work environment for better performance. Therefore, in the final analysis, it is the role of team leadership that often plays a critical role in the team being engaged or disengaged.

NOTES

1 Heskett, J.L., Sasser, W.E. and Schlesinger, I.A. (1997) *The Service Profit Chain.* New York: Free Press, p. 11.

2 Kaplan, S. and Norton, D. (1996) *The Balanced Scorecard.* Boston: Harvard Business School Press.

3 Becker, B.E., Huselid, M. and Ulrich, D. (2001) *The HR Scorecard: Linking People, Strategy and Performance.* Cambridge, MA: Harvard Business School Press.

4 Harter, J.K., Schmidt, F.L. and Hayes, T.L. (2002) Business-unit-level relationship between employee satisfaction, employee engagement, and business outcomes: A meta-analysis. *Journal of Applied Psychology,* 87: 268–279.

5 Ibid., p. 269.

6 Towers Perrin (2007/8) *Confronting Myths: What Really Matters in Attracting, Engaging and Retaining Your Workforce?* Global Workforce Study.

7 Robinson, D., Perryman, S. and Hayday, S. (2004) *The Drivers of Employee Engagement.* Institute of Employment Studies Report No. 408. Brighton: IES.

8 Schaufeli, W.B., Salanova, M., Gonzalez-Roma, V. and Bakker, A.B. (2002) The measurement of engagement and burnout: A two-sample confirmatory factor analytic approach. *Journal of Happiness Studies,* 3: 71–92.

9 See: Saks, A.M. (2006) Antecedents and consequences of employee engagement. *Journal of Managerial Psychology,* 21 (6): 600–619; Saks, A.M. (2008) The meaning

and bleeding of employee engagement: How muddy is the water? *Industrial and Organizational Psychology*, 1: 40–43.

10 For example: Cropanzano, R. (1993) *Justice in the Workplace: Approaching Fairness in Human Resource Management*. Hillsdale, NJ: Erlbaum; Greenberg, J. (1990) Organisational justice: Yesterday, today and tomorrow. *Journal of Management*, 16: 399–432; Sheppard, B.H., Lewicki, R.J. and Minton, J.W. (1992) *Organisational Justice: The Search for Fairness in the Workplace*. Lexington, MA: Lexington Books.

11 For example: Eisenberger, R., Huntington, R., Hutchison, S. and Sowa, D. (1986) Perceived organisational support. *Journal of Applied Psychology*, 71 (3): 500–507; Shore, L.M. and Shore, T.H. (1995) Perceived organisational support and organisational justice. In R.S. Cropanzano and K.M. Kacmar (eds), *Organisational Politics, Justice and Support: Managing the Social Climate of the Workplace*. Westport, CT: Quorum Books.

12 Settoon, R.P., Bennett, N. and Liden, R.C. (1996) Social exchange in organisations: Perceived organisational support, leader-member exchange and employee reciprocity. *Journal of Applied Psychology*, 81: 219–227; Liden, R.C., Sparrowe, R.T. and Wayne, S.J. (1997). Leader–member exchange theory: The past and potential for the future. In G.R. Ferris (ed.), *Research in Personnel and Human Resources Management, Volume 15*. pp. 47–119. Greenwich, CT: JAI Press.

13 For example: Konovoksy, M.A. and Pugh, S.D. (1984) Citizenship behavior and social exchange. *Academy of Management Journal*, 37: 656–669; Whitener, E.M. (1997) The impact of human resource activities on employee trust. *Human Resource Management Review*, 7: 389–404; Bradach, J.L. and Eccles, R.G. (1989) Price, authority, and trust: From ideal types to plural forms. *Annual Review of Sociology*, 15: 97–118; Clark, M.C. and Payne, R.L. (1997) The nature and structure of workers' trust in management. *Journal of Organisational Behavior*, 18 (3): 205–224; Miles, R. and Creed, D. (1995) Organisational forms and managerial philosophies: A descriptive and analytical review. In L.L. Cummings and B.M. Staw (eds), *Research in Organisational Behavior, Volume 17*. Greenwich: JAI Press.

14 Meyer, J. and Allen, N. (1991) A three-component conceptualisation of organisational commitment. *Human Resource Management Review*, 1: 61–89.

15 For example: Mael, F.A. and Tetrick, L.E. (1992) Identifying organisational identification. *Educational and Psychological Measurement*, 52: 813–824; and Wan-Huggins, V.N., Riordam, C. and Griffeth, R.W. (1998) The development and longitudinal test of a model of organisational identification. *Journal of Applied Social Psychology*, 28: 724–749.

16 For example: O'Reilly, C. III and Chatman, J. (1986) Organisational commitment and psychological attachment: The effects of compliance, identification and internalisation on pro-social behaviour. *Journal of Applied Psychology*, 71: 492–499; and Mael, F.A. and Ashforth, B.E. (1992) Alumni and their alma mater: A partial test of the reformulated model of organisational identification. *Journal of Organisational Behavior*, 13: 103–123.

17 Pierce, J.L., Kostova, T. and Dirks, K.T. (2001) Toward a theory of psychological ownership in organisations. *Academy of Management Review*, 26 (2): 298–310.

18 Seligman, M.E.P. (1975) *Helplessness*. San Francisco: Freeman.

19 Patterson, M., Rick, J., Wood, S., Carroll, C., Balain, S. and Booth, A. (2008) Review of the validity and reliability of measures of human resource management. NCCRM Report.

20 See for example: Heskett, J.L., Sasser, W.E. and Schlesinger, I.A. (1997) *The Service Profit Chain*. New York: Free Press; Rucci, A.J., Kirn, S.P. and Quinn, R.T. (1998) The employee-customer-profit chain at Sears. *Harvard Business Review*, January–February, 83–97; Wiley, J.W. and Brooks, S.M. (2000) The high-performance organisational

culture. In N.M. Ashkanasy, C.P.M. Wilderom and M.F. Peterson (eds), *Handbook of Organisational Culture and Climate*. pp. 177–191. Thousand Oaks, CA: Sage.

21 Koys, D.J. (2001) The effects of employee satisfaction, organisational citizenship behaviour and turnover on organisational effectiveness: A unit-level, longitudinal study. *Personnel Psychology*, 54: 101–114.

22 Schneider, B., Bowen, D.E., Ehrhart, M.G. and Holcombe, K.M. (2000) The climate for service. In N.M. Ashkanasy, C.P.M. Wilderom and M.F. Peterson (eds), *Handbook of Organisational Culture and Climate*. pp. 1–36. Thousand Oaks, CA: Sage.

23 For example: Schneider, B., White, A. and Paul, M. (1998) Linking service climate and customer perceptions of service quality: Test of a causal model. *Journal of Applied Psychology*, 83: 150–163; Schmit, M.J. and Allscheid, S.P. (1995) Employee attitudes and customer satisfaction: Making theoretical and empirical connections. *Personnel Psychology*, 48: 521–535; Johnson, J.W. (1996) Linking employee perceptions of service climate to customer satisfaction. *Personnel Psychology*, 49: 831–851.

24 For example: Gunter, B. and Furnham, A. (1996) Biographical and climate predictors of job satisfaction and pride in organisation. *Journal of Psychology*, 130: 192–208; Johnson, J.J. and McIntyre, C.L. (1998) Organisational culture and climate correlates of job satisfaction. *Psychological Reports*, 82: 843–850; Ostroff, C., Klinicki, A.J. and Clark, M.A. (2002) Substantive and operational issues of response bias across levels of analysis: An example of climate-satisfaction relationships. *Journal of Applied Psychology*, 87: 355–368.

25 Harter, J.K., Schmidt, F.L. and Hayes, T.L. (2002).

26 For example: Mittal, V., Kumar, P. and Tsiros, M. (1999) Attribute-level performance, satisfaction and behavioural intentions over time: A consumption system approach. *Journal of Marketing*, 63: 88–101; Zeithaml, V.A., Berry, L.L. and Parasuraman, A. (1996) The behavioural consequences of service quality, *Journal of Marketing*, 60: 31–46.

27 For example: Bolton, R.N. (1998) A dynamic model of the duration of the customer's relationship with a continuous service provider: The role of satisfaction. *Marketing Science*, 17: 45–65; Bolton, R.N. and Lemon, K.N. (1999) A dynamic model of customers' usage of services: Usage as an antecedent and consequence of satisfaction. *Journal of Marketing Research*, 36: 171–186.

28 Hennig-Thurau, T. and Klee, A. (1997) The impact of customer satisfaction and relationship quality on customer retention: A critical reassessment and model development. *Psychology and Marketing*, 14: 737–764; Verhoef, P.C., Franses, P.H. and Hoekstra, J. (2002) The effect of relational constructs on customer referrals and number of services purchased from a multi-service provider: Does age of relationship matter? *Journal of the Academy of Marketing Science*, 30: 202–216.

29 Gelade, G.A. and Young, S. (2005) Test of a service profit chain model in the retail banking sector. *Journal of Occupational and Organisational Psychology*, 78 (1): 1–22.

30 Lovelock, C.H. (1983) Classifying services to gain strategic marketing insights. *Journal of Marketing*, 47 (3): 9–20.

31 Gutek, B.A., Bhappu, A.D., Liao-Troth, M.A. and Cherry, B. (1999) Distinguishing between service relationships and encounters. *Journal of Applied Psychology*, 84 (2): 218–233.

32 Ostroff, C. and Harrison, D.A. (1992) The relationship between satisfaction, attitudes and performance: An organizational level analysis. *Journal of Applied Psychology*, 77 (6): 963–974.

33 Ping, R.A. (2003) Antecedents of satisfaction in a marketing channel. *Journal of Retailing*, 79 (4): 249–258.

34 Carlson, J. (1987) *Moments of Truth*. New York, NY: Harper and Row.

35 Babbar, S. and Koufteros, X. (2008) The human element in airline service quality: Contact personnel and the customer. *International Journal of Operations and Production Management*, 28 (9): 804–830.

CHAPTER 10

Cooperative Financial Services: Linking Ethics, Engagement, and Employer Branding to Business Model Change

CRAIG MARSH AND ROB WOOLLEY

10.1. Introduction

One of the areas of HR activity most commonly encountered in our research is that of employee engagement. Heskett and Schlesinger define the service-profit chain as "involving direct and strong relationships between profit; growth; customer loyalty; customer satisfaction; the value of goods and services delivered to customers; and employee capability, satisfaction, loyalty and productivity" Persuaded by the principles contained within the service-profit chain theory,[1] HR Directors are investing considerable time and organizational resources into creating systems for managing and measuring the phenomenon. In relation to the three core motivations to pursue an engagement strategy laid out in Chapter 9, the approach at Cooperative Financial Services (CFS) would be categorized as an internal marketing philosophy, underpinned by a belief that the service-profit chain applies strongly in a retail banking setting.

In periods of business model change, fundamental – and often long-held – employee ideas about how their work adds value, how their time should be spent, and how they should relate to the organization, may be thrown into confusion. Even the nature of the legal contract an employee holds with the company may change. The challenge, therefore, to HR Directors committed to the concept is how to develop mechanisms for retaining and improving employee engagement during this period of company transformation and individual uncertainty. This challenge may be said to be particularly acute when the organization in question is celebrated internally and externally for its strong ethical and value-driven approach to its stakeholders. When this challenge is your strategic imperative, what is the headline issue for HR and what is its must-win battle?

Aligning ethics, employee engagement, and brand

Headline issue:

Is it possible for an organization which places value on ethics and responsible business to continue to maintain employee engagement in a period of enormous restructuring and downsizing? And if it does, how?

Strategic imperatives:

The fundamental
challenge is how best to develop mechanisms for retaining and improving employee engagement during this period of company transformation and individual uncertainty.

HR Directors have to make difficult judgments on timing about (a) which stage of the change process demands what type of intervention and (b) the degree to which the agenda needs pushing at any given stage. If HR pushes too much, the organization may react by rejecting the people agenda. If it pushes too little, it abdicates its power and responsibility.

The HR strategy needs to alternate between hard and soft elements – elements of performance measurement can be introduced gradually and in a phased manner, engineering more sophisticated behavior. Redundancies may be taking place alongside leadership development.

Branding messages have to be evolved as the operational realities become more evident. Branding is only an authentic strategy where the company's values are shown to be central to the value proposition it offers to customers, where brand can be reconnected to history, where it can be supported at all levels and in all businesses, and where the organization will encourage debate across those levels, particularly through the diversity of participation. The resources necessary to do this should not be underestimated.

The order in which the HR agenda is delivered is essential. Employer branding simply does not work (seeds will be sown on stony ground) if the pain of restructuring has not yet taken place, if the company's strategy has not been clearly and consistently defined, and if the leadership of the organization has not already been transformed.

Must-win battle:

The leadership agenda must be unwavering, and perceived from the beginning as essential to bring about the necessary changes in culture which underpin the strategic agenda. The ultimate judgment on the success or otherwise of the soft and hard HR interventions is twofold: (1) Has the value proposition to the customer really changed? (2) Is the organization shown to be more agile in responding to its next strategic challenge?

In this chapter we will consider the question in the context of business model change at the CFS.

The key messages that emerge from this chapter

We argue that

1)   Business model change is an iterative process, during which time senior teams in the organization build understanding and clarify what it means for performance.

2) Squaring the circle, by aligning ethics, engagement, and brand, and maintaining the credibility of an ethical positioning while making some very tough commercial decisions, is possible – but only through becoming a performance-driven organization with that performance embedded in values.

3) Long periods of consolidation are often necessary to ensure this alignment, building an underpinning set of capabilities – the benefits of which may only be seen in 3 or 4 years' time. Maintaining belief in the interim period with inevitable ups and downs is a challenge.

4) Internal restructurings rarely go entirely to plan, and the inability of some people experienced in different operating styles can bring low even the best thought-out strategy. Even in the most ethical of strategies there is a "hard" HR agenda that must be dealt with – there is no nice way to deal with risk aversion, abdication of responsibility, misaligned accountabilities, skewed communication, structural deficiencies, and poorly targeted performance management.

5) As with most changes, therefore, a number of levers have to be pulled to "soften up" the organization and to make it more receptive to change. Dual processes of reinventing leadership (which includes exiting some leaders) and investing in new leadership are key ingredients in this. The result has to be a collective vision that can be signed up to. Persistence is needed for senior cadres to "get the message." Hard forms of performance management inevitably focus attention where it is needed.

6) Such traditional change management tactics have to be underpinned by what has been called "training for the long march" – the long-term strategic plans, the bomb-proof testing of contentious HR processes, and the problem-solving and education processes necessary to show people the path through complex organizational changes.

7) The confidence and authority of HR Directors – embedded in a collective responsibility – come to the fore. Planning for people issues proves to be an enabler of all the other business projects – this shapes the culture of the organization. If you do not get the culture right, then success is only short-term success and will not be sustained.

8) The sustainability of the strategic change requires – after the initial turbulence – a return to and validation of the originally embedded values. A reconnection with strategic principles is necessary.

9) The evolution of supporting HR processes becomes necessary. Performance management processes moved from a "what" to a "how" focus and the 360 degree process moved from purely developmental to rewards-linked. Internal and external employer branding initiatives were employed to reveal the links between customer needs of the brand and managerial and employee behavior. Emotional connection with the brand was reestablished.

10) Branding creates debates about brainwashing versus voluntary engagement with business logic. Only open debate and elaboration of – and mutual improvement in-key processes can defuse this.

11) The ultimate judgment on the success or otherwise of soft and hard HR interventions is twofold: (1) Has the value proposition to the customer really changed? (2) Is the organization shown to be more agile in responding to its next strategic challenge? The success of the latest merger will evidence this.

10.2. CFS: Background

This case study examines the issues associated with aligning ethics, employee engagement, and employer brand in CFS from 2002 until early 2009, in the run up to the subsequent merger with Britannia Building Society. Why is linking ethics, engagement, and brand so important? The Cooperative is undoubtedly one of the best known, and certainly one of the oldest, brand names in the United Kingdom. Formed in 2002, CFS is the group of businesses that includes The Co-operative Insurance and The Co-operative Bank including Smile, the online bank. In line with its origins in the cooperative movement, CFS is prominent in its claims to operate ethically, publishing, for example, an ethical stance whereby it clearly tells its customers who it will and will not do business with.[2] Since launching its ethical positioning in May 1992 it has succeeded in attracting customers who are concerned by the kinds of businesses their bank invests in. The values-driven foundations of the cooperative movement have also been important for attracting and retaining its employees, who have tended to be long-serving and loyal. Studies in the mid-1990s pointed to the differentiating aspect of the Cooperative Bank seeking to return to the values of its cooperative origins, and the positive effects on both customer retention and employee engagement.[3]

In the last few years the organization has undergone major changes. CFS itself was created in 2002 bringing together insurance, corporate, retail, and online banking. Since then change has been constant as these organizations, previously sharing little except the "cooperative" tag but having widely diverse strategy, processes, culture, and structure, were merged into a recognizably coherent entity. The process was not conducted without pain, as restructurings in 2003, and again in 2007 and 2008, resulted in large-scale reductions in workforce; in the most recent, 2,500 employees left the organization. The latter restructuring took place, however, in parallel with attention being paid to the brand, both internally and externally, as CFS rediscovered its roots in the cooperative insurance and banking movement founded in the mid-nineteenth century in North West England.

The detailed research for this chapter was conducted in 2007 and 2008 during which time we were able to track the business and HR logics. The chapter examines the issues associated with aligning ethics, engagement, and brand just prior to the significant merger with Britannia Building Society. The transfer of the business of Britannia Building Society to Co-operative Bank plc formed a strategic response to the credit crunch.

It is interesting to note as a postscript to this research that, perhaps contrary to what may be seen in some merger events, a similar business and HR philosophy linking these three issues clearly existed in both component organizations for several years before the merger, and will undoubtedly continue to drive HR strategy in the medium to long term.

After the merger, the new Chief Executive of CFS, Neville Richardson, stated:

... Trust has become a scarce commodity in other financial businesses of late and we aim to provide a genuine alternative to those disillusioned with shareholder owned banks. Ours will be an ethically-led organisation, part of a parent company which rewards members and is completely accountable to them.

In this chapter we will retrace the major milestones of the premerger change process in the original CFS businesses, as seen through the eyes of several key managers, including David Andersen, the former chief executive officer (CEO), and the HR Director. We will then investigate the role of branding and engagement as tools in managing business model change.

10.3. Business model change at CFS

Bringing two organizations together in 2002 – the Cooperative Bank and Cooperative Insurance Services (CIS) – saw the beginning of a long period of consolidation which accelerated with the arrival of CEO David Anderson in 2005. CFS had been created as a holding company to bring the two organizations together, but by the time of Anderson's arrival, it had been realized that the two entities could not really work together. CIS did not have any of the capabilities that would allow it to increase sales in the bank, or increase bank customers, or indeed sell banking products to CIS customers. The synergies that had been perceived as a strategic objective of the merger could not be delivered, and progress on change had stalled, especially in the Bank.

David Anderson recalls a Board meeting about 6 weeks after his arrival, which established a broad strategy for CFS expressed in a purpose statement, a definition of why the business exists: "to be a growing pioneering Financial Services Business bringing benefits to customers, members and communities through focus on fairness, value and social responsibility." As he says,

... you sense a lot of CFS values within that statement.

With this clearly defined, the next step was quickly to develop an aim – what CFS needs to achieve: and their vision, thus defined, is still "to be the UK's most admired Financial Services business." Having established this, the Board's task, to use the terminology the Board adopted fairly early on, was to develop, according to the CEO:

a target business model, a target operating model, a target culture model, and a target architecture model.

and to establish financially what the business needed to do to sustain future growth. Five targets were established to make the vision concrete and to ensure that, in 5 years, they would know what would have been achieved in pursuing the vision:

The original CFS targets

1. Profit generation to create a sustainable business
2. Market-leading colleague satisfaction
3. Market-leading customer satisfaction
4. Market-leading social responsibility approach
5. Membership growth

Only then did the Board – in the words of Anderson:

> . . . work this through to the change plan through a process of iteration.

The first part was working out the customer proposition; in essence this was to target, at least initially, the current customer base rather than going out and getting new ones. With this defined, the organization's structure could be tackled. The change of this aspect of the business model was far from straightforward. As Anderson says, there had been:

> . . . two or three different business models within the business – different value propositions, targeting different customers, and offering it in a different way, grouped by nothing but the co-operative name.

In its original conception, the idea was to "turn the model on its side." There had been two or three sets of management functions, classic organization "silos," remnants of the previously separate organizations, and consequently too many costs and inefficiencies inherent in CFS. So one person was placed in charge of each of the functions and of the customer-facing segments; and although cross-business systems and regulatory mechanisms were not in place, "we worked through that," says Anderson.
The result was a single business model, albeit operating in different sectors, that was focused back from CFS' target customers in terms of delivery of what they want; CFS was also clear on the capabilities they need to deliver the value proposition to customers – the product, the service, the levels of quality required, and the ethical positioning. This allowed the business to move on to widen the customer base to "conscience customers" in the larger Cooperative group – in other words, customers were clearly being targeted for their attitude rather than anything else. In the CEO's words:

> segmentation is shorthanded by the conscience of the consumer.

Key processes such as the core banking system were upgraded, involving "huge time and effort"; according to the CEO, the benefits of which would really only be seen in 3 or 4 years' time.

The change was significant. As one example of the degree of change, in 2005, 80 per cent of the general insurance business achieved its sales through field advisers; payment and queries were made through 120 field offices with no possibility of changing policies on the phone. By 2007, 75 per cent of insurance sales were on the phone or via the web, the number of claims centers had been reduced to six, the system for managing claims had been replaced, and the customer base has two-thirds different from 2 years' previously.

As is often the case, the internal restructuring did not go entirely according to plan, however. A structure consisting of two key commercial parts of the value chain, one dealing with distribution and service, and one with sector management and marketing, did not work even though "it should have worked on paper," according to Anderson, and it was abandoned in July 2007. It foundered on the back of a gap between the flexibility and autonomy needed to make it work and the command-and-control culture that largely existed within the senior team in charge. In the CEO's words:

> If you have an organisation where everyone is good at doing what they're told and not much else, then put them into a completely new structure and ask them to make up how it works, then it's perhaps not that surprising when it doesn't work.

However, a handful of people were brought in from outside, including a new HR Director, who were used to working in a much more flexible way, and the difficulties created by the twin structure were largely overcome.

The next stage of the process of change was dependent on two or three key commercial decisions to be taken (the subsequent merger with Britannia was one of these), so as a result planning horizons were relatively short; but some broad strategic principles were quite clear. Financially, the target was not to become the biggest player but to achieve sustainable growth; and the ethical positioning was also strongly defended. So for instance, no customer-facing roles were to be sourced from outside the United Kingdom. Executive activity was largely focused on streamlining cross-business processes – transactional work – referenced in the Annual Report as a commitment to strip out £100 million of costs by June 2008. But their attention would soon return to the delivery of results for CFS.

10.4. Ethics, engagement, and branding at CFS

We have already described how initial attempts at restructuring CFS internally were brought low by the inability of a group of people experienced in one operating style to cope with entirely different demands. From the beginning of the change process, the "people" element was identified as the key to making the change work. CFS was in a unique position with its very strong heritage – at least from the former cooperative bank – of ethical treatment of all stakeholders (described in the annual report as its "principles of value, fairness and social responsibility").[4]

A key challenge was to "square the circle" – maintaining the credibility of this ethical positioning while making some very tough commercial decisions, including – in the summer of 2007 – outsourcing a substantial part of its back-office functions, and announcing 1,000 redundancies across the business. In principle, the CEO was in no doubt that there was no dilemma to be resolved, even though he admitted it might initially seem that way:

> . . . we do require a lower return on capital than our competitors as a cooperative. Now we can either spend that on more expensive ways of doing things, or better return for our customers . . . although there is potentially a dilemma, if you believe that's what's required for the people who remain – it's either one thousand or it's ten [thousand] – it's not been so hard.

Cathy Wilcher, the HR Director until 2008, was primarily engaged in the change process. She defined the objective as "changing the organization from a paternal one to a performance-driven organization– with values." Recognizing, measuring, and driving high performance became the key priorities over the last 2 years for CFS. When the new structure was created in 2006, CFS had two broadly different approaches to managing its people. CIS, the Insurance arm, was "command and control"; dictated by qualifications and time serving, with little room for initiative or creativity, highly structured and hierarchical. The Bank, which was ethically driven and had already experienced change and downsizing a few years earlier, was nevertheless paternalistic and slow moving.

Senior members of the HR team in CFS who were interviewed at the time by Center researchers were in little doubt about the extent of change necessary in attitudes. An analysis of their responses showed that they identified eight existing challenges:

The eight challenges at CFS

1) **Risk aversion**
   "The company is risk averse, the company is going through hard times but you're still being paid bonuses, and still your distribution curve across the four scales – nearly everyone's achieved."

2) **Abdication of responsibility for people issues:**
   "They don't know what they're doing with their people unless HR tell them via an email. So from my perception I was saying "you're the managers, you're leaders, why aren't you doing this?" They were saying we need to have people performance as part of their

objectives. So they've not had that. They've not seen anything to do with people as an integral part of their role."

3) **A style of management considered to be "nice" rather than fair:**
"People like their immediate boss – probably because he's worked for him for years, they're mates etc and he certainly doesn't manage performance."

4) **Communication of key messages was skewed:**
"The strategy isn't clear, we don't tell people on the street, we're not open, we put a spin on communications."

5) **Levels of accountability and responsibility were wrongly positioned in the hierarchy:**
"Current thinking is that we as a business are performing one tier below where we should as a world class organization; our exec are performing as a tier 2, not doing strategic stuff, and our tier 2, they own up and they say they're probably firefighting."

6) **The company's matrix structure did not work well:**
"The matrix structure really just means we can blame someone else, we don't have the ability to manage it from the top down."

7) **Individual performance was not well managed or measured, nor linked to overall targets:**
"We don't tie performance back to business performance, and there's not enough done for those who are disengaged either to get out or do something about it, we're providing training for those who want to do something about it so the link to reward needs to be far stronger as well."

8) **There was a substantial amount of "disengagement" present in the company:**
"33 per cent of our people are disengaged and 20 per cent of those have no intention of going anywhere."

Much of the data for this evaluation of the state of CFS derived from two surveys – ECHO (Every Colleague Has an Opinion), an attitude survey, and OCI, an off-the-shelf organizational climate survey implemented by an external consultancy. The data from these two surveys provided the material for the first part of the People Program rollout, described below.

10.5. Making CFS receptive to change

The first part of the answer to this challenge was to invest heavily in the leadership of the organization, which was a relative novelty for CFS at the time. At precisely the same time as a thousand redundancies were being implemented in the summer of 2007, CFS was training a similar number of managers in an extensive program of basics in people management and leadership – every individual who had a responsibility for people went through the course. This was not however before 17 of the 40 managers at "tier two" – those reporting into the Executive Team – were "exited" from the organization because they were not considered to be capable of making the required change. According to Wilcher: "they were selected between the Board and the Executive, and there were members of the Executive among the 17. A very small number of people knew what was about to happen ... For a small minority that the investment required to get them to change [is too great] – we haven't got the time. So it had to happen."

A second part of the answer was to conduct a collective objective-setting exercise in which the top team agreed their objectives in common, shared these with the next tier who went through a similar process, and on to the 800 managers, team leaders, and supervisors through the rest of the company who met in a hotel in Manchester in a series of facilitated seminars. There was a great deal of resistance at first, from those who believed this to be a private, one-on-one affair, to those who simply did not agree with the process of setting any kind of objective, let alone collective; but Wilcher observed a gradual buy-in of the senior members of the organization which filtered down to the lower levels. A "tipping point" was met, as managers who were also experiencing the leadership training "got the message," understood the process, and became evangelists. Members of the Executive Team began to appear voluntarily at the lower-level managers' seminars, sending a strong message of commitment, to the extent that those who were not present began to lose credibility for their absence.

Central to the implementation of the second aspect – performance development – is a "vitality curve" forced distribution system for evaluating performance. The system was introduced in steps; in 2006 /07 performance was differentiated for the first time, but no one was force ranked (a term CFS did not use). By mid-year the ranking process kicked in, linking to a differentiation in pay and bonuses by the end of the year. Cathy Wilcher commented:

> 'You've got 100 people, if the curve of performance looks like that, we want you to force rank your people into 4 boxes – 50 in 'achieved', 10 in here, 10 in here, and 30 in here. You might say all my people are fabulous, but we'll say you have to distinguish "fabulous." '

There is no doubt that these steps, especially the focus on performance, engendered a great deal of resistance at all levels. As the HR Director says, "there was a long period when everything was being challenged." There was considerable thought invested into preparing the project however. As Wilcher noted:

> Before launching the 360 we got some actuaries to look at it and tell us all the things people would find wrong with it. And then we did it, we had the answers ready. Everything we did we trialled, we picked apart.

10.6. Signaling the capability transformation needed

Support from the highest level was crucial to the success of the "people program," especially in these difficult early days of the transformation, before new attitudes had entrenched themselves in the organization. The transformation of CFS' business model was framed in a cross-organization initiative called the "Summit

Program." The Summit Program comprised of a series of projects extending into all areas of the business and was oriented to achieving CFS' long-term vision of being the "United Kingdom's most admired financial services business." The transformation was conceived as a long-term plan, with key review points established for the end of 2007 and the end of 2009, each with a broadly defined set of outcomes.

The 7 projects contained in the Summit program include:

1. Building a better financial platform and banking system responding to FSA requirements and customer expectations;

2. Outsourcing of the administration of Life and Savings, where a lot of the processes are manual, to Capita – affecting some 700 CFS employees;

3. Understanding the customer better, being able to tap into their lifestyle and offer them information relevant to the stage they're at – advanced customer systems management;

4. "Target Operating Model" – how best to structure the organization to best meet the customer proposition rather than a historical structure that's grown up over time – what is the typical size and shape of a financial services organization?

5. "Customer front end" all about providing people in the call centers the full customer story. We want to create an "umbrella" of technology that enables them to say "I see you've got car insurance with us, do you know you can also have . . . "

6. Making sure CFS is 100 per cent compliant to FSA regulations in Insurance

7. The People Change Program – moving the business to a high-performing culture.

When the Summit Program was originally designed at the end of 2006, there were only six strands – those related to redesigning business processes and structures. Anderson originally intended that people issues would be an enabler of all the other projects and that it would be unnecessary to have a separate project for people transformation. The other six programs all have clear people-related implications – outsourcing, introduction of new technology, job changes, and so on. It became clear, however, that the performance and leadership agendas needed separate attention, time, and resources in order – in the words of Wilcher – to "create a high performance culture"; and so the "people program" was added some 6 months after the initial launch.

Anderson reflects on the importance of the "cultural shift" to the success of CFS' transformation:

I think that the policies that emerge from the HR space . . . they really shape the culture of the organisation and if you don't get the culture right then organisations may get short term success but they generally don't sustain it . . . it seems to me the ones that do well in the long term are the ones that have the HR strategy most integrated into business strategy.

For the CEO, the shape of the organization for the future, the nature of the people, where they come from, how they are developed – these questions, he believes, are as important to CFS' strategy as the question about which customers do they want. It is also clear that he has placed the HR Director in a central role in the nature of this transformation, attributing the work in transforming the performance of CFS' employees directly to her "confidence and authority." Equally as important, however, is the collective nature of responsibility in his senior team for *results*. He expresses particular pride in the fact that his leadership team now spends considerable amounts of their time understanding the culture of the organization using tools like OCI: "demanding their own bespoke surveys and devoting a lot of their own leadership time with their own teams developing responses to what it's telling them" as evidence of the success of the "people program."

The head of the CFS University, Rob Woolley, who led the effort on the leadership agenda, points out that this shift in attention on the part of the leadership team to the management of people and culture cannot be overestimated:

> if we could have created a category below bottom quartile, we would have been there – there was a kick up the backside to say "we are nowhere near where we need to be to be a modern high performance driven culture."

Anderson and Woolley both argued that it will take 3 or 4 years to embed the change in attitude and culture so that it would become "part of the DNA rather than something that's done to them." So what steps were taken at CFS to " embed" this cultural shift (prior to the later merger with Britannia)?

10.7. Embedding cultural change through leadership behavior and employer branding

Questions about corporate reputation and employer branding are examined in Chapter 11 when HR at McDonald's is analyzed, but for CFS the issue of branding was absolutely to the fore of their HR work. The core CFS values underpinning the brand were "value, fairness and social responsibility"; these, or something very like them, had existed as long as the cooperative movement itself. The values allowed colleagues, members, and customers to reconnect with the founding principles of the cooperative; they were a key differentiator in the market, and were used to create a powerful link between the company's business model, and its people agenda.

The Summit program, the overarching framework – and metaphor – used by CFS for delivering the change had four stages to it.

1. Clarify;
2. Catch-up;
3. Compete; and
4. Conquer.

According to Woolley the company was then at the "compete" stage with the work complete on vision, strategy, and establishing a platform for moving forward. The "compete" phase had two main elements to it with regard to the organization's people strategy: leadership and employer branding. A third strategic element to this phase, not dealt with here, was the introduction of a new banking platform, the largest investment the company had ever made; The CEO publically declared that the £170 million investment was a waste of money-without effective leadership.

A first key element of the change centered around leadership. Having spent around 12 months getting managers used to being measured on their delivery, and completing ranking of performance linked to differentiated rewards – the first time this had happened for the majority of the population – CFS then reoriented the expected outcomes of its leaders more toward "how" they deliver performance, as well as the results themselves. Up to 40 per cent of the 2008 performance bonus award to the top 170 leaders was based on their style of leadership. According to Rob Woolley:

> We're getting to the stage now with the leadership part that we're saying to people "we're not just going to measure you on your sales performance, we're going to measure you on your engagement, on your people and your leadership styles."

Engagement "scores" were a key element of this measurement process. Woolley was also keen to pursue measurement of what he refers to as "good citizenship," the willingness shown on the part of leaders to demonstrate their commitment to CFS as a whole, and the three values in particular, by becoming more visible across the organization and not merely "in their own silos," as he puts it.

The performance management rating of senior leaders has driven by a substantial, unified, moderation exercise from top down. The Executive Team at the most recent half-yearly review debated rankings from across the company – thus demonstrating their collective responsibility across the business – and changed them where they felt the ratings did not reflect the true nature of performance, an approach which could not have happened 12 months previously in the old "silo" mentality where senior managers would have fought to push "their" candidates for top ratings at the expense of others. Now, the exec, had a collective, and consistent, view of who the leaders were across the organization who exceed expectations; and thereby an agreed understanding of what "good performance" looked like in each area of the business.

In order to measure the all-important behavioral elements – including "good citizenship" – an indicative, rather than mechanical, approach was used supported by a 360 assessment. In 2007, the 360 had been purely developmental; negative ratings were excluded to avoid alienating managers for whom this was a huge change. In 2008, however, managers were to receive their true scores, and the evaluation would be underpinned at senior level by a target score for improvement being set ("your engagement score is 42, we want you to take it to 48"), and the improvement thus defined would be linked to a manager's performance pay for that period.

In the moderating discussions at exec level, the HR Director played a lead facilitating role, for instance by asking pointed questions of those leaders who have received high scores; on the citizenship rating, for example, they were challenged to prove whether the individual has supported cross-organizational initiatives out with their regular areas of responsibility, or had been in a local community project. The overall effect was that it is no longer acceptable, as it may have been in the past, for the company's leaders not to demonstrate active support the three core values.

A second key element of the next stage of "shifting the culture" was an internal branding exercise. At the same time as launching an external marketing campaign intended to create a single brand for the – at the time still relatively new and unknown – CFS organization, Woolley led the effort to send all CFS colleagues through a one day "going back to the roots" workshop on the Brand. The project consumed considerable time and resources and this alone gave a clear indication of the importance CFS places on it. Woolley described the learning outcomes of the workshop as follows:

1. To understand the business objectives and where we're going;
2. To gain insight into the brand and what it means for me and my customers; and
3. To understand the emotional connection I have with the brand and with other brands.

Two floors of the CFS office in Manchester were redesigned specifically to run the workshop, and some £2 million invested this year alone in the project. By the end of the year, all 8,000 or so CFS employees ("colleagues" as they are known in the company) had been through the workshop. It was embedded in the induction process for new employees (60 per cent of CFS employees arrived in the last 3 years), and a modified version ran for CFS' suppliers and partners, encouraging them to promote the CFS values in their operations. At least one supplier asked to run the same event for its own people.

The workshop was an impressive and innovative activity. Nine workshops were run in total. On any 1 day there were 60–90 employees attending, in a space which has a purpose-built cinema, an interactive gallery with touchscreens for researching information, and a breakout area complete with recliners, sofas, and coffee machines. Pictures of famous brands of all types, discussed in the workshop sessions, lined the walls. There was not a flipchart in sight. The day was run by internal facilitators drawn from middle management ranks, itself sending a signal about the commitment ("citizenship") needed from its leaders to CFS. Participants were diverse, drawn from all ranks and divisions of the company, and networking was an important outcome of the day.

Every workshop run in precisely the same way, and the three themes of value, fairness, and social responsibility were emphasized throughout. The style emphasized participation, informality and fun, as well as the serious messages embedded in the activities. Sessions included:

1. watching a DVD of the CEO describing the company's strategy and vision, and how the brand is central to achieving them;
2. participating in a research exercise to find out as much information about the company as possible using the interactive gallery;
3. answering quiz questions on CFS to obtain small prizes;
4. working collectively on a large mosaic using canvases and paints; and
5. understanding what a person who lives the brand looks like through a fictitious employee of the year ceremony

Clearly a criticism of this type of program is that it is essentially a brainwashing exercise designed to have all employees thinking and behaving alike; a comment heard regularly, according to Woolley, during the workshops themselves. He was sensitive to this accusation but defend the approach rigorously, arguing that the workshop encouraged, rather than stifled, active debate:

> The differentiation is between your own personal values and why you want to come to work and the company values. In answer to the criticism "you're brainwashing us" we say "no, we want you to consider what the company stands for and what we want our customers to see and there's a population who want to engage with us because of that."

The results certainly seemed to bear out his argument. People were asked to leave on rare occasions, but this was down to disruptive behavior rather than an attempt to stifle criticism of the process; facilitators went out of their way to take dissenters to one side and discuss their questions. There was, however, a hard edge to it, according to Rob Woolley:

> There are a lot of cynics – the people who've been here for 15 years and are time servers, who just want to earn their salary – they won't be here in 2 years, they can't be.

Some long-standing employees were clearly been converted to the cause; one phoned his local radio station to declare he had just attended the best day of his 15 years' service with the company.

10.8. Linking leadership and employer branding with business model change

One of the prime reasons for the change to the CFS business model was to exploit capabilities across the newly unified company. In the "old world," customers of the insurance company were treated entirely differently, and separately, from customers of the banking arm. In the new model, the engagement with the customer not only looked the same across the different cooperative businesses, but also the customer received advice on a full range of CFS offerings; something Neil Southworth, CFS' head of Strategic Planning, called "mixed package solutions": that is, offering the customer what they need at the time of life that they need it.

Thus the value proposition to the customer changed (a key criterion for identifying whether the business model has changed).

Logically, therefore, frontline employees needed to possess the knowledge, the skill, and the commitment to deliver this much broader offering effectively. We can see how the two key planks of the change process described in this section helped create the platform for the delivery of this new value proposition. Woolley was convinced that without reinventing the leadership of the organization much of this change would have been stillborn; the collective responsibility for performance now shown at the executive level was a necessary condition for the development of the cross-functional competence needed from frontline employees.

The employer branding exercise, which he described as "the cement which is poured over the new organization," is developed awareness of and commitment to this new customer offering. Without it, customer-facing staff and their support services would had no knowledge, let alone willingness to offer, products and services from a part of the cooperative network that was effectively a different company. Now, at least, the platform was built for the acquisition of a new type of "architectural" knowledge, to the advantage of CFS customers. A customer would not be able to tell the difference between a banking person and an insurance person.

One way of capturing vividly this change is the answer to the question: "who are your corporate heroes?" Two years ago, the answer would clearly have been the highly qualified technical experts, the actuaries who designed the sophisticated financial products and who defended their status rigorously as the heart and soul of the company. Move forward 2 years from now and the answer was quite different; 6,000 out of 7,000 people were selling CFS services. The corporate hero was the person who is engaging the customer.

10.9. Changes to the HR structure at CFS

The HR team at CFS itself underwent substantial changes in the 2 years even prior to the merger with Britannia Building Society, including a new HR Director (promoted from within, an important message to the organization about developing in-house talent), the recruitment of new senior team members, and a revised HR department structure. Former team members had to apply for new positions under the restructuring process, and at least one senior person didn't get through the selection process that this entailed. At the time of writing, a new HRIS was in the process of being implemented implying a substantial change in HR delivery to a self-service model. The department's service is currently delivered through a Business Partner role supported by four Centers of Excellence (see the discussion in Chapters 2 and 3 on HR Structuring). It has Centers of Excellence in

1) learning and talent management (the CFS University), comprising the engagement, brand, and leadership agendas);
2) operations (delivering eventually a self-service HR administration and employee advice line) and business partners;
3) reward, organization development, and employee relationship; and
4) resourcing.

The Heads of the Centers of Excellence report to the HR Director along with three senior Business Partners.

A key challenge for the HR unit as they support the change process in CFS is to apply consistency and conformity to the delivery of HR services supporting the strategic direction toward a unified branding and value offering to the customer, described above. The new IT platform is an enabler, but this move to consistency also represents a change in the role of the HR Business Partner (HRBP). Traditionally the agenda of the HRBP had almost entirely been dictated by the needs of the – highly independent – local business unit manager.

In the new model the skills required of the BP entail fitting the local business unit's strategy to the global HR agenda, especially at the inception of a project, and knowing precisely when to call on the services of the Center of Excellence to assist in service delivery to the line. The HR team has been recruiting people into the department who have a business background, so the capabilities required to perform this balancing act in the BP role or as the head of the Center of Excellence are no longer "purely HR."

10.10. The payoff: CFS performance in 2008

Did the changes deliver results? According to the CEO, sales by the end of the research process were up 30 per cent over the previous one; and over £90 million of cost savings had been made against a projected target of £100 million.

Although CFS was hit by the liquidity crisis that engulfed the financial sector in 2008, the bank's relatively low historical exposure to structured investment vehicles (£65 million) meant that the write-off (in 6 months to July 2008) was limited to £25 million.[5] The impact of the credit crunch on CFS has further been limited by its very low exposure to interbank lending, as it funds the vast majority of lending from retail deposits.[6]

On other measures, CFS turned in an impressive performance in 2008, despite difficult trading conditions. It reported a pretax profit of £73.4 million for the first half of 2008, up 93 per cent on the first half of 2007, and bad debts fell to £43.3 million from £53.2 million. The general insurance business was predicted to be in profit by the end of 2008 following a £33 million loss in 2007.[7] The bank has recorded a 65 per cent increase in the numbers of customers moving their current accounts to the Cooperative over the course of the year, increasing the total amount deposited by customers in personal accounts from £2.7 billion to £3.8 billion during 2008,[8] a phenomenon described by Anderson as a "flight to quality" as customers looked for reliable and low-risk brands to protect their savings.

At the same time surveys consistently reported that CFS was the United Kingdom's most admired financial services company, this at a time when the reputation of the sector is probably at its lowest. It topped polls by *Which?*, the former Consumers' Association, and beat Nationwide Building Society to top spot on a JD Power survey of bank customer satisfaction.

Internally, the data also pointed to a steady improvement in performance. The overall engagement scores for CFS in 2008 increased by 11 per cent, compared with a targeted increase of 5 per cent. Two areas of response appear to have had the most effect on this increase: "emotional attachment to CFS" has increased by 15 per cent, and "intention to stay with the company for longer than 2 years" increased by 7 per cent. According to Rob Woolley:

> These figures were achieved on a total audience of 6750 of our 7200 completing the survey. We believe this is proof that our internal branding programme is having the desired effect and also with more people wishing to stay this also has a bottom line impact on cost reduction.

10.11. Key messages for HR directors

The first key message concerns leadership and performance: getting the timing right. The HR unit at CFS has placed the performance development and leadership agendas right at the heart of the change process. These projects were instigated largely by the HR Director. A study of the history of the change process at CFS over the 2 years of study reveals how sophisticated were the steps taken in each phase; they involved making a difficult judgment about (a) which stage of the change process demanded what type of intervention and (b) the degree to which the agenda needed pushing at any given stage. Push too much, and the organization may have reacted by rejecting the people agenda entirely; push too little, and the performance and leadership agendas may have had no effect. In either event the change process itself would have been undermined.

Cathy Wilcher, when she was the HR Director, stood her ground in the Executive Team to defend the implementation of the people agenda when many in the team were actively against it, and when the CEO was wavering in the face of opposition. However she also knew that introducing a performance management process in one effort at the start of the restructuring would not have worked; so elements of performance measurement were introduced gradually over a period of 18 months, only at the end of this period culminating in the link between behavioral ratings and managers' pay. First, the emphasis was on what "good" looks like; then, on measuring it; finally, on rewarding it and holding leaders to account for improving performance.

When swift action was needed, however, it was taken. Even when redundancies were being implemented, leadership development was taking place;

more unusual was the fact that some of those departures were of very senior people. The attention to the leadership agenda was unwavering, and perceived from the beginning as essential to bring about the necessary changes in culture that underpinned the strategic agenda.

The second key message concerns the importance of employer branding. This is receiving more and more attention as part of the HR agenda, not all of it positive. The CFS case offers a good example of best practice in employer branding. Their model contains several elements which are making it a success:

– the clear links made between the branding exercise, the company's values, and the value proposition it offers to customers
– the reconnection of the brand to the origins and history of the organization
– the importance placed on the branding exercise being supported at all levels and in all businesses
– the encouraging of debate across those levels, particularly through the diversity of participation in the workshop and internal facilitation
– the need for substantial investment of resources into the program to make it work

Most of all, however, the importance of the order in which the HR agenda was delivered is essential. Employer branding simply would not work, in the manner of seeds on stony ground, had the pain of the restructuring not yet taken place, had the company's strategy not been clearly and consistently defined, and had the leadership of the organization not already been transformed (or at least was not in the process of undergoing a transformation).

10.12. Conclusion: Getting engagement right

Why have we featured the work carried out at CFS immediately prior to the merger as a case study in the book? Putting recent events at CFS to one side for a moment, there are important questions to ask about how sustainable and reliable are engagement strategies in the current, and near future, business environments. One of the more distinctive elements of the CFS case is how the organization is "bucking the trend": both of the upheavals to which the rest of the financial sector is subject to, and more specifically, in the way that it is apparently managing the risk of more value – adding long-term HR strategies being cast aside. For example, the CIPD's Chief Economist notes that ". . . the combination of hard times and diverse employee attitudes could test some engagement strategies to breaking point."[9]

Many engagement strategies will be found wanting in the months to come – the HR strategies were either not authentic, or were built upon weak and shifting sand. On the issue of authenticity and robustness, there are two reasons why, at CFS, the engagement strategy seems to have endured over time.

First, it is perceived at Board level as a necessary condition of a business strategy that itself is robust. CFS was able to ride the initial phases of the "credit crunch" business crisis, and through its brand positioning and reputation, capitalize on levels of trust within the population in order to attract business when many others were losing it. The linkage of engagement work to issues of corporate values and reputation therefore not only has both an evident business logic associated with it, but also an authentic ring (when employees judge the rhetoric of engagement talk versus the reality of organizational actions) to it that should enable the strategy to be stretched beyond any short-term breaking points.

Second, the engagement story at CFS appears robust when considered from a number of different perspectives. The dots really do seem to join up. As we have described, the sustained internal effort at employer branding and leadership development in turn support the external redesign of the Cooperative's image in its markets; the reconnection of a new generation of CFS employees with a very old value set has recreated a genuine sense of pride around the workforce; and the tough internal changes, including restructuring and downsizing, which were painful and occasionally messy at the time, appear in retrospect as a necessary rite of passage to enable the organization to develop a sustainable business model at exactly the right time.

Engagement, in these circumstances, is a message that employees can trust in. Chapter 11, using the example of McDonald's, moves on to examine how HR can help build a trust-based model of HR.

NOTES

1 See for example: Schneider, B. and Bowen, D.E. (1995) *Wining the Service Game*. Boston, MA: Harvard Business School Press; Heskett, J.L., Sasser, W.E. and Schlesinger, I.A. (1997) *The Service Profit Chain*. New York: Free Press. p. 11.

2 CFS website http://www.cfs.co.uk (accessed 23 May 2008).

3 Wilkinson, A. and Balmer, J.M.T. (1996) Corporate and generic identities: Lessons from the Co-operative Bank. *The International Journal of Bank Marketing*, 14 (4): 22–35.

4 CFS Annual Report for 2007, CEO's statement, p. 7.

5 "Stable image pays dividends for Co-op in credit crunch" 12 September 2008 http://www.creditman.biz/uk/members/news-view.asp?newsviewID=8958 (accessed 18 December 2008).

6 "Co-op Bank defies crunch" 11 September 2008 http://www.manchestereveningnews.co.uk/news/business/s/1066351_coop_bank_defies_crunch (accessed 18 December 2008).

7 From *The Times* 12 September 2008 http://business.timesonline.co.uk/tol/business/industry_sectors/banking_and_finance/article4735669.ece (accessed 18 December 2008).

8 "Co-operative Bank: Customers increasingly switching accounts" 10 December 2008 http://www.moneynews.co.uk/5866/co-operative-bank-customers-increasingly-switching-accounts/ (accessed 18 December 2008).

9 Philpott, J. (2009) Happy new year, anyone? *People Management*, 1 January, 15 (1): 22.

CHAPTER 11

McDonald's UK: From Corporate Reputation to Trust-Based HR

PAUL SPARROW, SHASHI BALAIN, AND DAVID FAIRHURST

Trust-based HR

Headline issue:

There is a shift taking place within organizations and their relationship with their consumers and employees, moving from a position where once driven by brand, marketeers, and a set of promises, they are now assessed on what they actually do. For consumers, the issue is moving away from being "about brand" toward being "about reputation."

Strategic imperative:

Having got the privilege of having a seat at the top table, the real judgment concerns how HR uses this seat. *Leading HR* requires courage to get the business to invest in potentially disruptive strategies and to be measured against this.

Corporate social responsibility without HR is just Public Relations. A poor employer brand reduces the return on investment both in targeted recruitment and in developing the competence of employees. Employer brands have to be visible, distinctive, consistent, transparent, and authentic.

HR has to put in place a platform of accurate perceptions (image) with regard to its employment proposition, upon which the organization can build its corporate reputation.

A strong degree of identification has to be built within the workforce to tackle negative associations, using a strategy built around the availability of information, personalized messaging, high-quality communication, and emotional appeal.

HR processes have to be linked up around the engagement theme, but there also needs to be a range of "pull mechanisms," that pull employees into the process of engagement.

Must-win battle:

In an information-rich digital world HR needs a different mindset. Consumers are listening to new channels, and are acting and changing their behaviors and purchasing power based on what people are saying. HR cannot control employee voice in the way that it used to. It needs to create transparency in the employee space.

11.1. Introduction: Strategic context for McDonald's UK

It is said that the sun never sets on the "Golden Arches." McDonald's is the leading global food service retailer with more than 32,000 local restaurants serving more than 58 million people in 118 countries each day. In the United Kingdom there are around 1,200 restaurants, employing over 72,000 employees, of which around 650 are operated by the franchises.

The brand "McDonald's" has become a synonym for globalization to an extent that economists use "The Big Mac Index" as a comparative index of the purchasing power parity (PPP) of a given country! Its brand name is anything but neutral; many love it, some love to hate it, but everyone has a view. Inevitably, over the years the company has been subject to criticism over various issues, and has always fought hard to protect its reputation. Probably one of its most iconic challenges has been it's fight to reclaim and rebrand the term "McJob" (BBC, 2007).[1] The term had entered common usage after it was defined in Douglas Coupland's 1991 novel *Generation X*, and by the mid-2000s in the United Kingdom it had become media shorthand for low-quality employment.

The Oxford English Dictionary had defined a McJob as a unstimulating and low-paid job, especially in the service sector. The term McJob is used to describe any low-status job – regardless of who the employer is – where little training is required, staff turnover is high, and where workers' activities are tightly regulated by managers. Most perceived McJobs are in the service industry, particularly fast food, coffee shops, and retail sales.

In 2006, McDonald's undertook an advertising campaign in the United Kingdom to challenge such perceptions of the McJob. The campaign, supported by research conducted by Adrian Furnham, Professor of Psychology at University College London, highlighted the benefits of working for the organization, stating that they were "Not bad for a McJob." When interviewed by the BBC in March 2007 about the McJob initiative, David Fairhurst (Senior Vice President, and Chief People Officer, McDonald's Northern Europe) said,

> . . . The definition is way out of date and indeed is insulting to the people who
> serve in our restaurants everyday . . . we think it is time to address that
> perception gap and put straight – with evidence – why we are a strong
> employer. 72% of our people are telling us through our opinion surveys that
> that are proud to work for McDonald's . . . there is a perception gap between the
> reality of the organisation and what is actually being delivered.

McDonald's was no stranger to battles for protecting its brand image, but this time they had a different strategy. In March 2007, Mark Blundell, HR Operations Director, explained the strategy:

> . . . When you see the evidence it's extremely persuasive, but our audience has its
> defences up . . . So we have to go to them, quietly and humbly (which has not
> been McDonald's normal style!) and share that evidence with them . . . because
> by sharing with people the reality of what working for McDonald's can deliver
> for its employees, and inviting them to come and find out more for themselves

we believed that we could change perception and prove to people that we are a good employer. In short, we chose to accept their cynicism in good faith, but humbly (because we're not perfect – just better than they think!) offer evidence to challenge their preconceptions.

We argue that

The key messages that emerge from this chapter

1) HR needs to position itself against the corporate reputation and employer branding activity taking place inside the organization.

2) To do this effectively HR must understand how it can move away from those activities associated with traditional employer brand management, toward a reputation management approach rooted in a trust-based HR strategy.

3) This is aided by the adoption of cross-disciplinary teams, of which HR are one part (but with an important and guiding voice).

4) A degree of courage on behalf of the HR Director, and a high level of transparency in the practices, becomes necessary if organizations pursue, as in this chapter, a disruptive communication strategy aimed at changing the nature of trust.

5) In turn this requires that HR provision meets a number of important preconditions that together form the basis of a trust-based HR strategy, including: creating a baseline of positive employee engagement and involvement; putting in place a suite of flexible work policies; making investments in training and education, underpinned by a philosophy of social mobility; operating democratic planning feedback processes joined up to engaging social media; and e-enabling core HR processes in ways that enhance the management of the employer brand.

Research on corporate reputation has long pointed to the power of reputational capital (defined as the difference between book valuation of an organization and its market valuation), noting that such capital has to be built on the trust and confidence of stakeholders in an organization – trust that the organization will act in their best interests. However, for reputation to be effective, in every interaction between the organization and its stakeholders (customers, employees, suppliers, etc.) "... the returns from maintaining an unsullied reputation must exceed the gains from violating trust and reneging on promises."[2] For Majken Schulz, Mary Jo Hatch and Mogens Holten Larsen[3] in their book *The Expressive Organization* the most obvious violations result from a series of possible misalignments. Strong corporate brands need to align three essential, interdependent, and largely intangible elements – an organization's vision, its image, and its culture. There are three gaps that can damage a corporate brand: between the stated strategic vision (of managers) and the reality of the corporate culture (as felt by employees); between the stated strategic vision and the perceived image of the company (by outsiders); or between the image and the culture. For Jez Langhorn (Head of

Talent, McDonald's UK) McDonald's starting point in building trust had to be image:

> ... Of those three facets, the strategic vision and the reality of the corporate culture in restaurants were more closely aligned. It was that third part – the perceived image – that was disjointed ... What we did on the employer branding work, was to say, first of all to our people, we recognise what's good and what we need to work on, and we're committed to doing that. But we also recognise your desire for us to tell your story better externally. So we're going to go out to the external world and say, "look, respectfully, we realise that you have some fairly strong views about us. What we want to do, metaphorically is to take you by the hand and take you across this perception gap and show you some facts that just might change your mind. We'll start that process with you.

Jon Miller and David Muir's work on *The Business of Brands* suggests that brand equity is based on four things: customer loyalty (repeat purchases), awareness (familiarity with the brand), perceptions (assessments of the expected quality that a brand will deliver), and associations (the images and ideas connected with the brand).[4] Using such distinctions, it was clear to the McDonald's HR team that their initial strategy, in addition to managing the corporate image (how an organization is perceived *now*) by narrowing the image and culture gap and readdressing external perceptions by communicating the reality of the employee experience both internally and externally, was also putting in place a platform upon which to build the corporate reputation (how an organization is seen as time goes on).

Events at McDonald's contain important lessons about *Leading HR*. The issue faced by the McJobs label was a problem of association amongst the external population. HR had to build a strong degree of identification amongst the workforce to tackle these associations. For Graeme Martin and Susan Hetrick, in their book *Corporate Reputations, Branding and People Management*, such identification is dependent on the availability of information, personalized messaging, high-quality communication, and emotional appeal. These all help create supportive employee behaviors.[5] For Charles Fombrun and Cees Van Riel in their book *Fame and Fortune: How Successful Companies Build Winning Reputations* the key judgment is whether an employer brand is visible, distinctive, consistent, transparent, and most importantly authentic.[6]

11.2. Initial resolve and purpose: Tackling employer reputation 2006–2008

We begin the story by returning to the challenges faced by the HR team at McDonald's UK as a result of employer reputation. The Sunday Express editor Martin Townsend commented in his column on 25 March 2007,

> ... one of the least attractive hangovers from an earlier, more class-conscious age has been the tendency, in Britain, to deride or patronise manual labourers ... and particularly people who wait at tables or serve food.

McDonald's considered the use of McJob in such a derogatory manner a collective insult to its 72,000 employees – an insult which was undermining the confidence of its people to deliver the levels of customer service customers expected from the organization. As a result, McDonald's UK decided to embark on a strategy that aimed to use what David Fairhurst described back in February 2006 as "evidence based reputation work."[7] Looking back over the initial work, he explained the strategy as follows:

> ... When we thought about this, we realised that by undermining the confidence of our people, the McJob myth was reducing the return on our investment both in targeted recruitment and in developing the competence of our people. Furthermore, as a progressive employer, we also felt a moral obligation to stand up for our people and the jobs that they do. So, since April 2006, we have undertaken a campaign to change the public's perceptions of so-called McJobs – and we have found that the strongest weapon in our armoury is evidence.[8]

This new approach was led by McDonald's UK's HR team and, reflecting some of the thinking in the employer branding literature outlined above, the strategy was as much inward directed as it was outward. It also drew upon a range of cross-functional expertise. At that time, Jez Langhorn had recently moved into the new role of Employer Reputation Manager. His task was not that of a standard communications expert using mass media to weave a positive image of the company. He reported to David Fairhurst, and much of his task was to execute Fairhurst's new approach to protect and enhance McDonald's UK's reputation. Looking back at the original task, Jez Langhorn explains,

> ... There is an old adage that you can continue doing what you've done in the past, but if you expect a different result then you're mad. There was clearly a need to do something new and David Fairhurst acted as a catalyst for that within the business. I think there was a strong desire amongst our franchisees as well to find a different way of telling our stories. Remember, our business is half franchised in the UK, and is moving to be predominantly franchised over the next three years. We have a responsibility to our franchisees as well.

Over the years McDonald's had been silently working on improving its corporate social responsibility. Its employees knew about these developments, and it was felt that it was now time to share this with the outside world, in doing so reflecting the shift taking place within the world of corporate reputation. David Fairhurst commented,

> ... There is a distinct shift in organisations and their relationship with their consumers and with their employees. Going from a position where organisations were very brand driven, driven by marketeers, and driven by a set of promises – what it's moving to, is less about what you say about your organisation, and more about what you actually do as an organisation. And

therefore, as a consumer it's moving from "about brand" to "about reputation". It's moving from promise to activity. It's moving from talking it, to walking it.

The new strategy, therefore, had to be based on trust; everything that the company did to fight the negative connotations attached to McJob had to built around the trust that the company had earned from its customers and the trust that company's employees vested in its work practices.

But the key question was how to do it? According to a MORI poll, other than the politicians and journalists, business leaders are the professional group least trusted to tell the truth.[9] There was a genuine trust gap between the source and the target – and it needed to be bridged. McDonald's new strategy, intended to bridge this gap, was to win this war of public perceptions.

11.3. Fundamental principles behind the HR trust strategy

From the outset, David Fairhurst was very clear that his efforts were not to be those associated with a regular public relations exercise. It needed to have more substance than propaganda. He laid out two ground rules:

1. Transparency and
2. Courageous HR leadership.

With regard to transparency, we live in an information-rich digital world. There are blogs for everything and dedicated websites where employees or customers can post customer reviews on anything one can imagine. Interactive online interfaces such as YouTube, Facebook, blogs, and other social networking sites work in both directions, and those interested can very easily get to every employee of every organization and see their collective views on anything. From an HR organization point of view, this requires a different mindset. Organizations are learning that they cannot control employee voice in the way that HR once used to do. They can no longer hide behind employment contracts pledging secrecy to company policies. In this new context, best practice is to have no secrets and total transparency about what the company does and how it does it. David Fairhurst explains the new world as follows:

> ... This model, from brand management to reputation management around trust, from what you say to what you do, is all being driven by transparency. And transparency is coming right into the employment space ... Not only are consumers listening to these new channels, but they're actually acting and changing their behaviours and purchasing power based on what people are saying ... what you have to be doing is making sure the experience is good in the first place.

Moreover, he argues that this new model for achieving and sustaining brand reputation is both an opportunity and a threat:

... This is no longer a world of managing an employer brand, where you make a set of promises, publicise them really well, and hope they stick. This is about creating a real experience that you know damn well is going to hit the business bottom line, either directly or indirectly. That's why reputation is so important.

David Fairhurst was also very clear that if his strategy was to succeed, then HR had to be more proactive and take a leading role in making the changes happen. In several public forums, he made it clear that:

... It is no good if you don't live up to what you are preaching about. You are on shaky ground if you are trying to build your reputation and you don't live up to it internally ...

... CSR (corporate social responsibility) without HR is PR.[10]

Consequently, he was never in doubt that there were risks associated with his strategy of total transparency. But he also knew that HR had to demonstrate leadership and show courage in its convictions:

HR is now having its day. The HR profession now talks about being at the centre and in the hot seat – and we have been crying out to be on the boards for years. We've now got that privilege. So now it is how we use it.

At McDonald's we needed the courage to break the silos down to get all our functions in one room ... Courage to fall flat on our face. Courage that we're the first on things: Family Contracts, the education stories. Courage to get the business to invest in some things we were going to do, and courage to be measured.

He was in no doubt that if his team was to succeed, they had to exhibit the courage to be measured against their promises and be ready for the consequences, good or bad.

11.4. What did McDonald's do?

At a macro level, McDonald's strategy had two facets:

1. Make active HR interventions that would help win employee trust; and
2. Use of effective internal and external communication strategy to counter the negative public perceptions being created about McDonald's and McJob.

But this double-pronged strategy itself rested on a number of important preconditions that needed to exist within the McDonald's work environment.

The preconditions for a trust-based HR strategy

1. In order to address misperceptions about the organization as an employer, there had to be a team that included individuals from every HR discipline as well as corporate affairs, internal communications, and an education team.

> **The preconditions for a trust-based HR strategy: (Continued)**
>
> 2. There needed to be a disruptive communications strategy to change the nature of trust.
> 3. There had to be a baseline of positive employee engagement and involvement.
> 4. The organization had to enhance its suite of flexible work policies.
> 5. It has also had to leverage its considerable investment in training and education, and demonstrate how this was underpinned by a philosophy of social mobility.

We explain how each of these initiatives set up a series of key preconditions for the move toward a trust-based strategy.

The first important precondition was that McDonald's needed to create structures and teams that brought together a range of expertise to the problem. Employer brand is a multidimensional, multi-departmental issue that requires strong internal communication so that an organization engages with its employees before it talks to the external world about the brand. Sometimes organizations have to do those things together. McDonald's created a multi-disciplinary Reputation team. From McDonald's HR this included Compensation and Benefits, Recruitment, and Training and Development. It also included Corporate Affairs, Marketing, Internal Communications, External PR (National and Regional), Advertising, and Education. Writing about such teams in 2008,[11] David Fairhurst commented,

> ... HR is a highly technical discipline, and it tends to structure itself around its specialisms: training and development, compensation and benefits, recruitment, organisation design, and so on. This must stop. To succeed in tackling the McJob myth we have had to work hard at dismantling these traditional silos within McDonald's. For example, the team addressing misperceptions about us as an employer includes individuals from every HR discipline as well as corporate affairs, internal communications and our education team.

He is of the opinion that:

> ... If as an HR function you try to think, "I'm going to fix our reputation," on your own, then you are very much mistaken. You have to cross the silos.

Jez Langhorn explains exactly how the cross-functional teams at McDonald's worked – how silos were avoided:

> ... When you come to set strategy, it would be very arrogant of us to think we have all the answers, which is why a steering group meets every two months to review strategy and of course correct if necessary. Their job is to look at what's coming up, to assimilate what the latest data is in the market, where we feel that the HR profession is going, what are the hot things around people issues, what is coming up, and how we can key McDonald's into that? We take a leadership position on some things. But equally, knowing and having remit to be able to

discuss anything that's upcoming, whether it's employment legislation or immigration ... [having a] cross-functional team helps us to do that. It keeps all the parts of the business engaged in what we're doing, so there's knowledge sharing amongst the McDonald's team.

As a result of both the work on employee engagement, and operating through cross-functional teams, the HR team at McDonald's learnt a lot from colleagues in Marketing – notably the way that they should plan and execute a promotion (see Chapter 9 for an outline of internal marketing approaches to employee engagement).

The second precondition was the use of disruptive communications. Mark Blundell, HR Operations Director, explained that:

> ... We proposed that a strategy of disrupting and challenging preconceptions in a quiet and self-effacing way should manifest itself in a series of in-store posters Why in-store? Because that's where we could achieve the greatest dissonance – customers standing at the counter looking at people they believed to be doing a McJob – but at the same time giving them evidence which challenged their preconceptions. It was a brave strategy – so one we had to validate before execution ... Because of the multi-disciplinary backgrounds of the Reputation team, we were able to "go live" externally through multiple channels: in-store advertising, press advertising, PR and conference platforms. This was replicated by a coordinated internal communications campaign.

David Fairhurst knew that for his trust strategy to work, the company needed to significantly alter the nature of the "trust bond" as it then existed, between the employees and the company. A new unwritten psychological contract was needed – one that underpinned the new trust bond. The company needed to first step forward and trust its employees more for them in turn to trust the company. The employees needed to believe that the company was making a serious effort to improve the quality of work life (QWL) and work life balance, not just because they had demanded it, but because the company believed that its employees must have it. The initial validation work showed some positive impacts, giving McDonald's the confidence to "go live" with the approach on a wider basis. By March 2007 the proportion of the workforce answering a series of key Viewpoint opinion survey items positively rose.

Improvements in employee attitudes

1. 62 per cent reported excellent earning potential.
2. 65 per cent reported opportunities to progress.
3. 74 per cent reported they had hours that suited their lifestyle.
4. 62 per cent reported good benefits.
5. 78 per cent reported an enjoyable and supportive environment.

These results represented positive increases in the order of 8–18 per cent from the previous year. Some of the new initiatives launched during this period of time had indeed been very disruptive of the old trust bonds and they challenged the institution. A good example was of this radical approach was the introduction of Family Contracts. Under this contract, two family members could swap shifts to accommodate personal needs. The contract allowed husbands, wives, grandparents, and siblings to job-share and swap shifts without needing to get the prior agreement of the restaurant management team. There was some concern expressed by commentators in the HR press about trusting people so much, but within McDonald's the benefits of doing so were clear: through the introduction of such initiatives, McDonald's was winning employees' trust.

The third precondition concerned the need to establish a baseline of positive employee engagement and involvement. David Fairhurst was convinced that if service-profit chain thinking applied anywhere (see Chapter 9 for an outline of the service-profit chain and its link to employee engagement), it was in the Quick Service Restaurant sector. Most of McDonald's employees are customer-facing and the success of the company rests on how these frontline employees treat the customers. An in-house research project conducted for McDonald's UK by the Centre for Performance-Led HR (Lancaster University Management School) found that customer satisfaction – as measured inversely by the number of customer complaints – was the most significant predictor of sales achieved by a given restaurant. David Fairhurst commented:

> ... What we know, from lots of research, is that the way in which the employees experience the business not only affects the way in which they deliver for that business – so the experience you get as a consumer – but it also impacts the way in which you as a consumer perceive that that employee base is being treated ... it impacts your consumer purchase.

Figure 11.1 shows the model that guides McDonald's thinking behind employee engagement.

Figure 11.1: The service-profit chain at McDonald's

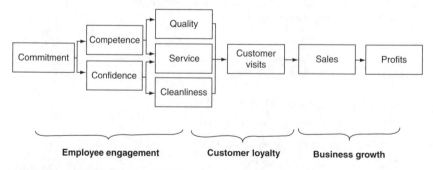

Source: Fairhurst, D. (2008) Am I "bovvered"? Driving a performance culture through to the front line. *Human Resource Management Journal*, 18 (4), 321–326.

Commenting In March 2007, Mark Blundell, HR Operations Director, explained that:

> ... To deliver the Quality, Service and Cleanliness that drives our business, our people need the Competence to deliver and the Confidence to deliver. The reputation programme was aimed at growing employee confidence by getting positive McDonald's stories into the media.

These views are echoed by the hard performance data that McDonald's collects. These data show how the three complaints measures (Quality, Service, and Cleanliness) do indeed sit in between the employee factors and company profits. Whatever the external perception about the hourly paid jobs at McDonald's, internally McDonald's is now very sure how vital these customer-facing frontline employees are for sustainable business performance. David Fairhurst has a realistic view about the role of such data:

> ... We can look for correlations. Now some of it is anecdotal, but the system believes it. I'm not claiming for a minute that the fact that we've had the highest sales in a decade and the fact that we have had excellent sales growth, is all down to HR. But a lot of it, and the business will tell you this, is down to the quality of employee engagement... I've done enough science to prove enough to get the investment. Would I like to go further? Absolutely. But I shall do it bit-by-bit, and be pragmatic and be commercial about how we do things.

Employee engagement management at McDonald's is also guided by their "Insight Map." The Insight Map identifies four areas that contribute to a rewarding job – recognition, respect, citizenship, and growth – and it looks at each of these across three levels – individual, team, and company. McDonald's believe that if an organization can create a sense of fulfillment in each of the resulting 12 "domains" outlined in Figure 11.2, then the individuals within that organization will be

Figure 11.2: McDonald's insight map

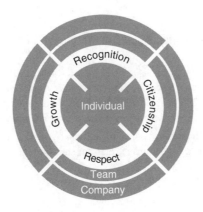

engaged and motivated to perform at their best for that organization because they will have a sense of empathy – a sense that, that "we are in this together."

The work on employee engagement and the adoption of cross-functional teams to improve both the quality of the thought process as well as the focus on internal marketing formed the bedrock on which McDonald's introduced HR practices that helped in sending an internally consistent message of McDonald's as an employer of choice. Their 72,000 employees represented a lot of "word of mouth"!

The fourth precondition was that McDonald's gave much attention to the issue of workplace flexibility. For most of the people who work for McDonald's, the context is a busy customer service environment, which commences trading at around 6:30 in the morning and closes late in the evening. McDonald's expects employees' to take responsibility to deliver on the company's promises to customers throughout the trading day. In return, McDonald's considered that its responsibility is to give its people the flexibility to fulfill their commitments and their aspirations outside of work. In achieving this, McDonald's realized that people need two categories of flexibility – what David Fairhurst calls "inflexible flexibility" and "flexible flexibility." Writing about this in 2007,[12] David Fairhurst explained these as follows:

> ... Some employees need inflexible flexibility to deal with the big, immovable commitments in their lives. Say a parent can drop their child off at school at 08:30, no earlier, and that after dropping the child off at school it takes 15 minutes to get to work. And say that same parent has to collect the child at 15:45. It is clear that the only workable shift lies between 08:45 and 15:30. Even a 08:40 start and a 15:35 finish will not do. No amount of persuasion or incentive will change the situation and as an employer we need to reflect this inflexibility in the hours we offer this individual. Other employees, however, need a completely different kind of flexibility to meet their commitments – flexible flexibility. It could be the varying demands of caring for an elderly relative, or meeting the fluctuating coursework requirements of a university degree. For these employees a rigid framework would be an obstacle rather than an enabler.

As a result an important range of inflexible and flexible programs are available.

Flexible programs currently in place at McDonald's:

1. In 2006 McDonald's introduced a Family Contract which in 2007 received the Working Families Innovation award and became a case study in an Equal Opportunities Commission report. This enabled McDonald's to showcase the initiative at a press launch with the Secretary of State for the Department of Trade and Industry.

2. Rotas are operated according to a weekly schedule system, and published 10 days in advance giving staff the opportunity to plan and request time off according to their needs;

3. In 2006 it launched an online community – called OurLounge.co.uk – cocreated with its employees, and signaling a number of initiatives such as the role of employers in tackling the United Kingdom's basic skills crisis. By 2008, 90 per cent of employees were using this site (from home as well as work) which meant that McDonald's were not simply able to convey corporate messages and business information, but could also use it as the platform for an online scheduling system which enabled staff to review and revise their rotas 24/7 from wherever they happen to be;

4. Parents can work during schools hours with holidays off, while students can work around college and university commitments, often transferring between restaurants during the holidays; and

5. A part-time scheme for restaurant management is available, which retains both the benefits of part-time working and the career benefits of a management position.

So, by enabling both inflexible flexibility and flexible flexibility, McDonald's UK has the potential, within the context of its business needs, to accommodate the non-work commitments and aspirations of all its employees.

The fifth precondition involves education and training. McDonald's is known for the emphasis it places on education and training of it employees and over the past few years, McDonald's UK has been working with the state-sponsored Sector Skills Council to turn its in-house training schemes into nationally recognized qualifications.

As a result, 9,000 will receive GCSE or A-level equivalent qualifications through McDonald's in 2009: 6,000 through the GCSE-level apprenticeship scheme championed by the UK Prime Minister Gordon Brown, and another 3,000 through the company's Shift Management Diploma announced in September 2008.[13] In March 2008, when commenting on the apprenticeship initiative, Jez Langhorn drew attention to the scalability of these programs – a factor that applies to much of their HR strategic thinking in general:

... Apprenticeships are something that we've been working on now for nearly two years, to get to the point where in April 2008 we'll launch a trial Apprenticeship in 80 of our restaurants. For McDonald's, everything is about scalability. When we launch an apprenticeship trial in 80 restaurants, it equates to over 1000 apprentices becoming qualified. Let's put that in context. BT's apprenticeship program, which has been running for 30 years, doesn't achieve 1000 a year. We can, just in our trial of 80 restaurants. When we launch it, there's the potential of us to deliver 10,000 apprentices a year within the next couple of years. We would then be, by far, the biggest provider of apprenticeships in the UK ... [This] gives us great opportunities, but is also a risk, because the quality has to be rigorous.

For McDonald's, the scale (and public visibility) of its HR work, creates a powerful tension. On the one hand, it can represent dangerous water for the organization, but on the other hand, as Jez Langhorn notes, it means:

... There's a big prize to be had for our people in relation to trust as well.

Not only is there an employee-trust dimension to such work, there is also a public-trust issue. The benefit of McDonald's training and education program extends far beyond what the company benefits from it. A recent report on social mobility by Leeds Metropolitan University, commissioned by McDonald's, found that 40 per cent of McDonald's employees had improved their levels of qualification. Almost all (96 per cent) of staff said the skills they gained would be useful for prospective employers in the future. The report concluded:

> ... Giving people the opportunity to learn practical business skills and gain transferable skills which can then be sold to other employers is possibly the most important factor in social mobility, especially when it is offered to those who might not have otherwise had the chance.[14]

The authors also argued that the company is playing a key role in aiding social mobility throughout the United Kingdom, as a result of its decision to actively recruit unemployed people.

The sixth precondition is the existence of relatively democratic planning processes that, in turn, enables "joined up" communication with the workforce through modern social media. McDonald's operates "Plan to Win" meetings as part of it planning process. It has five teams representing five core areas of the business and each of those groups comprises 10 members: a mixture of company employees and franchisees who work collaboratively and contribute to the Plan to Win meetings. In 2008, one of the issues the business wanted the team responsible for People to focus on was pushing knowledge down to employees and giving them a 3-minute conversation about McDonald's, helping to drive their knowledge, because they believe that knowledge drives engagement, which in turn will help the whole business. Jez Langhorn explains how these processes are linked up around the engagement theme, and how OurLounge, for example, operates as a "pull mechanism," pulling employees into the process of engagement:

> ... If you've got a 16 year old crew member who's working a Friday night and a Saturday, while they're doing their A levels to earn a bit of money, how do you engage with them? Things like "OurLounge" have to be fun and engaging, so when they're on there playing fantasy football – which we have 2000 people taking part every week – they're also getting some other messages, or talking about Math and English qualifications. So they're clicking on that, whereas they wouldn't go to those areas on their own. It is a joined up approach.

> ... Part of "OurLounge" has a section called "How About?", where you can make suggestions back to the business, and we reward them with vouchers and cash prizes. We get about 800 suggestions a month from our people, on a whole range of topics. Our Customer Service team filters those for us and they send them to each of the five teams. Anything to do with people will come through [to the HR strategy team] to share amongst the People team. You've got direct

access from a crew member in a store in Glasgow to the corporate office in Finchley in getting something on the agenda of the People team for the next meeting.

Finally, the seventh precondition concerned associated developments in employer branding, achieved mainly through the introduction of online recruitment systems. About 800,000 people a year apply to work for McDonald's in the United Kingdom, and they hire about 1 in 15 of these applicants. This represents a massive branding opportunity. It also means that the organization has to be very good at saying "no" to people. New systems were launched in 2008, designed to help the employer brand and to allow people to research McDonald's more thoroughly than they could do before. When McDonald's moved all of its management recruitment online in February 2008, it found that applications tripled, with no other marketing.

These seven preconditions, taken together, had a very significant impact on trust in McDonald's UK.

11.5. Reflections on the journey toward trust-based HR

Early work on the psychological contract at work gave attention to the nature of "trust" and the "cost of trust deficits."[15] Indeed, Diego Gambetta in his book *Trust: Making and Breaking Cooperative Relationships* defines trust as the specific expectation that the actions from an externality – such as an event, process, individual, group, or system – will be beneficial rather than detrimental.[16] In their contribution to *Trust in organizations: Frontiers of Theory and Research*, Douglas Creed and Raymond Miles argue that trust has three separate elements.

Three different elements to trust:[17]

1. Personal experiences of recurring exchanges creating ongoing expectations and norms of obligation about what is felt to be fair treatment (called *process-based trust*);

2. Beliefs about another's trustworthiness resulting from a perception of their expertise, intentions, actions, words, and general qualities (called *characteristic-based trust*); and

3. Trust in the integrity and competence of informal societal structures (called *institutional-based trust*).

McDonald's has had considerable success in its campaign to correct the misperception and labeling of all low-paid, low-skilled jobs as a McJob. The dictionary might not have changed its definition of the word yet, but McDonald's argues it has emphatically questioned its validity.

Was the strategy a success?

1. When potential job applicants were asked whether they would consider applying to McDonald's for a job, before the campaign, only 22 per cent responded favorably; but it rose to 31 per cent after the campaign.

2. As an indicator of the success of its HR changes and internal communication, the percentage of employees who said they would recommend McDonald's as an employer rose from 51 per cent to 86 per cent.

3. On the YouGov reputation monitor question of "Would you be proud to work for McDonald's," the positive responses rose by 15 per cent.

4. Employee turnover was significantly reduced. The turnover rate of employees is at a 30-year low and is half of the industry average.

5. When the education story broke in the popular press, McDonald's had a 10-point move on the "Brand Buzz" index – something unheard of in recent times.

The HR strategy has also clearly received support from the business. The HR function runs an annual opinion survey amongst franchisee owners, and as Jez Langhorn explains:

> ... The number one people issue for our franchisees, consistently for the last five years, has been them asking McDonald's to improve our employer brand ... Now, in the last two years – we have the highest rated positive response from our franchisees to the question, "McDonald's is working hard to change and improve our employer brand". It is the highest ranked question in terms of positive response, out of any questions about the business.

A year later, the performance improvement was sustained. In March 2008, Jez Langhorn concluded:

> ... Since we started our employee branding work, engagement levels have risen by 10% across the business. They were coming from a fairly high base anyway. You've got internal [opinion] measures [and] operational ones, because we know that engaged employees deliver better Quality, Service and Cleanliness to our customers, which in turn drives frequency of visit, which in turn drives profitability. We don't think that it's coincidental that the turnaround in our UK business, which started two years ago, is linked to our employer branding work. It's not the sole reason, but it's part of how McDonald's has turned around, and is turning around its reputation in the UK ... At the "Retailers' Retailer of the Year" awards – peer nominated by other retail organisations and voted on by them – McDonald's won "Revitalised Brand of the Year ... Business people recognise what the people agenda can add to a business like McDonald's.

The success of the HR strategy used to protect and enhance the company's brand reputation had many facets, but they were built around a common goal: to gain employee trust. Good news about employment in turn impacts customer trust:

... For 2007, the biggest source of positive stories about McDonald's in the UK was, for the first time ever, People. That in turn builds trust with our customers. We measure that through Fast Track, an internal measure we use that speaks to IEO (Informally Eating Out) customers.

As the YouGov monitor shows, employee trust rapidly spills over into trust from other stakeholders – for example, franchisees, customers, and peer organizations. Trust then, though needing to be fundamentally rooted in the employees of the organization, is a multifaceted issue. Again, Jez Langhorn explains:

... If you're looking at a business building trust, there are some very complex arguments about it. For McDonald's it's about our food and, our carbon footprint but it's also [fundamentally] about our people.

Figure 11.3: A model of trust-based HR

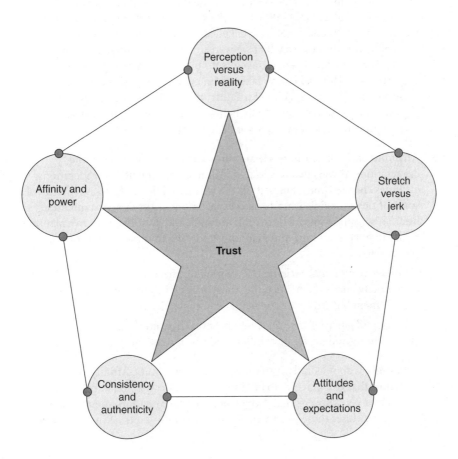

Once HR has mastered the trust agenda amongst employees, it is well placed to contribute thinking to solving the adjacent business trust issues outlined above. The HR strategy at McDonald's has been successful in creating trust in processes, the character of the organization and indeed also within surrounding institutions.

As a final piece of analysis, we ask how has this been achieved? David Fairhurst, through his personal experience in planning and executing this HR strategy, feels that there are five key aspects that are necessary to build a trust-based model of HR delivery (see Figure 11.3).

He articulates the five facets as follows:

1. ***Stretch versus jerk***: For any people strategy to work successfully, HR Directors must ensure that they do not use an intervention that "jerks" the existing work practices too hard; rather, an intervention that "stretches" practices in the desired direction is more likely to succeed. He believes that jerk affects trust, and if the trust is lost, it becomes difficult to regain it:

   > . . . What consumers hate is jerk . . . If you disrupt in that way you spoil the narrative, the trust goes down . . . It's exactly the same on the employment journey . . . We could not have talked about us becoming an education establishment in the way that we were, or about accreditation, three years ago. It would have been outrageous for our staff . . . and our training partners . . . [Instead] we've taken them on a journey of understanding – social mobility, the quality of training, the quality of our values and behaviours – to the point that when we do introduce it, it's seen as a pleasant surprise, but there's a logic to it, there's a story to it.

2. ***Attitudes and expectations***: He also draws attention to attitudes and expectations. Given current social–political–environmental considerations, attitudes change almost annually at the moment. HR needs to keep on top of some of these moving attitudes and expectations as they understand it the best. This again requires HR to look in future and do some proactive planning rather than keep looking and planning according to survey results of yester years.

3. ***Consistency and authenticity***: HR efforts must have a consistency and a feel of authenticity about them. Spending more money will not buy employee commitment but trust, consistency, and authenticity will.

4. ***Affinity and power***: David Fairhurst believes these are the prime drivers of trust. Affinity and power have influenced his strategy. He argues:

   > Affinity is about similarity, familiarity and proximity. Affinity is about people that you perceive to be similar to you, or who you know (or at least feel that you know) – that's why you get celebrity endorsement on adverts. And the closer these people are to you, the more you trust them . . . So we

use the voice and the ambassadorial ability of staff if we're going to tell a people story.

The power dimension, on the other hand, is about perceived control. In a consumer setting, people are more likely to trust businesses that have strong competitors rather than monopolies. Why? Because choice gives the consumer control and, therefore, power. If a supplier doesn't deliver, they can go to a competitor. You don't get that level of control with a monopoly. Similarly, people are more likely to trust the voice of an individual employee than that of a corporation – you can challenge an individual human being, but have less power over a faceless corporation.

5. *Perception versus reality*: Finally, HR Directors have to understand their starting point, understand the journey they need to go on, and be realistic.

> ... In businesses perceived to be better than they really are, HR have a lot of trouble on their hands – because the moment someone takes a close look at what they actually do, they find themselves exposed. The trouble comes because you can't manage reputation – you can't tell people what your reputation is. You can only help them to see the reality. So reputation starts with a principle of inherently doing the right thing, or at least trying to do the right thing – you've got to have an honourable intent [otherwise] you're in real trouble ... transparency will quickly expose you.

11.6. Conclusion

The success of McDonald's corporate reputation work and its subsequent pursuit of a trust-based HR strategy have important lessons for *Leading HR* in two regards:

1. The key skills that HR Directors need to possess to be successful in a business where – as we identified earlier – everyone has a view and

2. New modes of trust-based HR delivery.

For David Fairhurst, HR Directors have to put business first and HR second. Unless business comes first, HR becomes insular and inward looking. Its voice will not be heard. HR Directors also need to be good at marketing, understand brands, understand the media, understand government, and not be frightened of numbers. HR needs an understanding of the societal and institutional mechanisms that exist around their HR strategy and to take responsibility to manage them. In nonunionized work places, HR is the voice of the employees, and therefore should have the ability to win the trust of the employees.

Over and above these skills, HR Directors must exhibit courage, which will energize the whole HR team. They should not be afraid to go for bold HR changes when needed. They have to be confident but not arrogant.

Reflecting on his journey from corporate reputation through to developing trust-based HR, David Fairhurst believes that he had to count on a handful of strategic capabilities in his HR function. He argues that HR needs a number of modes of delivery in order to execute its strategy. Most of the time, when strategies fail, it comes down to how well they were planned and executed. Looking back over the development of HR strategy at McDonald's, he draws attention to six elements that were crucial for the success of his strategy:

1. ***Creating mechanisms to gather meaningful data***: HR needs to be more numerate and to have the ability to constantly monitor the efficacy of its interventions. Data help in giving the function an objective perspective on how things are going and if a course change is needed.

   . . . People think of discipline and think rigid, think military, think strict. I think we've got the discipline that we test things properly and we can scale things quickly. And we plan it, and we integrate it.

2. ***Building disciplines to analyze the data***: Many companies sit on volumes of data without knowing what to do with it. Data collection, and its analysis, should be a part of a preplanned research methodology. A post hoc analysis is more subject to erroneous interpretations and may result in self-fulfilling prophecies.

   . . . A lot of the employee surveys look backwards, they're historic. "Are you paid well? Are you OK about it?" It's functional. They're not about anticipating need and need states . . . A deficit of the function of HR has been a lack of research and a lack of insight. How many HR departments are doing more than a basic employee opinion survey? How many are deploying researchers to segment their employee base, understand their need states, and apply theory, apply innovation, test that innovation, use that discipline again at the back end to provide solutions that are for the future? Not many..

3. ***Be good at telling your story***: This analysis needs to be converted to a good "story" – something that employees look forward to and that external communications can confidently use to enhance the brand reputation.

   . . . It is almost like writing a novel – the story needs to be compelling for people to look forward to the next chapter.

4. ***Breaking down organizational and departmental silos***: HR alone does not have all the required skills set to plan, execute, and analyze a strategy that is touching all parts of the company. It needs partners from other disciplines and work as a team with a common super-ordinate goal. If need be, it must use external expertise to gain a deeper analysis of key issues. So the mindset needs a radical shift from working in silos to working more like an interdisciplinary team, cocreating the strategy and having common ownership for its success.

5. ***Designing early interventions to show results***: One of the big reasons for success of the HR strategy at McDonald's was that early interventions were low cost, but had a visible high impact. "Not bad for a McJob" was one such intervention that had 55-million OTS (Opportunities to See) in the UK media. Such impact creates confidence in the management team and provides the much needed freedom to operate and go for higher cost interventions. This too works on the principle of trust; early success makes the board trust the HR team. David Fairhurst acknowledges:

> ... I needed to make progress, I needed to make sound business cases, and I needed to get [the organisation] to give me resources to work with ... I was conscious every time that if anything I did in the early days didn't pay off, or any big mistakes, then resources would be likely to dry up ... I obviously chose very carefully what my early campaigns were going to be, what my early impacts were. I needed, ideally, low-cost, high-impact in the early days.

6. ***Relying on an air-traffic controller***: Finally, David Fairhurst believes that every HR Director needs to establish a functional position akin to that of an air-traffic controller.

> ... We make sure it's properly air traffic controlled. People would call it "organisational capability" but it's actually a collection of skills you've got ... a master planner ... It is the ability to look at the big picture in a very complex environment. It requires of the person in this position to be in control of a very chaotic situation without losing the rich flavour of its complexity but keeping things in control at all times. At McDonald's it was done by integrating the HR plans in the strategic calendar of the company so that there was a logical sequence in which a given intervention or policy followed the other.

The message for *Leading HR* from McDonald's is that the function does not need to know exactly what the journey will be, but needs to know how to keep the journey smooth, and to plan and design for this. It needs to know what the employee proposition is, what it is strong at, and the gaps in perception that exist. The function has to be quick at understanding the drivers of trust amongst its workforce, how to break down functional silos, and the analytical and operational disciplines that underpin the HR strategy.

NOTES

1 BBC (2007) McDonald's seeks "McJob" rewrite. See: http://news.bbc.co.uk/2/hi/business/6469707.stm Accessed 1 September 2009.

2 Roberts, J. (2004) *The Modern Firm: Organisational Design for Performance and Growth.* Oxford: Oxford University Press. p. 161.

3 Schultz, M., Hatch, M.J. and Larsen, M.H. (2002) *The Expressive Organization: Linking Identity, Reputation and Corporate Brand.* Oxford: Oxford University Press.

4 Miller, J. and Muir, D. (2004) *The Business of Brands*. Chichester: Wiley.

5 Martin, G. and Hetrick, S. (2006) *Corporate Reputations, Branding and People Management: A Strategic Approach to HR*, London: Butterworth-Heinemann.

6 Fombrun, C.J. and Van Riel, C.B.M. (2003) *Fame and Fortune: How Successful Companies Build Winning Reputations*. Upper Saddle River, NJ: Financial Times/Prentice Hall.

7 People Management (2006) Fast Forward. *People Management*, 9 February, pp. 26–31.

8 Fairhurst, D. (2008) Am I "bovvered"? Driving a performance culture through to the front line. *Human Resource Management Journal*, 18 (4), 321–326.

9 Lewis, S. (2003) *Corporate Brand and Corporate Responsibility*, MORI, January 2003.

10 See: http://www.mmu.ac.uk/about/publications/magazines/success/02-success.pdf, p. 8. Accessed 1 September 2009.

11 Fairhurst, D. (2008).

12 Fairhurst, D. (2007). A balanced model for sustainable workplace flexibility: The case of McDonald's. *Development and Learning in Organisation*, 21 (4), 16–19.

13 See: http://women.timesonline.co.uk/tol/life_and_style/women/the_way_we_live/ article5484886. Accessed 1 September 2009.

14 See: http://www.leedsmet.ac.uk/news/index_mrudd_McDonald's.htm. Accessed 1 September 2009.

15 Sparrow, P.R. (1998) New organisational forms, processes, jobs and psychological contracts: Resolving the issues. In P. Sparrow and M. Marchington (eds) *Human Resource Management: The New Agenda*. London: Financial Times Pitman.

16 Gambetta, D. (1988) Can we trust trust? In D. Gambetta (ed.) *Trust: Making and Breaking Co-operative Relationships*. Oxford: Basil Blackwell.

17 Creed, W.E.D. and Miles, R.E. (1996) Trust in organisations: A conceptual framework linking organisational forms, managerial philosophies and the opportunity costs of control. In R.M. Kramer and T.R. Tyler (eds) *Trust in organisations: Frontiers of Theory and Research*. London: Sage.

CHAPTER 12

Vodafone: Creating an HR Architecture for Sustainable Engagement

PAUL SPARROW, SHASHI BALAIN, AND PAUL CHESWORTH

Sustainable engagement

Headline issue:

The organization needs to build an "architecture" of supporting arrangements (policies, frameworks, and decision-making mechanisms) that can sit beneath the employee engagement strategy and be used to help the HR business partners and line managers deliver the results that they believe that they want.

Strategic imperatives:

Spending time with the chief executive officer (CEO) and board members getting a connection with them over the service-profit chain principles.

Cascading these principles into the rest of the organization by tooling HR business partners up with the arguments and building their influencing skills.

Setting up measurement systems on which management understands they will be judged and through which rewards will be impacted.

Employee segmentation: realizing that different categories of employees are looking for and need different things in the employment relationship before they offer discretionary effort. Do the due diligence to understand what the employees' understanding of engagement is and what they really need.

Using a common language framework in the organization so that you can engage employees with the business journey that is involved, and then put people plans in place that can be harnessed together through the use of this common language.

Building mechanisms that enable continuous improvement of the people plans and an ability to improve the capabilities of managers and influence their day-to-day behaviors. The manager makes or breaks your engagement strategy.

Sustainable engagement: (Continued)

Must-win battle:

Getting top-down support matters more than anything else in the engagement space. Unless you have leadership attitudes and behaviors at the top of the organization that are committed to the idea that employees' engagement can drive behaviors that provide a differential experience for your customers, then you are playing at engagement.

12.1. Introduction: The business journey

Vodafone has experienced remarkable growth having become the world's leading mobile telecommunications company within 25 years. In the financial year ending 2008/09, the company reported revenue of £41.0 billion, a 15.6 per cent increase over the previous financial year. Its proportionate customer base stood at 303 million, again an increase of 25 per cent over the previous year. During this rapid rise Vodafone has moved from being a conglomerate of acquisitions toward the formation of a singular identity – that of "One Vodafone." Much can be learned from the way in which it has managed its employee engagement strategy to sustain the rapid change and growth that have become the hallmark of recent years. We argue that:

The key messages that emerge from this chapter

1) In periods of relative stability, the challenge for HR is to provide the organization with an HR strategy that helps "future-proof" change (long-term investments designed to harness people's discretionary effort) by taking proactive steps to prepare for inevitable changes that lie in future. Time can be used to build identification with long-term strategic goals and a commitment to achieve immediate performance targets.

2) There needs to be a philosophy that ties key parts of the HR delivery model (in this case the design of Centers of Excellence/Expertise) to core business processes (in this case the logic was based around customer touchpoints, in other instances it might be the innovation process, etc.).

3) Organizations might underpin their engagement strategies with a common service-profit chain logic, but find unique ways of expressing the performance linkages and understand a simple "service-profit chain" logic cannot be applied to all business units – in many units it is best driven more by a logic of improving the business process, driving-up efficiency, and promoting innovation rather than generating pure profits.

4) Engagement can and should be used as a strategy for internal marketing, rather than one just for performance enhancement. In a business environment that requires rapid changes and a need for employees to accept and adapt to these new requirements, senior managers must first put effort into building business engagement with the strategy – and only then ask employees to engage.

5) The real value of designing HR around engagement is the necessary focus this creates around line manager and business engagement. This prior process of business engagement (educating the business about the ways in which people add value to the strategy and how engagement leads to business performance) is necessary before any engagement can be induced – a necessary condition.

6) HR has to put in place an "architecture" – a structure, systems, and processes – that enables this linkage. Business partner structures are another necessary condition. The protocols used to determine the relative power and information flows across the HR delivery model are crucially important. Engagement thinking can serve as a logic to explain how the elements of an HR delivery model (Centers of Excellence/Expertise, business partners, and service centers) must be tied together.

7) Engagement may therefore serve as important a role for the benefit of HR and design of its delivery systems, as it serves for the experience of employees.

8) Employee engagement is not a culture-free phenomenon. It means different things for employees in different countries, and execution plans have to be flexible enough to recognize and accommodate these differences. Vodafone estimates that around 85 per cent of the engagement drivers were local by nature, and only 15 per cent of the drivers had a global application.

9) Employee segments exist across various dimensions such as cultural dimensions of the operations that employees are involved with. There are different drivers for engagement not just across different operating companies and their national boundaries, but also within national boundaries but across different business units.

10) An engagement thought process transfers into global functions (i.e., it is not only relevant to directly customer-interfacing roles or business functions). However, complex internal structures mean that in practice any one organization might have dozens of different internal engagement models (i.e., the specific link between particular employee attitudes and performance works through multiple variations).

11) Engagement is fundamentally about trust in leadership – to work in synchronization with top leadership both the HR function and people at large need accurate and real-time information about how the line feels about the new initiatives.

12) As important as the measurement and targeting around engagement are the supporting elements (in this case engagement champions) that serve as a crucial link in establishing a two-way interaction between the leadership team and the line. These are politically difficult and very skill-dependent roles that serve a proxy organization development purpose.

13) Trust in leadership is the first casualty of rapid change. Important preconditions for engagement are clear lines of communication and employee involvement mechanisms in the good times that act as prechange "HR investments" that break down the internal barriers to identification with the business strategy.

Currently, the company employs over 72,000 people worldwide, and its recruitment strategy aims to develop and retain the most talented, motivated people aligned with the Vodafone brand essence. The goal is to provide a productive and safe working environment, treat people with respect, and offer attractive performance-based incentive opportunities.[1]

Vodafone has consolidated its presence in mature markets and expanded to emerging markets of Asia and Africa. It has three customer segments (Enterprise, wholesale, and individual consumers) and operates in four product areas (mobile voice, mobile data, specialist products for customers, and mobile solutions for organizational clients). It has five key strategic objectives: cost reduction and revenue stimulation in Europe; delivering strong growth in emerging markets; innovating and delivering on their customers' total communications needs; actively manage its portfolio to maximize return; and align capital structure and shareholder returns policy to strategy. There are no transformational changes in Vodafone's business model, but a general level of fluidity is necessary because it is highly susceptible to four forces: changes in technology; new entrants in the competition (such a providers of fixed-line services, or providers of other services such as VoIP); changes in regulations; and an increasingly aware, discerning, and a demanding customer with lots of options. Summarizing what this fluidity means, Matthew Brearley, the current HR Director UK, observed in 2009:[2]

> . . . The company's purpose of pioneering "connected living" for customers extends to its own people. That leads to a lot of work around embedding our brand values right across the organisation – to getting everybody to live and breathe those values.

This chapter melds together two strategic journeys within Vodafone:

1. Their adoption of an approach to employee engagement, originally within the UK business but then later broadened into a global strategy.

2. The relevance of – and management of – employee engagement as part of the global business transformation process.

Both stories provide invaluable lessons about *Leading HR*.

12.2. The one Vodafone transformation

Back in 2003, Vodafone was growing very rapidly and faced a positive business environment. Senior managers had much freedom and there was money to play with in the system. The environment was very entrepreneurial, with unlimited growth opportunities, and managers could develop the business and their careers at the rapid pace they wanted. However, senior management was conscious that this growth – through acquisitions and mergers – would not last forever. Sixteen core independent national operating companies looked more like a conglomerate of acquisitions rather than one company with a single identity and a common way of doing things. It was time for some serious changes.

Vodafone embarked on a "transformational journey." In October 2003, it launched a 5-year program called *One Vodafone* a key concept of which was the philosophy that you "*design once, deploy many times.*" This meant a shift in coordination and control. The design and architecting of core enabling systems,

Figure 12.1: The one Vodafone program

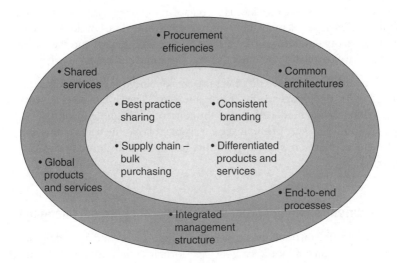

Source: Vodafone Analyst & Investor Day, 19 September 2005. Presentation by Andy Halford, CFO.

technologies, and business processes (see Figure 12.1) would be undertaken centrally and rolled out to multiple geographies. This would save on duplication of development costs in each country and ensure global consistency of products, services, and brand experience. Formerly separate companies would plan, buy, and operate as a single unit – a dramatic change from the past. It was an integration program spanning 16 countries, each with diverse people and markets.

Vodafone's scope for global economies of scale was compelling, but so were the HR challenges of such a transformation. Huge cultural and behavioral changes were necessary in order to realize a successful organizational transformation.

12.3. Leading the original UK engagement journey

Where did the engagement journey begin? As we begin the story in the United Kingdom, be aware that this global dimension was ever-present. In 2004, Paul Chesworth, now the HR Director Europe, had just joined Vodafone UK as its HR Director. He inherited a rapidly growing organization, but one with stable HR policies and practices. At that time there was no huge change agenda in Vodafone UK. The company was growing at a frantic pace with new acquisitions and mergers across the globe. The challenge, he felt, was to provide the organization with the basis of an HR strategy that would help "future-proof" it against the need to execute significant and ongoing business changes. He decided it was a good time to take some proactive steps on the people strategy in order to be prepared for the inevitable changes that lay in future. From the vantage point of 2009, Paul Chesworth recalled the challenge he faced in 2004 as follows:

> . . . We established a people agenda for the organisation focussed almost exclusively on driving differential levels of employee engagement. Vodafone UK at that time had some excellent HR policies and practices across the business, but we needed to assemble them into a really compelling employee proposition. Our overriding mantra was the service profit chain concept and the criticality of the positive correlation between our employee and customer experience .

The UK board and the new HR Director were convinced that there was a need for a more holistic people agenda for the organization. They established the Group's future HR operating model aligned to the concept of "High Performing Organization." The issue of employee engagement lay at the heart of this new HR thinking. The intention was to drive future business results through engaging their employees.

12.4. Vodafone's thought process and general approach to engagement

Vodafone had already developed considerable expertise at understanding their customers. As a part of monitoring their performance they utilized the concept of customer touchpoints, things about the customers that their research showed must be managed well to have a satisfied and loyal customer. Touchpoints had much in common with the ideas expressed back in the 1980s by Jan Carlson of SAS fame, who argued that there were "moments of truth" in the customer relationship where "thin slices of behavior" on behalf of the organization made the difference between a very poor or very good perception of service.

Using service-profit chain logic and thinking about these customer management concepts, Paul Chesworth came up with the idea of *employee touchpoints.*" The intention was to treat the employee as an internal customer and to see what needed to be done to have an engaged workforce. What he wanted employees to engage with was Vodafone's strategic long-term goals and a commitment to achieve the immediate performance targets.

> . . . We basically stole the idea from our marketing colleagues! Vodafone understandably is obsessive about the quality of our overall customer experience and when we think about our customers we think about the things we've got to get right in the form of "touch points". The customer touchpoints include things like the quality of our sales experience, our handsets, our network, our customer support services etc . . . So in the spirit of the service profit chain we decided to apply the terminology to our people experience and introduced the concept of "employee touch points." We then built our people strategy around the things we felt we needed to do to enhance our employee experience around the areas the company "touched" our people. We created six core touchpoints covering; the way we design and develop our organisation structures and job roles; the way we resource the structures, the way we grow and develop our people; the way we communicate and connect them to the business; the way we reward and recognise the contribution they make, and finally the quality of the working environment we provide for them.

These touchpoints represented a common language framework that could be used to hone the arguments to each different business and employee segment. Paul's HR team was clear that such an initiative – though driven from the top – had to start from the bottom up. In November 2005 a highly consultative process was put in place to design the Vodafone People Strategy (VPS), the driving principle of which was to arrive at a "deal" that had two sides:

1. The employee aspirations from Vodafone and
2. Vodafone's commitment to fulfill those aspirations.

The expectation was that if Vodafone kept their side of the deal and lived up to employee aspirations, employees would raise their game and fulfill their side of the deal by delivering the performance expected of them (see Chapter 9 for an outline of three different engagement strategies). The consultative process came up with a tangible goal of catapulting Vodafone UK into the top 25 per cent of comparable companies in terms of employee engagement.

12.5. Six employee touchpoints

Six employee touchpoints were identified as the drivers of the new employee deal, all reflecting the employees' relationship with Vodafone as an employer. From an HR perspective they could also be considered as six key HR practices that most influenced employee engagement at Vodafone. They are shown in Table 12.1.

The assumption was that Vodafone had to make a long-term investment, designed to harness their people's discretionary effort – the extra they can give if inspired to do so – making the difference to Vodafone's business performance.

Table 12.1: Employee touchpoints at Vodafone

Employee touchpoint	Realization
Organization and change	The employees expect from Vodafone that their roles and goals are clear; they had a clear sense of who their customers are; and that they understood the organizational changes as they occurred.
Resourcing	The job at Vodafone is attractive and there is enough internal progression to ensure a challenging career; employees expect the organization to support them as they change their roles or even when they leave the organization.
Communication and involvement	Employees aspire to be able to talk positively and confidently about the business and feel that their voice is heard and acted upon; also, it is easy to find out what employees need to know to perform at their best.
Learning and development	Employees expect to receive a regular feedback on their performance and aspire that the company will provide them the required training to continually improve their skills and realize their potential.

Table 12.1: (Continued)

Employee touchpoint	Realization
Reward and recognition	Employees expect the company to value their contribution and believe that the company recognizes their efforts through equitable rewards.
Safety, health, and well-being	Employees believe that Vodafone cares about their well-being and provides every possible support to promote a healthy lifestyle

Figure 12.2 shows the logic, which is embedded in service-profit chain thinking (see Chapter 9):

Figure 12.2: Service-profit chain thinking at Vodafone

12.6. Business partnering: A necessary condition

The thought process around employee engagement subsequently led to more sophisticated HR thinking within Vodafone UK and a fundamental transformation of the internal HR capability of the group. This new HR thinking could only be implemented through their line managers. In 2009, looking back on the changes that took place earlier, Matthew Brearley (now Director, Human Resources and Property, Vodafone UK, but in 2004 the lead HR Business Partner within the business who had come from an HR background in retail), pointed out:

> ... One of the fundamental principles was that line managers have to take accountability and we have to build line manager capability because the culture of the business is fundamentally built around the team ... employee experience is largely influenced by the local team leader or manager.

A major consequence of implementing the engagement strategy was the need to educate the business about what Vodafone really meant by engagement. The HR team was clear from the outset that the six drivers, by themselves, would not drive engagement. The line's capability to deliver locally on the six drivers was the only way to induce engagement within the employees. Only then would engagement translate into performance. So HR had to put in place an "architecture" – a structure, systems, and processes – that would enable the line to manage the touchpoints effectively.

To carry out the plan effectively, the first piece of the jigsaw for the HR function was to change their operating structure. Vodafone moved to a "three box" operating model (see Chapters 2 and 3 on HR structure and the approach to delivery models at Nestlé). Many organizations have struggled to execute this model, but at Vodafone, it has operated successfully, and has been key to the subsequent engagement strategy working effectively.

Back in 2007, Paul Chesworth had a clear view about how each "box" had to operate, and how the logic that tied each box together was driven by engagement thinking. As a starting point, Centers of Excellence (COEs) were formed around each of the six key touchpoints. These COEs had all the expertise that the line needed to know about their respective subject domain to be able to make sure that right policies, practices, and process were in place.

Besides these COEs, there was an HR Director in each operating company, supported by generalist HR practitioners who now operated as *business partners*. The Business partner was the prime contact between the customer base/leadership team. The COEs would never make contact with the customer base/leadership team without the approval of its business partner. The role of the business partners was to work with the people managers in the key areas to deliver the end-to-end requirements of the customer base. The new HR structure played a key role in enhancing the capability of the HR team. The business partners had a more enriched job role and were the all-important lynch pins between the line-managers and the COEs. They worked closely with the line-managers, understood their unique problems, and sought solutions to these problems from the COEs. As Paul explained it back in 2007:

> ... In essence the role of the HR Business Partner is to create and ensure execution of an impactful people plan designed to positively move the employee engagement dial. They are structured around the six touch-points but comprise people initiatives tailored to the requirements of any given part of the business. The bespoke nature of the plans is crucial as a compelling employee experience for our retail staff can look very different to the one preferred by our network technicians. Progress against the plans is measured through quarterly employee surveys which provide a very effective ongoing "pulse check".

As the success of the business partners rested on the advice given to them by the COEs, the COEs needed to be real experts in their fields. Again, Paul explained his thinking as follows:

> ... Our HR Centres of Expertise have a real obligation to ensure that the the policies, practices and processes within their "employee touchpoint"

remain leading edge. Where changes are necessary they need to be able to work collaboratively with the HR Business Partner population to make necessary improvements through the People Plan initiatives. I very much see the COE's as being key to the health of the current and future policies and practices within their domain area.

The COEs, along with the HR business partners, were then a significant "capability multiplier" for the HR function at Vodafone UK.

HR agendas, based on the six key employee touchpoints, were produced on an annual basis. The HR Directors would sit with the COEs to outline their views of what improvements, initiatives, and issues needed their attention over the next 12 months. The impact of the HR interventions on the customer base was benchmarked to audit the efficacy of the HR interventions. This was all pulled into a project plan with timelines.

The new VPS was a runaway success. Employee surveys showed significant improvement in engagement levels for Vodafone UK. Employee engagement went up from 69 per cent in October 2007 to 73 per cent in November 2008.

12.7. Initiating the Global Vodafone People Strategy: A common employee engagement strategy across one Vodafone

Encouraged by their early results, it was decided to roll-out the new VPS for Vodafone globally. This was a new game, with different challenges. HR at Vodafone UK could already articulate some important learning points from the original exercise that would prove valuable as they extended the UK employee strategy on a global basis.

1. *Employees as internal customers*: Treating the employee as an internal customer worked. The employee touchpoints had resonated very well with Vodafone employees. The word "touchpoint" had very high credibility. Employees knew the organization took customer touchpoints seriously, and they expected the same level of seriousness from the leadership to be given to "employee touchpoints." Employees did not perceive it as another fad or fashion. Vodafone convinced employees about the leadership's seriousness to enhance the employees' work experience through these touchpoints.

2. *HR function redesign*: Though there is much debate on the efficacy of the three box HR structure (see Chapter 2), it had worked very well for Vodafone UK. Vodafone did not frame its HR policy to suit the three-box model; rather, the three-box model was customized and implemented as needed for the success of its new HR strategy.

3. *Engagement strategy as a part of people strategy*: Though employee engagement had figured prominently in Vodafone's new HR thinking, employee engagement was not a stand-alone strategy. The HR team realized that for engagement strategy to work a host of other people factors needed to

be taken care of. It is important to identify what other people or policy issues need to be considered before employee engagement strategy is
rolled out.

Parallel to the engagement story of Vodafone UK, other significant changes were happening, all with significant HR implications not only for Vodafone UK but the whole of Vodafone. Changes at a global level proved invaluable when the Global VPS was rolled out. As Paul recalls:

> ... within Vodafone UK we had great success on this in the first couple of years, but also benefitted from a great deal of learning which we were able to leverage in the development of the Global People Strategy.

Vodafone UK had implemented the employee engagement strategy very successfully. Encouraged by the good results on the engagement index, plans were made to roll it out globally.

Vodafone's HR framework:

1. *Vodafone People Strategy Framework:* The global plan flowed from the VPS framework of six employee touchpoints that had been implemented and tested on Vodafone UK.

2. *Global Annual People Plan:* By November each year, a global annual people plan is prepared, structured around the VPS. It incorporated:

    a. The definitions of the prioritized global/regional initiatives for the coming year
    b. The definition of the key global/regional operational activities that will be the focus of the year ahead

3. *Local Annual People Plan:* Each Global Function, Region, and Operating Company (OpCo) leadership team is required to create their own local annual people plan by March each year, using the VPS template, which

    a. defines the implementation of global/regional initiatives and operational activities;
    b. defines key local initiatives and operational activities that will be the focus of the year ahead, designed to support the local business objectives and drive local employee engagement; and
    c. defines the employee engagement target the leadership team will work toward during the year, based on their goal of being upper quartile in their local market for employee engagement.

4. *Operational People Calendar:* Each Global Function, Region, and OpCo also designs an Operational People Calendar for all people managers. This articulates the annual schedule of operational people management activities to be executed during the year that support the achievement of the local employee engagement target.

The strategy had taken full cognizance of the fact that employee engagement was not a culture free phenomenon. It means different things for employees in different countries, and the plan had to be flexible enough to recognize and accommodate these differences. For Paul Chesworth, it was important that:

> ... We wanted to stay specific enough to articulate a common global employee proposition but stay generic enough for the those commitments from the employee and the employer side to translate, and be understandable across the 28 different cultures.

12.8. Developing intelligent global targets

Keeping in mind such differences across its various operating companies, the HR team created international working groups around each of the touchpoints; their task was to identify local and global drivers against each of the touchpoints on an ongoing basis. So not only there was a realization that there were different local and global drivers against each touchpoint, there was also the knowledge that these drivers tend to change from time to time and therefore needed regular monitoring.

To put the Global VPS in motion six two-and-a-half-day workshops were conducted. Every workshop began with a business update from the global strategy director. He would provide inputs like where Vodafone was competitive, what the business issues were, and where the organization was heading. The results from latest Vodafone Employee Survey (VES) were discussed and key issues identified. The drivers of each of the six employee touchpoints were discussed for each of the 28 countries. Paul Chesworth estimates that around 85 per cent of the drivers were local by nature an only 15 per cent of the drivers had a global application.

In initiating the engagement benchmarking, Vodafone took a pragmatic approach to targeted engagement improvements. Back in 2007, Paul explained his thinking this way:

> ... We have varying levels of employee engagement across our operating companies and culture clearly plays a part as over the last two years, the employee engagement index OpCo league table has tended to remain static. We are typically just outside upper quartile in most of our operating companies against the local benchmark, so 3–5 index points increase over the next couple of years would no doubt get us into the upper quartile. What we need to do now is intelligently determine what our short term targets are in each of our markets.

The question was how to establish intelligent targets. Simply asking for a 3- to 5-point index increase everywhere would not work. Paul explained:

> ... We're sitting down with our HRDs to do this. For example in Germany, our business will experience a significant amount of restructurings, so if you sit 5% lower than the national average in terms of engagement is it realistic to ask if this can be improved by 3% over the next twelve months? We will get a weighted average of the targets for each of our operating companies to ensure we have an

intelligent global figure. The bulk of the engagement levers are found locally, so it's very much about the local HRD being accountable for establishing and executing an impactful, locally tailored people plan and hopefully watching the results come through. It's an exciting way of operating and we have a great deal of (on the whole) healthy competition between the operating companies! .

The workshops provided what we would call "intelligent" local people plans. They also allowed the Opcos to design how their respective VES needed to be worded and measured. This resulted in a scorecard to measure the VPS that was benchmarked against the par engagement scores of high performance companies in their respective countries.

Looking back, it is clear that the planning workshops were of huge practical utility. They brought local intelligence into target setting for the engagement scores. Vodafone understood it was irrelevant to set global benchmarks, as there was significant difference in the drivers of engagement across various OpCos.

Another significant development was that the Vodafone survey slowly moved from being just an attitude survey to it now being a "Manager Index" (to measure line manager's performance). Work at Vodafone UK had shown that line managers were the key to implementing any people plan. The survey gave due prominence to this thinking, making the VES a more sophisticated tool in which the scores were a direct reflection of the OpCo's performance.

12.9. Globalization and organizational restructuring at Vodafone: A tough test for engagement thinking

We now develop a "case within a case" – the situation at Global Technology (GT) – to show how Vodafone's engagement thinking found broader global applicability.
We have chosen to examine events at GT for three key reasons:

1. As a function, it lay at the heart of changes triggered by the globalization process within Vodafone. Could engagement thinking help manage the strategic challenges it faced?

2. For Vodafone, using engagement thinking in a central global function created a new challenge. The organization had developed a sophistication in the approach within its UK Operating Company, but more than half of this OpCo's employees were directly customer-facing. Would the thought process transfer into a central global function, that interfaced mainly with internal customers and business-to-business networks?

3. By definition, lying at the heart at the transformation process, GT had to undergo difficult business changes, involving much redefinition of roles and rationalization. Could the approach to engagement operate in tough environments?

In order to understand how a global employee engagement strategy can work effectively, we now have to step back in time. There were inside Vodafone business changes taking place that meant that the performance of a number of central global functions was becoming both more visible and strategically relevant. Before the employee engagement strategy in the United Kingdom had gathered a head of steam, and certainly before Vodafone began to "export" its engagement philosophy on a wider geographical basis, important change initiatives were put in place. What happens in practice, as in so many organizations, is that one independent and apparently parallel strategic journey – in this case the globalization of Vodafone – ends up converging with another strategic journey – the touchpoints engagement strategy. No longer parallel, there is a point at which the two change processes suddenly become melded into a single test of HR's thinking.

GT is a key operation that was centralized as part of Vodafone's transformation program. It is responsible for all aspects of Vodafone's network, IT capability, Research and Development, and supply chain management. As Detlef Schultz, Global Supply Chain Management Director and CEO Vodafone Procurement Company Sarl, explains:

> ... In 2003 Vodafone decided to establish a function which was called global supply chain management. This was done because through the acquisitions, we had grown so much that there was a chance to take advantage of all the global scale and scope. Hence, this function was incorporated ... What we did back then is we started to establish some groundwork, and put the basic tools in place, which we didn't have, one of which was a spent analysis. We incorporated a spent analysis tool, which then gave us transparency about where we spent the money, with whom and by which operating company. We had never had this before. So suddenly you could add value and say, did you guys know that this supplier is the largest, or that is the third one, or this supplier does most of the business with that company ... The second thing we incorporated in 2004 was supply performance management. With that we gave the operating companies the lead function for some suppliers, and we incorporated global framework agreements, which provided a benefit for the operating company.

Through the centralization of functions such as GT (Global supply chain being one part of GT) and Global marketing, Vodafone could add value to the company. But this was not to be without its problems. The roles of people were changing and so too were the lines of reporting. Employee teams in these global functions were spread across the globe and had a totally different command and control structure compared to their compatriots in their respective OpCos. The changeover was not a smooth one. As Gianluca Ventura (the HR and Organization Director for Vodafone) recalls:

> ... Technology was moving (away) from being a central driving function of the company ... Now network coverage was the real issue. Some people started to ask "are we as important as we were in the past"? ... There was a little bit of general de-motivation and disengagement.

12.10. The employee engagement strategy at the global technology function

In September 2006, Stephen Pusey joined Vodafone as the Global Chief Technology Officer (CTO). He realized there was a lack of proper communication between the operating companies and what he called "the group in the middle," that is, a global function like Global Technology. The employee survey results for 2007 shocked the management team at Global Technology. From a very healthy engagement index of 71 in 2005, it had fallen to 53.5 by 2007.

This provided the organization with a wake-up call. Steve Pusey commented on the dilemma that people in global functions faced at the time – a sentiment expressed by most organizations as they globalize and learn how best to centralize and decentralize decision-making, coordination, and control:

> . . . We (employees in global functions) were very frustrated and de-motivated because the people in the middle felt that everything I tried to do [could be] blocked from shaping up. People in the operating companies felt "look at those idiots just meddling with what I do, you are better off without them!"

What did Vodafone decide had to be done? They had the historical success of Vodafone UK's employee engagement strategy. They believed the adoption of this thinking on a global scale, and especially within the GT business, could provide the solution to the turmoil that employees were experiencing.

Steve felt very strongly about the importance of employee engagement, but for him an employee engagement strategy was best run by the people and for the people. He was convinced that for the engagement strategy to work at a GT it had to be built through a bottom-up approach:

> . . . I always say . . . two ears and one mouth. If you listen to people they will tell you what they are looking for, if you listen hard enough.

The 2007 employee survey had highlighted some key concerns. For instance, trust in the leadership team was extremely low, although strangely trust in one's line manager was high! Steve surmised that the message was:

> . . . My manager is protecting me but my leaders are working against me.

The leadership knew what needed to be done, but the key issue was how to do it. Employee trust in its leadership had been lost. However, to regain it would be far from simple. Stephen Pusey decided it was time for a hands-on approach.

Steve identified the following core problems for immediate attention:

1. He needed constant feedback from the employees on his engagement strategy – once a year annual survey was too distant for immediate actions. The feedback needed to be more elaborate, qualitative, and rich, rather than just quantitative numbers.

2. There was a need to involve people from the line to work in synchronization with top leadership – people who had more accurate and real-time information on how the line was feeling about the new initiatives.

3. The leadership had not only to buy-in to the new strategy, but had to make an effort to convince everyone that it was their top agenda and was not just "eyewash."

With issues in mind, Steve Pusey launched a range of initiatives.

The first was the Pulse Group. He initiated another survey. This time, however, the focus of analysis was on the verbatim comments that employees gave, rather than the actual engagement scores. The idea was to identify what exactly had gone wrong, and then put in motion appropriate corrective measures. He hand-picked a working group to manage these data and provide oversight to the change process. This was called the Pulse Group, whose role was to conduct pulse surveys. Unlike the annual Vodafone People Survey, the Pulse Survey was short and targeted, taking the employee pulse on key issues at regular intervals. The Pulse Group was used to tackle the most difficult, emotional, or worst scores – anything from "we don't understand our strategy" to "you don't communicate enough" – and to establish tangible actions against them.

The second was Engagement Champions. The GT leadership also put in place a team of people who acted as the "engagement champions." This group had two roles:

1. to feedback to the leadership team on how the interventions to improve employee engagement were being viewed by employees, and what their *real* concerns were (the concerns that likely triggered their survey answers) and

2. to play the role of an ambassador in their own teams for engagement matters.

They served as a crucial link in establishing a two-way interaction between the leadership team and the line below. But the leadership team put much effort into listening and addressing the concerns of the employees. The leadership needed to win back employee trust, and was being seen to leave no stone unturned to do so. Engagement champions were proud of their job; their voices were not just being heard, they were promptly acted upon. Like change champions, they were key to the success. They enriched the bottom-up information, a process much needed during the initial stages of any strategic intervention. As Sam Hoblyn (the Business Partner, Vodafone Information Services) comments:

> ... They were going back into their business, helping the managers with their own results and briefing but getting the data about what's going on and feeding it back through to Gianluca, into the team that was providing some colour to the various results. Interestingly, their role has continued to develop so there they were, very hands on, literally taking the survey results to the manager and saying, go on then, what are you and I going to do about this?

Being an engagement champion was not an easy task. Though some volunteered, others were picked by managers. At times they felt like the "jam in a sandwich" – squeezed from both ends. The Champions did not have an easy role. Judi Grant-Johnston, one of the GT Engagement Champions, recalls that the reason why the scores in GT were so low (i.e., when they had fallen back to around the 50 per cent mark) was that there was a basic fear around job insecurity. When the new team came in, this fear slowly subsided – the new team rotated people more and avoided the need for any mass rationalization – but there were still important issues to solve. The 50 per cent score was also an average – scores were very variable at business unit level – from teams that had almost zero scores to teams that were very positive. The engagement strategy had both a strong top-down element to it, but had suddenly switched to a bottom-up "you solve it" approach. In dealing with pressures from both directions, the Engagement Champions had to make sure they did not miss the "hard to move" issues, that is, everyone would just go for "low-hanging fruit." They knew too that some managers would be instrumental, either thinking "get my scores moved up, but *you* do what it takes to move the scores and figure it out *for me*," or thinking "please keep this away from me!" In many instances, the managers or leaders may be part of the problem. No one was incentivized to deal with the perennial and more thorny problems – so they had to make sure these key issues were not ignored. Equipping the Champions for their role was a mission-critical task.

The third cornerstone of success was visible leadership and visible action. As a personal initiative, Stephen Pusey ensured that he did not let his engagement champions down. In the first year of intervention he personally attended big town hall employee events to let employees and engagement champions know that he cared for the issues. In the second year he became more subtle. He remained a visible leader, but one with a hands on approach. He met employees in smaller groups of around 50 people to get close and more intimate with people down the line to assure them that their concerns were being met.

Was this, however, just a glorified change communication exercise? We believe not. The processes put in place enabled the GT leadership team to break the information it gathered around employee engagement into tangible interventions. Steve implemented his engagement agenda as follows:

> . . . I broke the strategy down into tangibles, that what you could touch and then I used the working groups to come to me with recommendations for change, and got the management to endorse them . . . Then I would get on the road and endorse it.

Visible leadership and visible action were both quintessential ingredients.

12.11. Communication, trust, and identification

For the employee engagement strategy to work so well at GT Vodafone, a number of things had to be handled effectively. The leadership's commitment to the cause and its belief that such a strategy works best though a bottom-up approach had obvious benefits. The most critical lessons are as follows.

First, there were clear lines of communication. All the information gathered through the surveys and fed up and down the management structures by the engagement champions created a proper and direct channel of communication. This eliminated the grapevines that might otherwise have become established. The engagement champions had all the relevant information that had importance for employees, with this information coming directly from the leadership team. This not only gave the engagement champions a lot of credibility, but helped address key employee issues in a short time. The time gained through these clear lines of communication helped reinforce the employees' belief that changes at their workplace were a direct result of their suggestions. They had a feeling of instrumentality over their own work environment.

Second, in organizational change, they recognized the importance of having people on board. Employees had therefore internally accepted the changes being carried out in their functions. As Gianluca Ventura points out:

> ... In the end, the measure of the success of the program, was our capability to deliver change in a measureable way – having people on board.

This employee involvement was the first step toward employee engagement; the engagement strategy ensured that GT did not leave the people out of the business equation.

Third, there was trust in leadership. This had been the first casualty in the rapid changes being carried out within GT at Vodafone. The engagement strategy was successful in restoring that trust. In Stephen Pusey's words:

> ... You have to pick the honest brokers to be your transients – which are the employees themselves. If you can get them to look at the problems, pull these problems out, champion them, [then instead of] giving you all the rubbish that goes with [the problems generated by major change processes] instead we got a "here was the problem, you have got to tackle it" approach.

The leadership believed that it was the employer's responsibility to convince the employee that they cared about them. The surveys validated this – they showed that the leadership had done a good job in improving their scores on trust and care.

Fourth, time was taken breaking down the barriers of identity. One of the most difficult issues faced by the GT function was that it had a workforce of around 2,000 employees, across 7 nationalities. The new employee engagement initiatives brought a feeling of community among this multicultural group. They were successful in implementing joint programs with teams from a range of nationalities and were largely successful in breaking down the barriers of identity between the operating company and the centrally managed GT group. This had hugely positive implications for the VPS.

HR had understood that for their strategy to succeed at the global level, they needed to consider engagement as a culturally loaded construct. It needed sensitive cultural interpretation, provided by a culturally diverse team drawn from various nationalities that Vodafone operated in.

In the final analysis, the proof of success is in the end results. Did the effort and initiatives pay-off resulting in improved engagement scores? Let us take a look at the scores that were announced in October 2008. Steve Correa, HRD-Global technology confirms:

> . . . Our overall Engagement scores improved by 5% basis points from 64 to 69. In addition our Manager's index moved 6% basis points from 63 to 69.

Equally important to note was that with the exception of one OpCo (partly explained by ongoing restructuring) all OpCo's had either sustained and in most cases significantly improved on both Engagement and Manager's index. Analyzing the results in GT Steve Correa comments

> . . . The results show that there is a significant increase in employee's understanding of our strategic direction as well as increased confidence in the leadership team. Another clear message was that employee's recognised that we are in a changing environment, and that they feel that we are getting better at supporting them through change. We have also been seen to be improving in team working and collaboration as well as in attracting, developing and retaining our people. The improved results are a direct result of the efforts invested by line managers, the HR team across Opcos, the critical roles played by the engagement champions and increased communications.

Looking ahead, he comments,

> . . . In the past year, Vodafone Technology has embarked on a Global Technology Transformation programme that will dramatically alter the platform architecture and positively influence the way our end Customers will engage with each other. This will mean significant changes internally, in the way we think, act and work with each other We achieve the business benefits of change through ensuring our people understand the need for change, are engaged and committed to its success and are treated with dignity and respect throughout. In this, employee engagement is key.

12.12. Conclusions

Vodafone has established a sound case for employee engagement as an instrument for improving business unit performance. As with all the cases in this book, the story does not end where the case ends. The future holds challenges that will test even the most recent lessons. This is especially relevant for an organization like Vodafone, which is still under considerable pressure to change, as a consequence of being in the technology business. Vodafone will need to continually reinvent itself and the way it does its business – adopt fluid business models. Vodafone has learnt that an engaged workforce is a prerequisite for a successful business change. This fact has sunk in well throughout Vodafone's hierarchy, and engagement scores continue to be monitored closely and regularly.

Looking across the two journeys that Vodafone has been on – formulating and maturing their employee engagement strategy within a lead OpCo such as the United Kingdom and then applying the strategy across global businesses – we believe four important learning points serve as key conclusions:

1. The role of employee segments;
2. Flexibility of plans;
3. Business engagement is a necessary precursor for employee engagement;
4. The role of leadership.

12.12.1. Employee segments

Vodafone is a huge organization operating across 28 different countries. Employee segments exist across various dimensions, but the two that Vodafone has rightly identified are employee segments along cultural dimensions (that can be captured through national boundaries); and segments that are due to the operations that the employees are involved with (such as retail and technology). There are different drivers for engagement not just across different OpCos and their national boundaries, but also within national boundaries but across different business units. With regard to the latter, Matthew Brearley explains:

> ... Technology may always come out as our lowest engagement area, but part of that is that a lot of technical people are introverts. And introverted people take a lot to express an outward expression of engagement. You go to sales, or to retail, you only need the touch paper and they're off ... and they're much more likely to give you very high engagement scores. So segmentation [means] you must implicitly know the different parts of your employee base. When we target, some of the rewards propositions we put in place, the career development, or the development solution, might be different by area. Recognition is a great example ... you would not recognise retail sales people in the same way that you recognise technology engineers.

Interviewees within Vodafone leadership also agree that the engagement strategy did not follow the simple "service-profit chain" logic for all its business units. Vodafone worked with this logic in the retail parts of the business – in the UK Operating Company more than half of the employees are directly customer-facing – but understood that this model did not apply as directly in the case of Global Technology, which is not directly customer-facing. In these units the engagement strategy was driven more by the logic of improving the business process, driving-up efficiency and promoting innovation rather than generating pure profits.

Therefore, an astute understanding of the employee segments existing within its business helped Vodafone come up with a more flexible and pragmatic engagement strategy. This lesson holds good for any company that operates across various national boundaries and has value generated through quite different business units.

12.12.2. Flexibility of plans

HR at Vodafone dealt with these employee segments by building flexibility into its people plans. For example, various OpCos can fine-tune their local people plans based on the local drivers of engagement existing in their culture and economy. Even the measurement and benchmarking of the engagement index is localized and previewed against the level of employee engagement existing in matched industries in a given country. This flexibility is an important ingredient for the success of the Global VPS.

12.12.3. Business engagement is a necessary precursor for successful change

Vodafone learned the hard way in some of its businesses that not taking the employees on board "before" the change process starts can lead to difficult consequences. Fortunately, the leadership at GT soon realized this, and went in for an inclusive and consultation-based change program rather than a dictated one. This brings out another perspective of engagement. It can and should be used as a strategy for internal marketing, rather than one just for performance enhancement. In a business environment that requires rapid changes and a need for employees to accept and adapt to these new requirements, senior managers know that they must first put the effort into building business engagement with the strategy – and only then ask employee's to engage. Although much of this chapter is about the HR strategy and the mechanisms put in place to build employee engagement, senior leaders at Vodafone had first built a high degree of business buy-in to the necessary strategies. Stephen Pusey was very aware of this need – he quips:

> ... You can take a horse to water, but you can't make him drink ... Even as recently as last month's Technology Board I said it's not what we can do technically – because technology knows very few boundaries ... What I need debates on is how far does the team feel comfortable in going – and we will push it [employee engagement] to only that boundary.

12.12.4. The role of leadership

The most important lesson, therefore, to be gained from Vodafone's journey on implementing their people plan is the central role played by the leadership in a successful implementation of any such plan. Though HR may be the coordinating function of such a strategy, at the end of the day it is the line and the leadership up and down the line that has the ability to implement their plans. The use of engagement champions, business partners, and line managers, along with the higher leadership that was shown from formulation to implementation of the plan, was the hallmark of Vodafone's people strategy. A visible leadership buying and backing the plan is a must for engagement strategy to work. In the absence of such leadership, the strategy runs the risk of being used by the cynics as hollow talk and just management rhetoric. Such a view can be immensely counterproductive and can only be countered if the employees believe that the strategy has actual meaning, with the required backing from people who matter.

Vodafone is not standing still, despite what it has already achieved with its employee engagement strategy. It is operating in a very fluid business sector that is constantly reinventing itself almost on a daily basis. Change is the norm, and its employees will need to always stay ahead of their field to stay competitive. An engaged workforce will be more ready to change and adapt because it understands the realities of their market and the challenges that their leaders face.

NOTES

1 Vodafone Annual report for the year ended 31 March 2008.

2 Arkin, A. (2009) Fully charged. *People Management*. 4 June 2009, pp. 21–23.

CHAPTER 13

The Future Scenario for Leading HR

ANTHONY HESKETH, PAUL SPARROW, AND MARTIN HIRD

13.1. Introduction

Future scenarios for *Leading HR*

Headline issue:

People issues will lie at the heart of most strategy execution problems, but in the world we are moving into, strategies are only going to get more sticky, complex, paradoxical, and people-centric.

If HR does not manage its own destiny, either events or aspiring competitors will manage it for them. How should the HR function evolve, what will the market require from their services in future years, and at what price, and will market logics be the only dominant show in town?

Strategic imperative:

HR needs to look at the complete *set of business models* that might impact the sector the organization is in. It needs to analyze, in real time, which models require HR investments now as an insurance premium, consider what capabilities are needed to get the chief executive officer (CEO) into each business model, but also to then get them out of it.

It needs to be direct *commissioners* of service rather than simply being direct *providers* of service. HR needs to understand how it is enabling the organization to achieve its goals, and working with different people across different organizations to improve businesses and how organizations manage and broker relationships with other organizations.

It needs to determine what should be commoditized or customized and what will remain key. It needs to decide whether it, or other specialist houses, should be the ones to develop skills in risk mitigation alongside smart ways of analyzing, detecting patterns in, predicting, integrating, and modeling the relationship between the competitive environment, business, and people data

Must-win battle:

What will remain of the future HR function once stripped of many traditional service lines? Can HR demonstrate the foresight to take control of the many people-related issues that may be solved through action outside the function?

In covering these issues, there are a number of key messages:

The key messages that emerge from this chapter

1. The future of the HR function in modern and future organizations is in a precarious position, a position not of its own making, and certainly not under its own control.

2. The HR function will transform in size, scope, and content over the coming decade.

3. Against the dramatic scaling back of the HR function's workforce there have been a number of debates: Should HR be *at* the table rather than *on* it? Should HR remain inside organizational structures? Or should HR be insourced to a shared service center (SSC) delivery centre with its own P&L?

4. As organizations break up and redeploy their service lines to realize cost efficiencies, and release new value streams, many service lines are returning to the functions from whence they originally came, or they are being scaled and leveraged by third-party providers.

5. In asking whether this situation will change in the future we have to ask whither: labor markets, trust, and economic factors with regard to future sourcing options, and the reputation of HR?

6. Whilst many labor market trends are clearly evident, and will be played out over the next decade, in terms of macro HR issues, there must remain much uncertainty over how trust will affect future labor market behavior. Societal mindset (the factors on which employee behavior will depend) can change where there are significant shocks to the system, such as collapse of the financial system or the symbolic actions of organizations.

7. HR functions are also having to second guess what the market will require from their services in future years, and at what price. Organizations will continue to seek both price *and* quality differentials aided by the standardization of a global understanding and benchmarking of quality assurance.

8. New service delivery platforms will lead to a new economy of access to information market places. This access and the quality of information will be negotiated and jealously guarded by either host organizations and procurement third-party constellations.

9. The outsourcing of HR services will rise from 30 per cent of organizations currently to a much higher proportion. Although caution is advised, some estimates have suggested the figure could approach as high as 75 per cent. Ultimately, the level arrived at depends on the extent to which you believe organizations are driven by economic logics, or by strategic leadership and end-user behaviors.

10. The strategy curve is simultaneously increasing in both frequency and amplitude. Economic cycles will have little impact on this imperative. The future of HR is less a debate about the standing of the function, but much more about HR's capability to meet the challenges of strategy execution.

So what should we expect to see as we look forward to the next decade? Let us begin with the charge that we are seeing the death of HR.

13.2. The death of HR?

> ... I think all this change signals the end of the HR empire, not the end of HR activities. The senior HR executive is not endangered, but the HR department is; and that senior executive might not even be a "professional" or specialist in HR, just a savvy leader who knows how to connect people and strategy. There will continue to be high-level executives dedicated to people and strategy. There will continue to be high-level executives dedicated to people or to workplaces or to culture and values, but there will be a shrinking department under them, and a lot of specialists once in HR but now reporting to finance, IT or corporate relations. Rosabeth Moss Kanter[1]

Some have managed these transitions particularly well, others less so. This is perhaps as well summed up as anybody by the old *Talking Heads* song "Once in A Lifetime." The song depicts an individual – a man in this case – awakening from a deep sleep to find himself in a beautiful house, with a beautiful wife. Impressed with his seemingly new surroundings our hero asks himself, "Well, how did I get here?" Dedicated followers of HR fashion have been asking themselves the same question. Most appear to agree on the same single causal factor: relevance.

The question then turns to what might make HR relevant not just now, but in the next decade or so? In this chapter there must be an inevitable amount of crystal ball gazing. Some will want to challenge our view, whereas others may question the evidence-base on which we make our claims. Long-term predictions have the luxury of being free from empirical scrutiny. But the flip-side of prediction is also in play: without cast-iron evidence, leaders are less likely to transform their HR functions on the predictions of several academics.

Therefore, we pull together much of the thinking we have undertaken for the Centre for Performance-Led HR member organizations. Inevitably, these organizations, too, have invested time and considerable resource into anticipating the future direction of their markets and the concomitant required changes in the HR function. The ultimate test will arrive in 2020, which is an interesting hypothesis, given Rosabeth Moss Kanter's observation that many HR functions will have been eradicated by then! Prediction Number 1, then, is that HR will undoubtedly be living in interesting times!

Much of the debate about the potential "Death of HR" stems from the questions asked about value and the management of this value across different sourcing choices. Chapter 1 argued that articulating how HR contributes to the creation, improvement, and leveraging of value, especially through the reconfiguration of business model change, represents the central challenge for today's HR Directors.

The future of the HR function in modern – and also future – organizations is in a precarious position, a position not of its own making, and certainly not under its own control. The HR function has seen its numbers slashed, with the traditional benchmark of one HR person per 100 destined to fall to as many as 1:500 by the end of the decade.[2] Five years ago BT openly talked of moving their HR function through the "hop, skip, and then jump" transformational process of first shared services then to a third-party provider where 600 HR staff could deliver the company's global HR services to its 108,000 employees, where 14,500 previously did so.[3] As the economics of HR service delivery continues to change, moving forward to 2020, the HR function will not be that which has brought us to today.

Of course, predicting the preferred or actual level of future outsourcing is problematic. There are contrasting prognoses whereby:[4]

> ... some industry analysts and media pundits ... translate the findings into painful trade-offs: cost savings vs. growth, speed vs. quality, and organisational cohesion vs. knowledge and innovation. Others suggest outsourcing is in a death spiral ... a decline fuelled by structural risks, questionable cost savings, and multiple complexities

Others point to:

> ... lucrative outsourcing deals, impressive benefits and uncapped growth projections" and "level[s] of strategic and operational flexibility unattainable through other means.

Judgments are therefore being made by senior managers about cost reduction, risk reduction, and capability building. These judgments are based on the existing perceptions about what should be classified as commodity-like and esoteric activity, and what should be replaced by more value-adding activity.

Drivers such as cost savings, improved service quality, IT investment and access to technology, improved process efficiencies, global process harmonization, strategic reorientation of HR, and improved business agility are driven by both economic and political arguments,[5] with one driver being given precedence over another at one point in time, as senior managers learn about their future business models and threats to organizational performance.

Four core sourcing strategies

1. *In-country insourcing* describes the situation where the supplier–customer relationship is still formalized and contracted, and activities are sent to an overseas location (generally for reasons of cost efficiency), *but* the activities are still performed in-house, such as in one of the organizations' own subsidiaries or a service center. The responsibility and delegation of tasks to the service provider means that the service center is still what is called an internalized "client-entity."

2. *Global insourcing* describes the situation where the redesign and reconfiguration of activities and processes to become more efficient and effective allows some geographical flexibility over the location of the activity. For economists, ownership of

10 per cent of offshore operations constitutes direct foreign investment between a parent operation and an affiliate.

3. *Outsourcing* describes situations when a third-party provider is used to carry out the activity, with the production of services purchased externally, but still within the same country. Higher profitability may be achieved by using fewer in-house resources. It is defined as "... a discontinuation of internal production (whether it be production of goods or services) and an initiation of procurement from outside suppliers."[6] HRO involves "... the purchasing by an organisation of ongoing HR services from a third-party provider that it would otherwise normally provide by itself." [7]

4. *Offshoring* describes a particular type of specialization in which the production of services or goods is moved overseas. Offshoring involves a broad range of tasks that are executed by a firm in another country, ranging from the establishment of a foreign subsidiary to a relatively arm's length relationship with another firm.[8] More arm's length relationships tend to involve a more explicit practice of contracting with individuals or companies in foreign countries to perform work that might reasonably be conducted domestically. Offshoring is best defined as "... the act of transferring some of a company's recurring internal activities to outside providers, who are located in a different country and market economy, under a formal service contract."[9] Offshore transactions also typically involve two parts: a transfer of *responsibility* for the operation and management of part of an organization; and a *guaranteed provision of services* to the client organization by the vendor for a time period. Given the distances involved in offshoring, the factors of production are rarely transferred to offshore sites, but the services, processes, and decision rights are.

Theory, however, rarely aligns with the pragmatic judgments that are made by strategic actors – the CEOs, Finance Directors, Operations Directors, and HR Directors. The challenge they face is that:

> ... The extent to which each (core competence) ... is singularly both necessary and sufficient to justify the ... choice has never been satisfactorily squared ... Ambiguity still reigns on how to establish what, and what not, should be seen as core. Is it what we do best? Is it what creates value? Or is it related to the strategic importance of the activity in relation to changing industry requirements?.[10]

Current responses are therefore complex. Each of the forms – and indeed the hybrid combinations of these forms that are pursued – offers a different contribution to parts of the value chain.[11]

Differentiated decisions

Organizations currently make very differentiated decisions, involving choices about

1. sourcing (for example, cosourcing with one or multisourcing with multiple vendors);

Differentiated decisions: (Continued)

2. different support strategies (for example, fix-and-keep in-house, rehabilitate and retain, enable capability building within the client or indeed the vendor operation, outsourcing with a reverse option, through to complete divestment)

3. contractual arrangements, which may be benefits based (whereby payments are linked to realized benefits) or may be cosourced (where vendor revenues are linked to client performance); and

4. location of resources, which may be distributed (where the vendor has teams both on shore and offshore) or dyadic (independent client and vendor operations).

HRO arrangements come under multiple regulatory regimes (referred to as contract complexity or density), and attention is therefore given to the nature of governance and risk mitigation that accompanies any particular outsourcing solution[12] in order to mitigate opportunistic behaviors by the vendor, avoid over-dependence on the vendor, and allow flexible responses to changes in the environment. Governance arrangements are based on two control mechanisms:

1. Formal contractual relations in the form of bundles of obligations, incentives, rewards, and penalties. Does the chosen governance arrangement mitigate against all the potential contractual hazards?

2. A range of complementary social mechanisms such as trust, reputation, and what has been termed "the shadow of the future."[13] Does the specter of potential future economic trends and scenarios act to coalesce attitudes around alternative futures, which can then act to ensure self-regulation?

There are also global differences, which show geographical differentiation in HRO expenditure and market volume, different preferences for insourcing versus outsourcing across geographies, cultural differences in service perception (and so different pull factors with regards to use of services), and different institutional contexts that surround the attractiveness of sourcing and shoring options.[14]

Despite this complexity, we believe the underlying trends that will shape the path to 2020 are already evident. Against the dramatic scaling back of the HR function's workforce there have been a number of debates:

1. Should HR be *at* the table rather than *on* it?[15]

2. Should HR remain inside organizational structures?

3. Or should HR be insourced to an SSC delivery center with its own P&L?[16]

Many have viewed the SSC as merely being the precursor to full-blown outsourcing of the HR function as in the case of BT, and then P&G, BAE SYSTEMS, Dupont, and Unilever. Data from HRO advisors, Equaterra, estimated that even by 2007 in excess of 4 million employees were being supported by third-party HR providers with a total contract value in excess of $20 billion.[17]

Despite such scaling back, conversely we have seen the expansion of the HR function into a number of areas previously the domain of other functions such as payroll and pensions (from Finance & Administration [F&A]), IT-enabled HR systems or Enterprise Resource Planning Systems (ERPs) from the IT function and now procurement, and occupational health and a whole raft of different "back office" services.

Therefore, as organizations seek to break up and redeploy their service lines in ways that enable them to realize major cost efficiencies, and release new value streams, many of these service lines are returning to the functions from whence they originally came, or they are being scaled and leveraged by third-party providers.

This has raised significant questions concerning what now remains of the future HR function, once stripped of all of these service lines?[18] Is this situation going to change in the future? To answer this we have to ask

1. whither labor markets?

2. whither trust?

3. whither economic factors with regard to future sourcing options?

4. whither the reputation of HR?

13.3. Whither labor markets?

Current forecasts anticipate the following developments, each of which will challenge future HR provision:

1. *Increased granularity of the labor market:* Top-end professional jobs will be knowledge and intellectual capital based, creating a three-tier workforce: workers will either be innovating, producing, or selling. Some refer to this as the "innovation-production-implementation continuum" or the distinction between knowledge work and knowledge work*ed*.[19]

2. *A search, if not a war, for Talent:* Traditionally this has very much been waged on the field of the high-value-added skills of knowledge workers, but similar intense levels of competition are being waged by organizations for middle-ranking and some lower-level skilled labor. This has been intensified by the global explosion of human capital acquisition in both developed and developing economies. For example, in the United Kingdom it has been accepted that long-run productivity has more to do with intermediate level skills development.[20] Nearly 20 per cent of the productivity gap between Germany and the United Kingdom is explained by the skills gap, and 10 per cent of the gap with France. Most of this gap occurs at intermediate skill level and not high talent, and there are strong regional cluster effects for productivity. Skills supply strategies will need a stronger focus on

intermediate level skills and organizational investments in human capital will become focused around productive hubs, not spread around.

3. *Understanding new pools for talent:* Demographic realities are forcing organizations to focus on strategies designed to retain older, skilled, and more experienced workers, and compete for scarce talent at the top end of younger labor markets, including graduates from emerging markets with a relatively high capability-low cost tag, or a mobile graduate elite who encourage organizations to compete for their services. Attention has been drawn to changes in both supply and demand factors such as:[21] the volume of migration; the shift toward skills-related immigration systems; the globalization of a number of professional labor markets (such as healthcare and information technology); an increase in demand for skilled expatriates to help build emerging international markets, even as the world economy is in general decline; temporary and short-term access to specialized talent to assist the execution of overseas projects and to develop emerging markets; and the need for highly mobile elites of management to perform boundary-spanning roles to help build social networks and facilitate the exchange of knowledge necessary to support globalization. These all provide renewed energy to talent issues, but seen through an increasingly global lens.

4. *New skills to manage global capability and knowledge:* Whereas old traditions saw International HRM merely as an extension of the conventional HR agenda, a new agenda points to different ways in which skills issues, and their management, will be handled by firms at the transnational level. The opportunity for skills arbitrage now extends to the whole of the labor force. The process of skills creation and skills utilization is complex and will lead to "skill webs," where organizations will relate to their suppliers, generate levels of trust in the relationships they establish, may seek to protect their core capabilities, or may share them with suppliers in order to improve their performance.[22] Multiple skills supply strategies will be pursued, ranging from: contract expatriates; assignees on short-term or intermediate-term foreign postings; permanent cadres of global managers; international commuters; employees utilized on long-term business trips; international transferees moving from one subsidiary to another; self-initiated movers who live in a third country, but are willing to work for a multinational; international employees active in cross-border project teams; immigrants actively and passively attracted to a national labor market; domestically based employees in a service center but dealing with overseas customers, suppliers, and partners on a regular basis; and skilled individuals working in geographically remote centers of competence or excellence that is, serving global operations that may be remote, but through the use of talent and expertise that has been internationally mandated.[23]

5. *Shifts in the power of employer brand:* Many people are simply eschewing less intrinsic or less "branded" forms of employment in favor of more workable and aesthetically pleasing working conditions and environments. As organizations continue to build global customer-facing brands, they will[24]

address pressures to meet international governance standards, transfer best practice, and develop global performance standards and HR business processes that can be adapted to technological solutions and outsourcing, then they use employer branding as a tool for creating a sense of "corporateness" among often decentralized operations and as a key means of differentiating themselves in domestic and overseas labor markets. This process will see changes in the balance of global integration toward local authenticity and maximum employee voice.

6. *Radical redesign of work:* This has continued to unlock productivity, value-adding, and innovative processes and practices, with a dramatic reduction in working hours and increased empowerment with wider adoption of the European model for empowerment through learning and development.

7. *Digital Taylorism:* In this, the processes of reengineering and process scaling and commoditization will increase the value curve toward jobs currently seen as secure.

8. *The emergence of the boundaryless or portfolio career:* Here, the average US citizen has already worked for nine separate organizations by the age of 32. For many, periods of engagement and disengagement with an organization are becoming shorter duration and more surface-level. Demise of the permanent contract, where employees will increasingly have, simultaneously, more than one work role, more than one employer, and multiple main sources of income. Identification and engagement with any one employer will become more problematic.

9. *An economy of experience (social capital):* This economy has emerged for market-savvy executives and managerial elites who can now command significant salaries for acutely scarce skills and capabilities, and for the possession of networks and reputation within this network.

10. *Transparency of financial information means that more employees will be able to cost the value of their (or their teams') contribution:* The short-term salary-depressing effects of economic recessions aside, this will continue to force idiosyncratic/ market-breaking deals at ever-lower and broader levels of the organization.[25] Unlike the debate at the beginning of the decade, however, the pressure now will be to prove the benefit/ performance manage such deals whilst balancing perceptions of fairness (a major predictor of employee engagement behaviors) in the majority.

11. *Increased positional competition:* As more employees acquire requisite levels of human capital, individuals' labor market strategies are evolving, making recruitment processes and their transparency and accuracy more important.

12. *Shift to team-level management reward:* In order to incentivize speed, firms will need to pace the performance of more and more strategic teams with shared/gainshare rewards and wealth packages. Fast-paced project teams (in areas where innovation is important) are well aware of their business benefit. Already more detailed and decentralized finance and information systems

have made it easier for R&D teams to assess their worth to their organization; if needs are not met, whole teams may move from one firm to another.

13. *New models of reward:* There will be a significant increase in individual negotiation for reward and recognition programs for those who can still evidence the benefits from their talent, which in turn will generate intense demand for transparent and democratic evaluation and performance management processes. A challenge in the immediate postrecession world will be to rebuild the balance in rewards systems, given the recent criticisms of greed and value destruction built into some executive incentive systems versus the need for pay cuts and freezes and flexible work deals in other parts of the workforce.[26] Commentators are giving more attention to questions about rewards for failure, internal pay equity, and links between performance-related pay and total rewards management and performance. Questions are being asked whether experiments in financial participation seen during the recession will see new gainshare and rewards mentalities applied beyond strategic teams.

14. *Beyond idiosyncratic dealing/ negotiations:* High talent with specialized skill (engineers, geo-scientists, etc.) may well become owned by other players. Universities are expected to have their own institutes (consider current biotechnology centers) and will lease out expertise. High expertise staffing agencies or other forms of brokerage (mobility agents) will negotiate the best deals for these skilled employees as they will be in high demand (even if governments increase supply of graduates in relevant areas, experience levels will still be important).

15. *Personal support services:* By implication, current internal career broker models (consider those that have traditionally been seen for high-value employees such as expatriates) will be supplanted by a need for individual employees to network into the external brokers; HR functions will have to make on-project assessments of such employees in order to entice them into more permanent relationships; join-us negotiation arrangements will be very idiosyncratic needing flexible sets of personal support services to be offered.

16. *E-enablement of HR:* This has already intensified the recruitment space, in terms of speed, volume, and complexity. New skills are emerging on both sides of the labor divide to negotiate this new phenomenon. These in turn are being complimented by a number of new e-enabled workforce providers and agencies, generating new market places and networks within particular domains of expertise.

17. *A "winner takes all" game theory market is now dominant:* Here, what winners win, and losers lose is changing. In a labor market characterized by *relative,* not absolute employability, there is no prize for second place. A new "fear of falling" is coming to characterize established middle-classes, as their cultural heritage of access to elite human capital is slowly eroded by mass higher education, and economic collapses that impact knowledge workers.

18. *Aging Workforce*: People are working for longer periods of their life, but shorter hours during the working day due in the main to other commitments. In the United States, 35 per cent of all workers say they provide regular care for a parent or in-law over the age of 65 in the last year. A "Sandwich Generation" has emerged which has caring obligations for working people both above (their parents) and below (their children) their own life-stage.

19. *Eldercare:* This is slowly overtaking childcare as the big work/life issue. Childcare is often financially subsidized by nation states; care of the elderly remains a major gap in provision with major negative impact on people's (especially women's) propensity to work.

20. *Shifting workforce values:* Seventy-five per cent of working parents put family friendly working hours ahead of other benefits. Many view large scale MNCs to have universally failed in their capacity to accommodate such requirements, whereby a commercial 24:7 working model has not been matched by caring facilities.

21. *Increased correlation between corporate social responsibility and economic issues:* This has increased focus by employees, customers, and stakeholders on issues of environmental, diversity, and CSR concerns branding and defining where we want to work, who with, and even who to invest in.

22. *An end to presenteeism*: This technology will enable flexible and virtual working to increase with less people requiring office resources for less time.

23. *Increased costs of absenteeism:* Costs due to stress are estimated to triple.

24. *Business leaders:* They will be younger and their profile more diverse. Diversity concerns will focus on the need to reflect the new geographies of operation within senior decision-making processes and forum.

13.4. Whither trust and its impact on labor market behavior?

In terms of macro HR issues there must remain much uncertainty over how trust will affect future labor market behavior. Societal mindset (the factors on which employee behavior will depend) can change where there are significant shocks to the system, such as collapse of the financial system, symbolic actions of organizations, and so forth (Peter Cappelli has called this image inertia[27]).

Imaging Inertia theory

In his 1999 book *The New Deal At Work: Managing the Market-Driven Workforce*, Peter Cappelli presented an intriguing model of how employees appeared to be adapting to the new employment contract. His outline, an *imaging inertia* theory, was based on the

Imaging Inertia theory: (Continued)

assumption that altered perceptions endured throughout generational cohorts. This perspective argued that employees did not make decisions or judgments purely on the basis of a rational cost-benefit model. They relied instead on recalling previous experiences in similar situations – imaging – and based their decisions on what happened then. People who had experienced the hardships of the Great Depression often felt insecure throughout their whole lives even when they had become wealthy. The generation that grew up assuming that their employer was responsible for careers similarly never forgot the waves of downsizing. Their children, the next generation of workers, also did not forget. Their images of work had been forever altered. What will be the images – and the new inertias – associated with a collapse in confidence in market-based HR?

The fundamental issue for employers and employees alike is one of fairness in this new deal. HR will have to investigate and establish the new contours of fairness. But what is fairness? For example, the credit crunch provided new impetus into the thorny question of pensions, retirement age, and age discrimination. Given that the age of disengagement from work for many has little to do with official retirement age, questions have been raised about the ability of employees to find and maintain high-quality employment until the age at which they retire. This then raises questions about societal attitudes to older workers, about career paths, and about access to quality work. It also raises questions about the transfer of risk – risks generally being transferred from governments and organizations to individuals. When you transfer risk, complex issues about fairness follow. Is it fair on the younger generation not to address the pensions time bomb? Is it fair on older employees who signed up to a "deal" based on current market value of salaries, foregone benefits and so forth, to then take away promised future (pension) benefits? Are these hardships being applied fairly across all classes and segments of employee? But then is it fair to expect lower service employees to have reduced entitlements and to pay for more generous pensions of older employees? This then moves HR into the next set of questions, which are really based around making judgments around "total rewards." What is the real value of the formal short-term and long-term incentives, the benefits offered, and the subsidized costs of employment? If employees are made aware of what they really get (or do not get!), will they be able to rationalize what is going on in the labor market and make appropriate adjustments?

As we look to the future, it is clear that

1. Some HR functions are better equipped than others to raise these issues.
2. In the next 10 years we will see many innovations as HR functions try to address the complex questions of relative fairness.
3. They will need to base these judgments on the best evidence that they can marshal about the impact of such HR adjustments.

4. The credit crunch brought to a head long-standing questions about the relative performance contribution of different segments of employee.

In addressing this agenda, it is possible that recent economic events might have created new images – helpful and unhelpful – that are yet-to-be-played-out in future employee behavior.

13.5. Whither the economics of HR service delivery?

Not dissimilar to futures in the financial market place, HR functions also find themselves having to second guess what the market will require from their services in future years, and at what price.[28] The future price of HR services is uncertain. The only certainty is that the cost per transaction is falling, both in terms of the people costs that HR services attract – largely through the economies of scale brought about by e-enablement – and, the rationalization of HR functions as more processes are shipped to lower cost geographies. Organizations will continue to seek both price *and* quality differentials aided by the standardization of a global understanding and benchmarking of quality assurance.[29]

By 2020 we will have seen considerable development in both the nature and quality of interactions between employer and employee. However, central to the debate over the delivery of HR is the question of transaction cost economics.

A distinction if forged between the hierarchical form of process delivery that takes place inside organizations (when services remain internal to a company) and the market form of process delivery (where external providers compete to deliver services).[30] Transaction cost economics postulates that market forms of delivery by external service providers are more efficient than internal, organizationally owned services.

In line with this recent evidence from McKinsey, the distinction between transactional and tacit forms of interaction is crucial to understanding the combination of complex processes such as HR and its future scalability via information technology.

The nature of interactions is changing however. In their broadest sense, interactions involve "the searching, coordinating, and monitoring required to exchange goods or services."[31] There is a crucial distinction between *transactional* or rule-based interactions (which can be scripted or automated) and *tacit* or complex interactions (which involve a higher level of judgment, more ambiguity and drawing on tacit or experiential knowledge). In terms of delivery the latter require highly skilled, and consequently higher paid individuals.

Figure 13.1 captures current thinking on how delivery is differentiated on these lines. Through the application of IT and process mapping, many feel that far more HR interactions can be e-enabled, in part to eliminate low-value-added transactional activities. This process of scaling has created the *One2Many* or HR transactional process outsourcing market place, such as payroll, benefits, and administration, which in turn has been mimicked by SSCs or insourcing to realize efficiencies and keep cost savings in-house.

In the immediate future, however, a similar level of scalability is being applied further up the HR value chain, as technology enables the quality and speed of

Figure 13.1: Emerging markets in value, complexity, and HR interactions

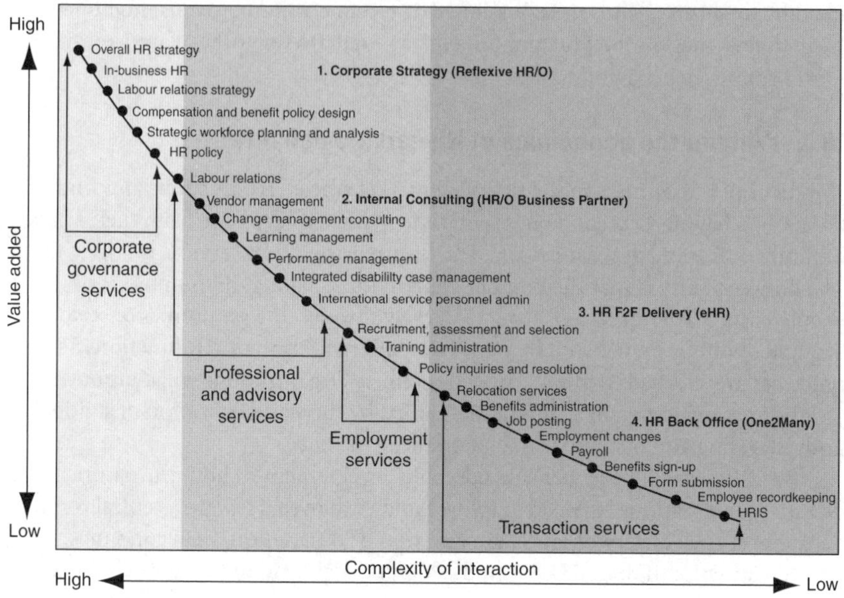

Source: Hesketh (2006; 2008). Reprinted with permission.

Face-to-Face (F2F) service delivery centered round employment services. Employment and transactional services largely comprise the new and evolving e-enabled HR(O) market place that is now served by a multitude of ERP service providers (such as SAP, ORACLE, etc.). The implication is that

1. the future will involve further progress up the value curve, with the scaling of professional and advisory services, as development enables service providers to extend the breadth and impact of tacit interactions via new and emerging technologies;

2. this scaling, and possible outsourcing of such processes to third-party providers will not just enable organizations to enjoy short-term efficiency gains in providing such services, but they will also be able to focus on the higher-value-adding tacit and strategic activities involved in corporate-level HR.

Cynics describe such a process as the devolvement of HR activity to the line and employees themselves in order to reduce the costs of delivering transactional HR services. Advocates of this approach will point to a new cadre of middle and senior managers capable and prepared to handle people issues supported by powerful, yet highly centralized e-enabled system of HR. This new "push to pull" HR market place will enable employees to have more control over their own HR interactions (e.g., completion of life census data, greater autonomy over, and access to expert help with, pensions and wider investment portfolios).

Again, by implication:[32]

1. Investments need to be made now to grow the need amongst employees to take such self-management responsibility

2. It should not be assumed that the ethics and desirability of self-management are the same across the diverse cultures and geographies that organizations will operate in.

These new models also have implications for the traditional Ulrich 3-Box model. They offer the possibility of HR removing itself from the equation, with external providers dealing directly with line managers and providing the information and coaching support around the employment relationship.

Going forward, these new platforms will lead to a new *economy of access* to *information market places*. This access and the quality of information will be negotiated and jealously guarded by either host organizations or procurement third-party constellations. It will be seen as a new source of competitive advantage in the talent market place.

Many organizations will have initiated new internal centers, think tanks, and networks to manage proprietary HR expertise necessary for long-term performance-driving processes – strategic competence, innovation, consumer insight, productivity, and partnership learning.

Emerging evidence also suggests that a talent strategy of e-enabled and ubiquitous service delivery generates a performance differential. Research from McKinsey estimates the variability in company-level performance of those streamlining transactions to focus on higher value, tacit processes to be in the order of 50 per cent measured by revenue or EBITA (earnings before interest, taxes, depreciation, and amortization).[33]

The increasing commoditization of processes, partly through developments in interaction and design and the technical possibilities of scaling, is leading to new pressures on the HR function, all of which have a clear impact on the employee value proposition (EVP).

The problems of aggregation:

1. *Adaptation*: maximizing local relevance. Organizations should expect that as they diversify into, or enter into strategic collaborations, they will have to protect these new businesses from early "corporate death" and that this will depend not just on clear strategic insight and technical skill but on organization design and development skills.

2. *Aggregation*: Major pressures are now apparent to realize evident economies of scale through standardization. Leaders who fail to demonstrate suitable levels of aggregation and efficiencies, as, for example, measured by benchmarks of operational costs for the Function, risk losing their positions. But employees are especially wary of cost-cutting exercises, notably HR outsourcing, as, too are customers.[34]

The problems of aggregation: (Continued)

3. *Arbitrage*: the exploitation of differences at different points of processes. Hierarchies of processes through which additional value can be realized and structural and operational risks can be mitigated by HR services delivered in "extended organizations."[35]

The bottom line here is that HR will need to enable Enterprise First Behaviors. The HR function itself now needs to be direct *commissioners* of service rather than simply being direct *providers* of service. HR needs to understand how it enables the organization to achieve its goals, and how it works with different people across different organizations to improve businesses and how organizations manage and broker relationships with other organizations. We believe this will require four areas of activity:

Four activities to become commissioners of service:

1. More focused selection and assessment of business model capabilities in a wider range of role (with associated developments to the resourcing toolkit).
2. Strategies to make sure that line managers can make more with what they have (so ensuring work processes and toolkits that engender creativity, innovation, and entrepreneurial skills).
3. Alignment of all HR practices and processes (and other key financial and information processes) to the development of appropriate climates (at team and function level).
4. A service-oriented mindset is the key to releasing additional value lines as organizations shape the interactions they have with their people – internal as well as external.

Not only must HR professionals be expert in the new value-driving HR advocated by Dave Ulrich and others, but they must also have a rich-set of service-oriented capabilities (see Table 13.1).

There are two ramifications of this development that relate to the qualities needed by HR professionals themselves:

1. Relating to the labor scarcity of these new capabilities, HR service-providers hold the view that the residual supply of these capabilities has now dried up. Apart from the obvious benefits of arbitrage, it is no coincidence that many back- and mid-office service suppliers have headed East to the deep and as yet untapped pools of relevant talent.
2. These dynamics between service providers of HR will have been played out by 2020. Currently the likes of Accenture, Capita, IBM, and Hewitt are in direct

competition with mainstream organizations for HR professionals with the requisite capabilities. McKinsey's *The Dearth of HR Talent* has only served to pour flames on what was already more than the smoldering fire of talent scarcity.[37]

Table 13.1: The necessary 9: The new service-oriented capabilities

Capability	Definition	Driver
Service orientation	Focusing on delivering the services my customer contracts for.	Focus on CRM and e-enabled service experiences of (internal) customers.
Process mastery	Proficiency with the scope, impact, policies, and procedures of the process(es) I perform.	Convergence of cross-function business processes onto a single process delivery platform.
Using resources	Making sure of the right use of people, process, and technology to deliver services.	Meeting increasing client expectations and leveraging available legacy resources.
Knowledge management	Locating, accessing, sharing, and assembling knowledge from a range of sources in order to improve performance.	Differentiation through continuous capability stretch and utilization aligned with the business contexts of clients.
Career management	Maximizing my career progress.	Retaining key employees and servicing human capital management and development.
Commercial understanding	Finding and acting upon opportunities to create more value for my customers and my company.	Aligning service delivery with the service expectations and requirements of customers.
Performance orientation	Understanding and linking how well I perform with the quality of service provided to the customer.	Prioritizing particular aspects of service delivery in order to maximize the performance requirements of clients.
Risk management	Recognizing and evaluating the impact of a range of internal and external factors upon successful delivery.	New levels of sensitivity to potential risks experienced by clients in the delivery of their services.
Relationship management	Understanding the importance of good relationships with customers, suppliers, colleagues, and management and using these relationships to drive better performance.	The increasing importance of networks and business interactions across different client and service-provider platforms.

Source: Hesketh and Kops (2007). Reprinted with permission.

Figure 13.2: Capability index: The overall capability areas of HR and F&A compared

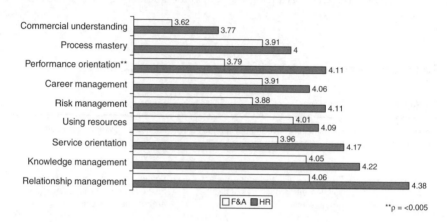

Source: Hesketh and Kops (2007). Reprinted with permission.

This tight labor market is further exacerbated by an apparent synergy between the capabilities required to deliver the different services, of which HR is only one.[36] There is growing evidence for a "Conversion Thesis" that those who can deliver world-class finance and administration services can also provide world-class HR (see Figure 13.2 above). Figure 13.2 identifies nine abilities that the delivery team – on an individual basis – must exhibit in order to insure that the promise of outsourcing and internal shared services operations are delivered. Crucially, the nine capabilities may vary in importance across all service delivery teams, but each is common to all of the different service domains, be they IT, Finance, Procurement or, crucially, HR. Figure 13.2 above shows that comparisons are made between the capabilities of different teams in HR and Finance and Administration, there is little to choose between them. HR leaders can currently draw some comfort from the observation that the only significant difference between HR and F&A lies in HR's greater orientation to performance. However, closer scrutiny of the data above also reveals that whilst HR functions may be more oriented toward performance, but both they and F&A functions have difficulty marrying this mindset with commercial reality. This is a *clear future development need* toward 2020.

Expansion in functional demand for the same capabilities coincides with a dip in the appeal of a career in the back offices of large-scale organizations to those with the capabilities future HR requires. McKinsey express caution about HR's future capacity to deliver service-orientation, and conclude:

At first glance, this model may appear to be fine, but the lines have not be drawn clearly enough when it comes to execution. To deliver on what the business needs, HR must put its own house in order, starting with the skills and capabilities of its staff.[38]

13.6. Whither HR functional reputation?

So, whither HR's reputation? In Chapters 2 and 3 we raised the complex issues associated with executing and indeed then globalizing an Ulrich delivery model. David Ulrich notes that the breaking up of HR into a "3-Box Model" has served to "let some operational aspects of HR fall through the cracks."[39] Chapter 2 outlined our own research into the implementation issues associated with this model. However, many see Ulrich's more recent work on leadership brand as a symbolic break with the HR function. Ulrich himself suggests HR now needs to evolve in order to, "deliver value in ways that have meaning to the receivers, not just the givers."[40]

As the labor market trends make abundantly clear, the solution to the problems raised will often lie outside the remit of existing HR functions, or if to involve them, will require radically different ways of thinking about the most appropriate roles, structures, and processes that must be brought under HR influence or control.

It is clear that HR Directors face significant challenges in ensuring that their function can muster sufficiently talented professionals to manage the forward agenda. They should not assume that, for example, that it will be their internal centers of expertise or excellence that will employ the best HR Leaders. HR Leaders may equally well be developed in outside organizations specializing in, and combining, the following functions:

1. General consultancies, sporadically designing generic people-handling processes, that is, things that end with an -ing (changing, legalizing, protecting, advising, organizing, designing, branding, communicating, assessing, resourcing, rewarding, engaging, benchmarking, etc.). Today, many HR functions uninspiringly equate these functional processes or expertise areas to internal centers of expertise or excellence. The reality is that many of the -ing processes rely on the skills that benefit from cross-organization insight, and so much more of this activity may still yet be able to go outside.

2. There will be a widening plethora of specialist houses offering value-added but discretionary services (smart ways of analyzing, detecting patterns in, predicting, integrating, and modeling the relationship between the competitive environment, internal business and people data, and providing additional services to manage risks, etc.). Their analytical tool skills will be key, but only a few analysts may be needed to understand what a pattern of data really means. Whether HR functions will chose to, or can afford to, own such specialists is a moot point.

3. HR service providers will be fewer in number, but will have learned how to deliver more than just scale benefits for component HR processes. They will have advanced up the value chain, offered HR system and process design

affording modularized levels of employee-intelligence, integrated HR-IS-Finance services, and will have more global capability. They will face the challenge of advancing entry-level HR skills up through meaningful career paths, but these HR careers will be distributed across widely varying geographical hubs.

A new onus on HR?

With all of this fluidity within and without organizations will come a new onus on the organization and its HR function to

1. maintain a longer term view. Rather like the new breed of industry regulators, they will find themselves overseeing all those parties and partners involved in people-related aspects of their own business model, regulating both internal and external HR systems, ensuring they perform in line with the overall goals of the organization. They will not just equate internal centers of expertise to existing HR processes, but will need to initiate internal Centers of Excellence, think tanks, and networks that can manage the proprietary HR expertise necessary for long-term performance-driving processes – such as strategic competence, innovation, consumer insight, productivity, and partnership learning;

2. direct attention to how they can shape the interactions between employees, organizations, and perhaps following current rhetoric, customers; and

3. build their social capital with all the stakeholders who will be called upon to engage with the HR issues (beyond employees this means governments, CEOs, business functions, individual talent, and unions). The power of each of these stakeholders will wax and wane over the coming years, but any one of them may have the power to dethrone HR.

13.7. Conclusions

What have we said throughout the book about the current challenges facing HR? Chapter 1 established the agenda that we returned to throughout the book. We argued that in order to understand *Leading HR*, we must give consideration to three things: the range of business issues that are leading HR into new roles and new contributions; the *Leading HR* processes and practices that need to become embedded into the business; and the ability of HR Directors to lead HR as a function or as a capability within the organization. We have addressed the question of strategic capability throughout this book, showing how this turns on how HR can help the organization to understand how to implement strategy from a people perspective. More than ever HR Directors must engage in and use the language of strategy in order to demonstrate the value of their function. What ties all the chapters in this book together is the drumbeat of business model change. In the near-future, innovation will define the business environment for business leaders, whether this be innovation in strategy, business model, products, services, or organizational design. We painted a picture of executive demand for new and fast-evolving business models. These will continue to be driven by three analytical fundamentals: what creates customer value, what drives costs, and how to maximize profit? People, however, are the common denominator for all three of these strategic imperatives. This language of strategy, however, sets a challenging agenda for HR functions.

Chapter 2 entered into a discussion about HR delivery models, and in particular the genesis of ideas behind the current adherence to Ulrich-based structures and the challenges faced in working with these structures. Chapter 3 used the example of Nestlé to explain the complex evolution of HR delivery models. Chapter 4 then picked up the drumbeat of business model change, and drew attention to the current frenetic state of the HR function in relation to different degrees of change, and different political spaces the function finds itself in. We laid out the numerous transitions it has to manage, both on behalf of the business and on behalf of itself. Chapter 5 provided an example of these transitions at NG Bailey.

We then addressed and unraveled a series of key HR capabilities that have to be built in order to establish a *Leading HR* function. Chapters 6, 8, and 9 described three key activities and capabilities that we see as necessary for *Leading HR*. The first of these concerned the traditional issues of power, reputation and influence. We outlined what we called a Golden Triangle between HR Directors, CEOs, and CFOs. The second was to build an organization design capability—we termed this architectural design given the new combination of skills and levels of analysis that the capability implies. The third was the ability to reverse engineer the performance recipes that are used to demonstrate some linkage between employee engagement and organizational performance.

Chapters 10 to 12 then focused on a range of strategies necessary to handle the following issues: linking ethics, employee engagement, and brand (drawing upon experiences at Co-operative Financial Services); moving from the management of corporate reputation through a model of trust-based HR (drawing upon experiences at McDonald's); and creating an HR architecture for sustainable employee engagement (drawing upon experiences at Vodafone). These chapters bring together the actions and perspectives of the key players involved in the HR strategy.

We argued that the activities outlined in each chapter should be viewed as a totality that, if all are present, provide for a high level of proactivity within the HR function. However, few HR functions, at the present time, would have "mastery" of all the capabilities outlined.

We have also drawn attention to general trends in labor market behavior, the way that future trust might impact such behavior, the economics of HR service delivery, and the reputation of HR, that will have independent and combined effects on the future of HR.

On all this we can agree. However, we must confess to remaining areas of debate. Returning to the "Death of HR" discussion earlier in this chapter, we draw attention to two competing "lenses" through which we might think about this.

Ultimately, the future facing HR may come down to the view that you chose to take about how organizations actually work.

The first lens that we have used is the economic/services arbitrage/and outsourcing view. Based on a logic of economic rationalism, CFO views about how organizations should judge value-added, and data about the economics of IT and technical delivery, this scenario leads us to the view that services higher up the value chain can also be provided externally, and that the residual (strategic) activity can be "returned home" to (newly people-savvy) line managers. We have developed these arguments in this chapter, and see an inevitability about many of the structural and service responses that this will force upon HR.

But of course economics is not the only logic that shapes history. So there is a second lens that might come into play. This comes from a strategic leadership/political/behavioral view of organizations. This lens would argue that despite economic logics, organizations, their leaders, and end users do not necessarily behave rationally. A combination of strategic behaviors can always override, or attempt to stand in the face of, economic logics. We are reminded that back in the 1980s various prognoses about the future of HR concluded (wrongly!) that HR had a time-limited future unless it rose to the strategic challenge. In the days before mass outsourcing/IT-enablement it was argued that top-level HR Director positions were already going to people from outside HR (so limiting senior careers in HR), lower level work was routine and could be designed out, and finally that the "stuff in the middle" (the bread-and-butter activities such as performance management system design, selection system design, etc.) only needed periodic expert knowledge and so would be done by the generic HR consulting houses. A bleak picture of the future of HR was presented. Yet in the next 10 years the number of people working in HR, and the perceived professionalization of HR grew massively.

What happened historically? Might this happen again? Looking back in time, it became clear that many CEOs, strategists, and service designers did not think and act rationally when planning their own organizational changes. In practice they have multiple mental biases, and they factor-in multiple contextual judgments. They factor in political considerations and their own "agrandissement" goals. They will look for all the things that the change management literature draws attention to – layers of support amongst fellow executives, willing coalitions, and project champions. They will pay premiums for this political support if the gift is in their control, and it is not too embarrassing to be seen to do so. Moreover, they know any financial figures are manipulable and may be used on either side of an argument. Skilled in creating a rhetoric and a narrative on either side of the balance sheet, they can use financial figures to their favor, or override them as they see politically fit or bearable by stakeholders.

There is also the question of end-user behavior. It is not just the behavior of service designer of service brokers that will shape future HR. Will end users, for example, line managers looking for HR Business Partner support, or staff taking up (or not taking up!) self management, create new and noneconomic patterns of behaviors? Currently unmeasured and "under the radar screen", there will be seen to be a cost to these behaviors, not picked up by current HR capital metrics. For example, line managers, despite the dictates of the organization, HR delivery models, and their own role dictates, might still want a "dogsbody" HR Business Partner to clear up their mess. Just as much as a CEO often wants an HR Director to help clear things up for them, line managers and employees may still want personal dialogue. Employees might rebel against what they could perceive as the "commoditization" of their talent and of their service desires. They might perceive reductions in personal service, especially, on issues that go beyond the things that even a more personalized-service service center could ever give them. The need for hand-holding and for HR to act as a fair juror may yet keep alive the need for dedicated HR staff within businesses, despite the economics and technology.

In this scenario, then, organizational behaviors may yet create new counterbalancing drives, which politically driven senior managers – HR Directors included – may sense and see a need to respond to. The costs of HR, recession aside, may drift up again, or simply get transferred around the organization under different budget and activity headings that hide them, and as long as overall finances are positive, who will go to the wall taking away too much service? They can just manipulate control systems to hide the reality.

So, in the final analysis, we accept that arguments about the Death of HR should be seen through two different sets of lenses – one says you are dead no matter what in a decade because of the logics of economics and service delivery, so become a business/line manager people-savvy person, and outsource the rest of the activity. The other says things will not happen according to economic, service, and technical logics, so build the necessary coalitions now and take on the most visible "new" business projects that will enable you to sell and market your wares.

Whichever future may come to pass, what is evident over the next 10 years is that the sequential planning process historically put in place by HR Directors to support business strategy planning and decision-making processes – creating the strategy, building the facilities and capabilities to support it and its implementation over say a 5-year period – is giving way to "real-time strategy," where a decision or transaction made by the CEO (or a broader collective of senior managers) today determines organizational, and consequently HR's strategy, tomorrow. For right or for wrong, the strategy curve is therefore simultaneously increasing in both frequency and amplitude. Economic cycles will have little impact on this.

The origin of this intensity is not (just) how frenetic (we use the word freneticity to convey its sense of energetic mania) the HR function is. Upstream from HR, CEOs are forced to come to terms with the twin drivers of modularization and innovation. The recent McKinsey dialogue[41] about the ability to create high profits per employee and to cope with the challenge of complexity argues that the world of CEOs is no longer one characterized by a linear value-chain of innovation, production, and protection of value-adding activities. CEOs are now having to identify value in three-dimensional terms or value constellations, where different modular forms, designs, or constellations of their organization are seen to offer new and exciting opportunities for the rapid release of new value.

Against this backdrop, the current freneticity of the HR function makes more sense. The future is less a debate about the standing of the Function, but much more about HR's capability to meet the challenges of strategy execution. Many of the ideas in this book hopefully help us to formulate a more reliable way of understanding how HR is faring in this, its number one task.

NOTES

1 Moss Kanter, R. (2003) Foreword. In M. Effron, R. Gandossy and M. Goldsmith (eds) *Human Resources in the 21st Century.* New Jersey: Wiley, pp. vii–xii.

2 Davis, S. (2003) Is this the end of HR? In M. Effron, R. Gandossy and M. Goldsmith (eds) *Human Resources in the 21st Century.* New Jersey: Wiley, pp. 239–244.

3 Accenture (2003) BT Case Study.

4 PriceWaterhouseCoopers (2007) *Outsourcing Comes of Age: The Rise of Collaborative Partnering.* London: PWC, p. 3.

5 Sparrow, P.R. and Braun, W. (2008) HR outsourcing: Drivers, success factors and implications for HR. In M. Dickmann, C. Brewster and P.R. Sparrow (eds) *International Human Resource Management: Contemporary Issues in Europe.* London: Routledge.

6 Gilley, K. and Rasheed, A. (2000) Making more by doing less: An analysis of outsourcing and its effects on firm performance. *Journal of Management*, 26: 763–790, p. 764.

7 Hesketh, A. (2006) *Outsourcing the HR function: Possibilities and Pitfalls.* London: Corporate Research Forum, p. 1.

8 Harrison, A.F. and McMillan, M.S. (2006) Dispelling some myths about offshoring. *Academy of Management Perspectives*, 20 (4): 6–22.

9 Hunter, I. (2006) *The Indian Offshore Advantage: How Offshoring is Changing the Face of HR.* Aldershot, Hants: Gower Publishing, p. 2.

10 De Vita, G. and Wang, C.L. (2006) Development of outsourcing theory and practice: A taxonomy of outsourcing generations. In H.S. Kehal and V.P. Singh (eds) *Outsourcing and Offshoring in the 21st Century: A Socio-Economic Perspective.* London: Idea Group Publishing, p. 4.

11 Chakrabarty, S. (2006) Making sense of the sourcing and shoring maze: Various outsourcing and offshoring alternatives. In H.S. Kehal and V.A. Singh (eds) *Outsourcing and Offshoring in the 21st Century: A Socio-Economic Perspective.* London: Idea Group, pp. 18–53.

12 Barthélemy, J. and Quélin, B.V. (2006) Complexity of outsourcing contracts and ex post transaction costs: An empirical investigation. *Journal of Management Studies*, 43 (8): 1775–1797.

13 Ibid.

14 See: Sparrow, P.R. and Braun, W. (2008); Budhwar, P. and Cooke, F.L. (2009) HR offshoring and outsourcing: Research issues for IHRM. In P.R. Sparrow (ed.) *Handbook of International HR Research: Integrating People, Process and Context.* Oxford: Blackwell.

15 Becker, Huselid and Ulrich (2001) *The HR Scorecard.* Boston, MA: Harvard Business School Press.

16 Hesketh, A. (2006).

17 Lepak, S. and Palmer, T. (2007) HRO lessons from early adopters. *Human Resources Business Review*, 1 (1): 23–34.

18 For debates on the future of the HR function and the 3-Box model see Hesketh, A. (2008) Should it stay or should it go? Examining the shared services or outsourcing decision. *Strategic Outsourcing*, 1 (2): 154–172.

19 Brown, P. and Hesketh, A. (2004) *The Mismanagement of Talent*. Oxford: Oxford University Press.

20 O'Mahoney, M. and De Boer. (2002) *Britain's Relative Productivity Performance: Updates to 1999*. National Institute for Economic and Social Research Final Report to DTI.

21 Farndale, E., Scullion, H. and Sparrow, P.R. (2010) The role of the corporate HR function in global talent management. *Journal of World Business*, 45 (2). (In press).

22 Ashton, D., Brown, P. and Lauder, H. (2009) Developing a theory of skills for global HR. In P. R. Sparrow (ed.) *Handbook of International HR Research: Integrating People, Process and Context*. Oxford: Blackwell.

23 Mayrhofer, W., Sparrow, P.R. and Zimmermann, A. (2008) Modern forms of international working. In M. Dickmann, C. Brewster and P.R. Sparrow (eds) *International Human Resource Management: A European Perspective*. London: Routledge, pp. 219–239.

24 Martin, G. and Hetrick, S. (2006) *Corporate Reputations, Branding and Managing People: A Strategic Approach to HR*. Oxford: Butterworth Heinemann; Martin, G. and Hetrick, S. (2009) Employer branding and corporate reputation in an international context. In P. R. Sparrow (ed.) *Handbook of International HR Research: Integrating People, Process and Context*. Oxford: Blackwell.

25 Rousseau, D.M. (2001) The idiosyncratic deal: Flexibility versus fairness? *Organisational Dynamics*, 29 (4): 260–273.

26 Brown, D. (2009) Fairness: The ultimate reward goal. Opinion Paper OP16, *Institute for Employment Studies*, May 2009.

27 Cappelli, P. (1999) *The New Deal at Work: Managing the Market-Driven Workforce*. Boston, MA: Harvard Business School Press.

28 Hesketh, A. (2008).

29 Davenport, T.H. (2005) The coming commoditisation of processes. *Harvard Business Review*, June, 101–108.

30 See: Williamson, E. (1975) *Markets & Hierarchies*. New York. Free Press.

31 Johnson, B., Manyika, J. and Yee, L.A. (2005) The next revolution in interactions. *The McKinsey Quarterly* (4): 21–33.

32 Sparrow, P.R. and Braun, W. (2008).

33 Johnson, B., Manyika, J. and Yee, L.A. (2005).

34 Ghemawat, P. (2007) Managing differences: The central challenge of global strategy. *Harvard Business Review*, 85 (3): 58–69.

35 Aron, R. and Singh, J.V. (2005) Getting offshoring right. *Harvard Business Review*, 83 (12): 135–149.

36 Hesketh, A. and Kops, D. (2007) *The Necessary Nine*. New York: Hackett.

37 Lawson, E., Mueller-Oerlinghausen, J. and Shearn (2005) A dearth of HR talent. *The McKinsey Quarterly*, 2: 13–14.

38 Ibid.

39 Ulrich, D. (2007) In the hot seat. *People Management*, 28 June, p. 28.

40 Ibid.

41 Bryan, L.L. and Joyce, C.I. (2007) *Mobilising Minds: Creating Wealth from Talent in the 21st Century Organisation*. New York: McGraw-Hill.

Index